FOAL

America's Moment

America's Moment

Creating Opportunity in the Connected Age

A Book by Rework America

THE MARKLE ECONOMIC FUTURE INITIATIVE

W. W. NORTON & COMPANY *New York • London*

Photograph on p. 23 by Austin McAllister; photograph on
p. 247 by Julian Mancuso; all other photographs by Matthew McDermott.

Pictures on pp. 114 and 115 © 2015 DAQRI LLC.

All line drawings by Suits & Sandals, LLC.

For information about permission to reproduce selections from this book,
write to Permissions, W. W. Norton & Company, Inc.,
500 Fifth Avenue, New York, NY 10110

For information about special discounts for bulk purchases, please contact
W. W. Norton Special Sales at specialsales@wwnorton.com or 800-233-4830

Manufacturing by Courier Westford
Production manager: Julia Druskin

ISBN 978-0-393-28513-0

W. W. Norton & Company, Inc.
500 Fifth Avenue, New York, N.Y. 10110
www.wwnorton.com

W. W. Norton & Company Ltd.
Castle House, 75/76 Wells Street, London W1T 3QT

1 2 3 4 5 6 7 8 9 0

Contents

Preface

BY ZOË BAIRD

Everyone has a meaningful place in the new economy.

What you hold in your hands is a call to affirm that statement—a call to participate in perhaps the most vital undertaking for America in the 21st century.

Together, we are in the midst of the biggest economic transformation in a hundred years. It has disrupted the expectations—and even dreams—of millions of Americans. The defining challenge of our time is making sure that all Americans will be included in this transformation.

This is personal for me. My mother was a Rosie the Riveter in the Brooklyn Navy Yard during World War II. She and my father were so proud that their daughter graduated from college even though neither of them had college degrees. They were able to find a place in the American economy and achieve their American Dream. But if they were starting out today, would the same be true? I have two children who are growing up in this world transformed by technology and globalization. It's my deepest hope that they will live in a time of optimism and shared opportunity.

Yes, there are many who have grabbed hold of the new economy and built incredible businesses and careers. But there are many more who don't know where to find opportunity in this new digital networked era. They have lost faith.

That's because they are uncertain about the future. They don't know what to tell their children about how to prepare for the jobs of the future. They don't know which diplomas or credentials will be meaningful anymore. They don't know whether their skills will be recognized or valued. They don't know how to match up their education with the businesses looking to hire—and for that matter, businesses don't know how to effectively connect with the most qualified workers. They don't know which technologies will be essential to the workplace. They don't know which industries will be created, destroyed, or transformed.

This book offers an agenda for action that takes the very forces causing the change—technology and a networked world—and turns them into the tools we need so that all can prosper.

This is a prescription that also comes with a warning: if we don't embrace new ways of doing things—right now—we will soon hit the point of no return, and the American Dream might vanish for all but a few.

We have been here before. A century ago, America was going through the greatest economic transformation and technological revolution in its history. Cities sprang up overnight, and traditional farm life disappeared for many. There were extremes of wealth and poverty. Then came the Great Depression, which left a third of America, in the words of Franklin Roosevelt, ill-housed, ill-clad, and ill-nourished.

Only when our leaders began to embrace new approaches for a new world did the American Dream achieve real meaning for the majority of Americans.

In the decades that have passed since, no other era has achieved the scale and significance of the economic upheaval of the early 1900s.

Until today.

The transformation of the past 20 years—as our nation has moved through the information era into the digital age—has turned the world upside down once again.

One hundred-year-old industrial buildings now house 3-D printing companies. Farmers are using sensors and tablets to irrigate their crops. STEM education, once the province of only a select few jobs, is now, more and more, a prerequisite. Individual entrepreneurs—using tools that were the stuff of science fiction even 10 years ago—are starting businesses that are changing the world. But many others are left out.

The troubling reality is that doubt and despair have corroded our collective economic prospects and our trust in the promises of our democracy.

How can there be so many paths to opportunity with so few people traveling them?

As a nation, our leaders and all of us need to recognize the profound transition we face. We have to focus on what we must do to help Americans succeed now, and what we must do to prepare our country for what comes next.

That's why, at the Markle Foundation, we have made it our purpose to inspire and enable leaders from all sectors to create new paths for good and meaningful work in the digital economy so that all Americans can dream again.

In the absence of that national conversation, we decided to start one.

We convened a group of remarkable people who know the challenges and potential solutions from their own experience: some of our nation's most successful corporate CEOs, leading technologists, inspiring faith-based leaders, passionate educators, innovative government leaders, celebrated management gurus, and many more from across the political spectrum.

We asked, What can we do today, to make opportunity available for everyone tomorrow?

Our answers are contained in this book. They were generated

by all of us and were artfully woven together by our colleague Philip Zelikow.

Our agenda for action is not just a policy prescription, though it is that too. It is a practical agenda created by people on the ground for actions we can take today in every community around this country. It includes:

> • *Preparing people to succeed.* In the modern economy, information, power, and the ability to make things happen are all distributed, rather than concentrated. So why are people's capacities judged solely by old centralized markers like a high school or college diploma. Why, in this day and age, is just one diploma the goal? Why not many rapid and affordable diplomas that are better matched to today's career paths? Why isn't lifetime learning—accessible affordable education for all people—the norm? It's time we ensure that careers are based on what you can do when you are ready, and not a single path you failed to take at the only turn in the road.
>
> • *Using the reach of the Internet and data to innovate jobs.* We have at our fingertips the power of Internet-based platform marketplaces, and the enormous potential of data and analytics—but they are still exceptions to the norm. We need to fully integrate them into mainstream work and upgrade jobs so that, empowered with information, we develop millions of more valuable workers—and train a new generation to succeed within that context as second nature.
>
> • *Using technology to match employers and workers.* There are millions of middle-skill jobs around the country that aren't being filled. CEOs cannot connect with trained and talented workers. Too many potential employees are in the dark about these positions, or don't know what

skills to gain. We have to use the power of the Internet to make the job search transparent and based on competency and new credentials. We have to match people with opportunity.

• *Transitioning to a "no-collar world."*[1] The old system of credentialing talent is antiquated. Blue-collar, white-collar—it's a hierarchy that doesn't accurately reflect people's abilities, and handcuffs employers to ineffective metrics when trying to find new workers to fill open positions. Job categories, and the skills they require, are changing every day. We require new ways of categorizing and credentialing talent—one in which no worker or employer is limited by arbitrary delineations.

Forward-thinking leaders have already put many of these ideas into practice in some corners of the country and economy. The examples are here, and they are already paying dividends. It is our task to identify them, scale them up, and turn them into something that can benefit all Americans.

When we first began the Rework America initiative, we started the conversation by asking each of our members a simple question: "What is your American Dream story?"

All of the assembled leaders had their own versions of the American Dream story, but all shared one common theme: all of them got to where they are today through perseverance and hard work, but also because of the help of others.

For the next generation, will that hard work be enough? Will those opportunities be available? Will our children be able to tell their own American Dream story?

We think, yes.

In the midst of all this transformation and upheaval, the one thing that hasn't changed is the fundamental belief that has driven this country since its inception: that the American Dream should be within reach for everyone.

We can do this. We have so many tools at our disposal. We are more connected, and more networked, than ever before. But the only way we can translate that into real success tomorrow is by starting to rework America today. This is America's moment.

This book is meant to start that urgent conversation. It's meant to shine a light on the ideas and policies that will secure our economic future. And, most importantly, it's meant to bring people to action.

So it is in that spirit, and in that hope, that I leave you with two questions as you read.

What is your American Dream?

And what are you going to do to make the American Dream possible for everyone?

This is our time to act.

Zoë Baird
CEO and President
Markle Foundation
New York City
February 6, 2015

Chapter 1

To Bend History

America and the world are in the early stages of an economic revolution. The smartphone in your pocket, the website at your fingertips: these are small parts of it. Americans—and people the world over—live in a historic age of transition.

The last time Americans experienced change on this scale was more than a hundred years ago. Then they were coping with industrial revolutions. This time it is a revolution defined more by technological leaps and globalization as networks and data travel the world. Many Americans are benefiting from it, charged up by a wealth of knowledge and possibilities. So far, though, the possibilities have not opened doors for the majority of Americans. They can see that the world is changing but also feel understandable uncertainty about what comes next.

There are many versions of a similar story. For decades, as the U.S. economy has grown, income and wealth for the large majority of Americans have not grown with it. Wages have suffered even more than job growth. Adjusted for inflation, the median U.S. household now has a lower income than it did in 1996.[1] Wages as a share of national income are now at an all-time low. Some 50 percent of Americans have a real household income of about $52,000 or less, a median that has been fluctuating around this number since the end of the 1980s. After the financial crisis and Great Recession from 2007 to 2009, the slow recovery has improved the economic circumstances of only a small minority of Americans.[2]

Or, to take another version, there has been "a great decoupling."[3] Productivity growth was once coupled to growth in incomes and employment. The linkage to both has been broken for at least 15 years. The implicit bargain that gave workers a steady share of the productivity gains has unraveled.

America is creating jobs, but not enough of them. Millions of Americans have withdrawn from the labor force, are no longer seeking work at all (and therefore do not show up in the usual headline unemployment rate). At the same time, American employers are having trouble filling millions of middle-skill jobs.

The powerful forces of technology and globalization driving this transition need not pose a threat. They can offer a historic opportunity. Imagine the America you want to live in: with good meaningful jobs and ways to prepare for them, opportunities to build businesses, the excitement and not fear of innovation, a chance to create a better life for oneself. This is the America you want your children to inherit.

We must recognize that this will not happen without a vision of the America we want to create. It will not happen without leaders who see how these strategies can change the way Americans do business, create and find work, and prepare themselves for the future. At this rare turning point in the history of our country, no one should be a bystander.

When the members of this initiative first met, the Reverend Calvin Butts, the pastor of New York City's Abyssinian Baptist Church, evoked the founding language of the United States. He had grown up in the Lillian Wald projects in the Lower East Side of Manhattan. His father, he told us, "was a butcher by profession. His mother was a simple servant." He had seen a lot of changes.

But he did not think the American Dream had changed. To

him it was still the same dream he had learned about as a child in public school, reciting the founding documents of the country. "I never thought the dream was about trying to be more successful than my parents were materially. I never had an idea that it was about one generation doing better than the next." To him the essence was in the "prophetic and poetic" words of the Declaration of Independence on the inalienable rights to "life, liberty, and the pursuit of happiness."

In a time of great change, it is not the dream that has changed. And that dream need not be out of reach. Instead, Americans must seize new ways to attain it. This book will show that the opportunities for fulfilling, stable, and, yes, exciting careers exist and that the tools are at hand.

No magic wands, these are blueprints for actions that have to touch many parts of a big and complicated economy and society. Arriving at this economic turning point, all in a leadership position must ask himself or herself, What am I doing that will help enable Americans to take advantage of these new opportunities and restore the American Dream?

Americans in an earlier age remade their country to cope with the industrial revolutions. Americans in this one can rework America for the digital revolution.

As before, the agenda will touch many areas of American life. Once again, the leaders must come from every part of American life. It is time for Americans to get ready and gear up for this transition. It is our turn.

American Dream

What is the American Dream? Almost all the answers have always had something to do with two ideas. One, of course, is opportunity. The other is responsibility.

From the time they discovered the new land, European settlers were awed by both the opportunity and the risks. When John Winthrop wrote his famed 1630 sermon to his Puritan flock on their journey to the unknown new world, he preached to them about a "city upon a hill." But he was not thumping his chest with pride. He was giving them a warning.

We are fashioning a community, he told them, where "the eyes of all people are upon us." If we fail, our "shipwreck" will make us a laughingstock, "a story and a by-word through the world."[4]

That mix of opportunity with responsibility set the tone for much in American political culture. Success would need *risky efforts*: crossing oceans, crossing plains, risking money, risking lives. That meant responsibility.

In return, the system should offer *fair chances* to participate. That was the opportunity part. The original American system was always one of "try, try again." It was about fresh starts. It was in America that bankruptcy relief would begin replacing debtors' prisons. America would give people repeated chances for a meaningful life.

The American Dream thus also came to stand for a *freedom to experiment*. Social reform, self-improvement: these are constant motifs all through the country's history.

In a 2013 survey the definition of the American Dream that attracted more support than any other was "to have freedom of choice in how to live one's life" (75 percent). The least favored definition emphasized the ability "to become wealthy" (29 percent).[5]

In return, the country offered a *context of abundance*. At first there was the land. Then there was the abundance of personal possibilities, of reinvention.[6]

Throughout American history, leading thinkers have seen the dream threatened and put forward ideas to save it. This theme—threat and salvation—is the narrative line of the bestseller that first popularized the term "American Dream." The book, by James Truslow Adams, came out in 1931, while the country was in the depths of the worst economic depression in American history.[7]

Entering one of the few truly fundamental periods of change in the history of America's economy and society can be scary. So it is a comfort to know that Americans have been there before.

Each time, Americans had to consider how to renew their hope in the American Dream, using the tools that the new era gave them. How to remake business? How to remake education?

This Revolution in Historical Context

During the first two hundred years that European settlers lived on the eastern fringe of North America, most of them were farmers. Almost all lived on a farm or in a village with fewer than a thousand people.

Few went any farther from a sustaining sea or navigable river than they had to. Into the early 1800s most people in the new United States of America lived within 50 miles of the Atlantic seacoast. Thinking about economic growth, those Americans were preoccupied with two concerns: safely getting new land and the conditions of Atlantic trade.

The circumstances of Americans began changing in fundamental ways during the early 1800s. By the 1820s several changes were becoming obvious:

• The country had grown vastly larger.
• It was now possible to move people and goods vast distances, even on land, at a manageable cost. Historians call this the "transportation revolution." In America this meant canals, steamships, and then, above all, railroads.
• The "factory" method of production began to take off, having arrived from Britain at first mainly in New England, using steam engines as well as water mills.[8] The Americans early became known for using their machines to offer state-of-the-art ways to process cotton and build firearms (Eli Whitney was involved in both developments).

By the 1820s the founding generation was passing from the scene. Americans wondered aloud whether they were still worthy of what they had inherited. A mere republic of quarrelsome land-hungry subsistence farmers did not seem very fitting.

Public and private leaders called for a shift from a culture built around subsistence farming. They argued for an America remade to thrive with capitalist production and a market revolution.

The leading proponent of a broader political and economic vision for this new "American system" was Henry Clay. Often citing the example of the Kentucky plantation he managed with his brilliant wife, Clay thought farmers should also be businessmen, as he was in selling the hemp he grew on his own farm. Clay sought to avoid panics, like the one America had experienced in 1819, caused by overreliance on foreign markets.[9]

Flocks of journalists and opinion leaders elaborated and spread the basic elements of Clay's thinking: stronger governments to make "improvements," reliance on markets in a great American *union*, tariff barriers, and cautious western expansion.

These causes marked the "national Republicans" of the 1820s, the Whigs who came next, and the Republican Party built from the wreckage of the Whigs. They molded thinking about the American political economy for the next hundred years.

Andrew Jackson and his successors in the Democratic Party framed their own agenda by how they agreed or disagreed with much of this. For example, most Southern planters were enthusiastic supporters of a more market-oriented agriculture, but using slaves to grow cotton for factories in Britain and consumers around the world, they usually opposed tariffs on trade.[10]

So Americans then argued about how to remake their country in this revolutionary age and preserve the American Dream. The issues of "markets and manufactures" that characterized this first American economic system were understood and debated everywhere.

Americans discussed issues like freedom of labor and the problem of Southern slavery; issuance of money, credit, and the control of banks; sectional economic divides, like those between North and South; sale of public land; tariffs on imported goods; government sponsorship of "improvements"; and encouragement or regulation of railroads.[11]

In this older era, Americans debated economic subjects at a remarkable level of detail and understanding. Students stuck in a history class today might roll their eyes if a teacher turns to a topic like the "bank war" or the "gold standard." But issues like those fired the emotions of generations of ordinary Americans from the 1820s through the 1920s.

Why? Were people back then just so much better educated and informed? No. But to them, these topics were not abstract. To a farmer, currency issues were about the price he would get for his wheat. Local merchants and farmers wanted thousands of local institutions ready to extend life-giving loans. Banks were therefore vigorously regulated to limit the power of distant financiers.

In education, this first American economic system emphasized individual opportunity. It stressed self-improvement. It was an age when "the cult of the 'self-made man' was universally accepted in America . . . that the key to success lay within."[12]

For many people of that era—and the present one—an embodiment of these ideals was Abraham Lincoln. Lincoln grew up on the frontier. He had no formal education to speak of. His great gifts were acquired on his own, in a life of reading, reflection, and practice.

Lincoln thought Clay was a great American. He found in Clay and Clay's system models of American character and statesmanship. In Lincoln's day this American system was much more than economics (a word then not much in use). It was about how to build an American way of life.

Americans of Lincoln's generation believed they were breaking from their parents (Lincoln was estranged from both of his natural parents). In this new market world Americans had to fashion their own identities.

They had to educate themselves outside of formal institutions in every sundry way they could. It was a time when "library companies, literary societies, mutual improvement associations, [and] the grand American adult education program called the lyceum flourished."[13] It was not a land where formal credentials were necessary badges of entry.

Men like Lincoln—or the ex-slave Frederick Douglass—were held up as exemplars of the self-made man. Education in this age was considered the development and discipline of the person as a whole. It was seen as a matter of moral self-instruction as much as any mastery of technical skills. Lincoln himself did not talk much about his log cabin beginnings. He spoke instead about the duty to build a balanced character, to build a balanced country.

For Lincoln, containment of the slave power was necessary to protect such an American Dream. And if destruction of the slave power was the only step that could save the American union, he would lead it.

The Second American Economic System— "An Era of Mass Production"

As a new kind of American union was slowly rebuilt after the Civil War, the circumstances of the American and world economies changed yet again in deep and lasting ways, obvious to all. The second economic revolution set the terms that would dominate the rest of the 19th century and almost all of the 20th.[14] Americans experienced it as

> • the rise of mass production, ranging from much more steel to canned goods to Coca-Cola to automobiles and beyond, with the supply chains, mass marketing, and distribution that went with that;
> • greatly improved communication, through the cabling of America with telegraph and then telephone service;
> • the rise of giant companies and the professionals operating them, seeming to touch every facet of life;

• the urbanization of the nation, as most Americans moved from the countryside into towns, cities, and then many large cities; and

• the harnessing of new forces—electricity and the electromagnetic spectrum—and many new materials developed by industrial chemistry, including biochemicals (like aspirin) and petrochemicals (like plastic).

As they had before, back in the 1820s, Americans began arguing about ways to remake their country. The issues of the earlier American system, the one of "new markets and manufactures," had not yet disappeared. But as the older issues faded, the newer ones came more into the foreground.

Most of the economic topics that moved to the center of attention more than a hundred years ago remain there today. Among them are the power or control of big business, including "trusts" or monopolies or "utilities"; the power or control of organized labor, including unions; immigration (business was hungry for the labor it brought); farm versus city (once a defining topic, receded now); public education; provision of health care; and government regulation of products and working conditions. These issues all arose out of arguments about how to adapt to the era of mass production and the mass consumerism that came with it.

There was also, always, the hardy perennial about taxing and spending by the national government. But after the 1930s the content of the argument shifted. Government spending became not just an instrument to do something else, like build a road. It became a policy in its own right as spending—on anything—was seen as a way to manage the economy and its business cycles by stimulating or slowing mass buying, "aggregate demand."

From this point of view, the objects of the spending are secondary, except for arguments about how well they promote or "multiply" aggregate demand. Experts in the new field of economics called macroeconomics, which emerged in the 1940s and 1950s, then argued about the instruments to be used to achieve these mass effects—spending, tax rates, or interest rates.

In this American system of the "era of mass production," Americans either embraced or mourned the rise of big institutions. Both sides agreed that these large hierarchies seemed to dominate much of what they could do.

Before the Civil War only about 7 percent of American manufacturing had existed as corporations; by 1900 that figure was 69 percent. In the 1870s a future Republican president (Garfield) warned of a coming "industrial feudalism." At the end of the Civil War, "I found that I had got back to another world," says a wistful veteran, wounded at Gettysburg, the title character in William Dean Howells's *The Rise of Silas Lapham* (1885). "The day of small things was past, and I don't suppose it will ever come again in this country."[15]

But by 1938, as big business was still a lightning rod for controversy in much of America, researchers went to "Middletown"—Muncie, Indiana—and found that "Mr. and Mrs. John Citizen of Middletown, U.S.A.," seemed to like big business. "They mention nearly twelve times as many good points as bad points about ninety leading corporations." The once-resented telephone giant AT&T was generally praised for its service, and only 4 percent considered it an unfair monopoly.[16]

Notions of education and self-improvement changed too. The era of mass production was also in awe of scientific progress. Americans deferred to professionalized experts who would call for "rational," efficient solutions to problems.

The great problem solvers of this era were not in the Clay/Lincoln mold of the self-made individual. Instead, at this high tide of deference to expertise (between, say, about 1900 and 1960), Americans would often look for answers from rigorous investigators, austere and dignified lawyers, and engineers.

This was another age in which Americans had to reinvent the jobs they did every day. Millions filled new professions, like those of "engineers" and "public school teachers," that were practically unknown in 1850. Children no longer ran the machines. Common laborers, many of them illiterate, were trained in the new high schools and by their employers to fill new kinds of jobs with titles like "welders" or "machinists" or "electricians." A huge new kind of educational system had to be built to train both the scholars and the workers.

How Did Americans Rework Their Systems?

In these first two eras of economic revolution, when Americans remade their country and argued about ways to do it, how did the great changes occur? In other words, if we need to remake our country again in order to restore the American Dream, are there lessons for how we might expect to do it now?

A conventional way Americans think their systems have been remade takes the form of stories in which entrenched interests are eventually overcome by the power of the people, usually led by a charismatic president. In this view the slave power was overcome by Lincoln, the greedy robber barons were stayed by Theodore Roosevelt, the capitalist disorder was taken in hand by Franklin Roosevelt and the New Deal, or the welfare state hydra was laid low by Ronald Reagan.

Whatever their merits, these stories overlook much of what is most interesting about how Americans actually reworked their country in the past. These older summaries, "positing a clear-cut battle between the 'people' and the 'interests,' [have] long been rejected" by historians "as too simple a framework for an extraordinarily complex era of political and social change."[17]

What the historians found instead is more complicated and at the same time more interesting. In many practical ways, Americans remade their country by fashioning alliances of private and public interests, working in concert. Such alliances were usually found on *both* sides of the political arguments.[18]

As the French traveler Alexis de Tocqueville observed in the

1830s, Americans would join or create associations of all kinds—
profit seeking, nonprofit, professional, voluntary. To remake
America, to get really large-scale jobs done, the work had to
involve coalitions. These groups sought out allies here and there in
the relevant agencies of government.

Innovators found that, in order to take off, they needed political order. That was not a new pattern. At the start, right after
the innovation starts turning things upside down, there would be
the "normal characters of a frontier town . . . the pirates and the
pioneers, the tinkers and the traveling salesmen." But then, the
Barnard College president Debora Spar has noted, someone usually called for the sheriff.

"Frequently," she writes, "the worlds of business and politics are
described as belonging to wholly different spheres." Not so. It is
right there, on the technological frontier, where "markets are actually created, where industries spring to life and then settle, eventually, into some kind of ordered existence," that order needs some
help. "As this process unwinds, power is distributed and structures
are established. It is a hugely political enterprise, even if governments are not actively calling the shots or regulating commercial
activity."[19]

A common view of American history is that back in the good
old (or bad old) 19th century, the state was a weak player in the
economy. Laissez-faire reigned. Not so.

Government in that era was not large in size, but it was the
indispensable partner to large private initiatives. This was the
period in which state and federal government gave about one-fifth
of all the land in Minnesota to the railroads. Governments like
that in Minnesota also issued bonds to finance the railroads. Minnesota was not unusual.[20]

The auto and truck roads were developed in another enormous alliance. This one had a larger role for governments—local,
state, and federal—which assumed the road cost. They were in
league with private interest groups (like freight companies and the

Teamsters union), with the occasional private-chartered turnpike thrown in.

Another competitor for the railroads was air transport. Air travel got off the ground on a large scale in America with the aid of subsidies during the 1920s and 1930s. These were coming from the federal Post Office Department, so the airplanes would carry high-priced, faster "air mail."

Again and again, when Americans remade their country, they built and used these private-public alliances. Whether the new systems were telephone networks, public schools, or electric power, one finds stories like these.[21]

Nowhere was this clearer than in changes in education.

> • The era of markets and manufactures had a culture of self-improvement. Thus it was the era in which Americans started a "high school" movement and founded hundreds of tiny, private colleges. A network—mail delivery of newspapers and magazines—was seen as the main way for people to teach themselves. Because it subsidized such distribution of the written word, the Post Office seemed—to Edward Everett Hale in 1891—the "most majestic system of public education which was ever set on foot anywhere."[22]
>
> • The era of mass production had a culture of training tens of millions. Thus it was the era in which education was more centralized in larger institutions. Public high schools became the norm, the university movement took off with its professional graduate schools, and everything—curricula, credit units, and credentials—was standardized for mass production and mass marketing.

Today Americans are so far removed from the last great age of re-creation, that we forget that a great, conscious effort is needed in order to think anew.

A Different Kind of Revolution

A hundred years ago Americans were buffeted by an economic revolution that was transforming their country. Their collective response harnessed the industrial might of great American institutions—corporate giants, a government with the largest office building in the world, big schools, towering hospitals. Business models relied on mass production. Institutions were centralized. People had to fit themselves into the system: its workplaces, its structures, its timetables, whether in business or education or health care or government.

Our current revolution is different because a networked world is inherently less centered and more distributed. This revolution can be more about empowering individuals, rather than institutions. It is "user-friendly." It is a revolution that asks first, What capabilities would people like to have at their fingertips? Then, What solutions will give them that capability?

Instead of making people come to the institution, the "system," and fit into it and its products, the networked economy will press many institutions to reach and fit every individual. That is why Americans should work to unleash the potential of individuals, networked with each other and the world. If the older revolution was about our mighty structures, this one is about the might of our combined talents, organized and deployed with unprecedented flexibility.

To thrive in this era, Americans have plenty of new tools and new openings that have also come with technology and globalization. Americans will choose how to take advantage of them, guided by their values.

Rather than ask, Will the robots take our jobs?, we ask, What jobs can Americans perform if they are empowered by these machines? And how can Americans get ready to take advantage of new opportunities?

Rather than ask, Will our jobs be outsourced or offshored?, we ask, What new markets and global supply chains can Americans share?

In the first generation of technological change, the initial reaction is to think, How do we automate what we do today? In the next generation of change, the one we are entering now, we should also ask, How can we invent what we want to do tomorrow?

The first kind of thinking is more obvious. The second kind is more important. It is the kind that put the smartphone in your pocket. It is the thinking that creates new sorts of business, new ways of finding fulfilling work, and new ways to prepare for what is next all through our lives.

Our Values

This brief sketch hints at the possibilities we will explore in this book. We hope that, in reading it, you are inspired, or provoked, or want to start filling in areas that seem incomplete. If you have any of those reactions, you are at least looking ahead, imagining futures. You are joining us in thinking about how to rework America by means of the new tools coming to hand.

Our vision is about unleashing individual potential. To do that, millions of Americans may find new roles and opportunities—often helping others or being helped along the way.

Our vision is not mere speculation. The tools are already coming into use or soon will be. The money is there.

Reworking America is a great challenge, in every sense. The details are vital. And just boosting overall GDP is not an adequate goal. The bar must be higher. The American Dream is about opportunity for all, not just a few. In this revolutionary era we believe the greatest and most durable successes will flow from the broadest possible empowerment of Americans to realize their potential.

- We care about the large majority of Americans who are feeling left behind. Today we associate the highway to success with a college education. But most Americans either do not go to college or are unable to complete a degree. Although higher education should be more inclusive, even it is no panacea. Nearly half of the college degree holders in their 20s are unemployed or underemployed.

• Good work provides predictable, steady income as well as self-satisfaction. We want as many people as possible to see opportunities to participate productively in ways that are meaningful to them.

• We want all Americans to be able to prepare for a world of constant change, able to learn new things or retrain in the most flexible and affordable ways throughout their lifetimes.

• The American Dream has always been about opportunity for all, rewards for effort and ingenuity, fresh starts, and second chances. We want to rebuild the American Dream so that it works for people who now feel disconnected from the benefits of the emerging networked world, who feel left out from this new era in America's history.

• We call on compassionate leaders from every part of American life to join this effort to rework America. Partnerships with governments will be vital. But Americans cannot wait for leaders in Washington to tell them what to do.

Economic growth is good. It is not good enough, though, if most Americans believe that the opportunities ahead for themselves and their children are steadily narrowing.

We discussed some of these statistics at the beginning of the chapter, about income and the "great decoupling" of productivity gains from income gains. A further version of the story is what the University of California at Berkeley economist Enrico Moretti calls a "Great Divergence." He starts by comparing communities once demographically analogous—as Albuquerque and Seattle were in 1978 while the little start-up company Microsoft was based in Albuquerque. He then follows how the paths of different cities, like Albuquerque and Seattle, have diverged in the decades that followed.

Beginning in the 1980s, "America's new economic map shows growing differences, not just between people but between communities." On the one hand, there are thriving communities built around various kinds of innovative producers and the multiplier effects from those nuclei. On the other hand, there are communities, growing farther and farther apart, "stuck with dead-end jobs and low average wages."

Such differences have always been present. "But today the difference among communities in the United States is bigger than it has been in a century."[23]

There are a number of ways to measure real, broad improvement, improvement that most Americans experience in a more dynamic economy that creates good jobs that pay well.[24] Some of the most revealing indicators of success will be found less in aggregate GDP numbers or in measures of the unemployment rate. Better measures will be surveys of public attitudes, the scale of net job creation, the number of young firms, evidence of rising median income, signs of a fluid labor market, growing attainment of adult job skills, and the participation of young people in the workforce. In all these measures, the trend lines have been going down at a troubling rate for a number of years, often for decades.[25] Success, five or ten years from now, should mean that trend lines like these have changed direction and are moving consistently the other way.

There are many numbers for observers to track.[26] But we agree that to rework America and renew the American Dream, indicators of American economic opportunity should change course. They should trend up, not down.

To Bend History, Change the Odds

One of our members, the former Utah governor Michael Leavitt, likes to tell a story of a child being shown how an old clock works. When its back is opened, the child is bewildered by all those wheels and connections, all in motion. The kindly clockmaker points, though, to the big gears. It is those big gears, he explains, that turn all the little ones.

This book points to some of the big gears in America's economic future. We believe that the American (and world) economy is in a *transitional period*, of a kind and scale that comes along every hundred years or so.

We believe the systems of the old economy have become *mismatched* with the emerging new economy. The mismatches are creating a sluggish economy, out of gear, limiting opportunity. It is not so much the overall size of the economy that is the problem, more its shape—too much here, not enough there.

We cannot predict a specific set of outcomes. The historical changes in motion are far too large and sweeping for us to be able to do that. Nevertheless, one of our key premises is that we can shape these outcomes, not merely wait to be shaped by them.

Our strategy is to use the new tools to change the odds to favor our values. To be more exact, our strategy is not to change just one set of odds. Fixing the mismatches can radically change the odds of success in tens of millions of individual American stories. In each of those stories the odds might change at several stages in a person's life and in the life of a business. Do that, and then play for the breaks. We are too humble to predict the results, but do that, and America can again become a country full of promise and possibility.

The two goals we suggest—more opportunities for good work, more pathways to valued careers—can be advanced with strategies for business development and personal development. We think these strategies make sense because, in the emerging networked economy, it has never been easier—in theory—to start and grow a business. It has never been easier—in theory—to find and get the education or training you need, anytime, anywhere, throughout your life. So, in theory, the strategies are workable.

Our job, then? Nudge reality for all Americans closer to the theory. In this book we will offer six strategies for action to pair up reality and theory.

For business development and more opportunities for good work:

- ***Connect to a world of buyers.*** Get ready for a world economy about to more than double in size. Use the openings for much more digitized commerce that play to American strengths in producing goods and especially services that are already valued around the world, bringing billions of potential new buyers to Americans' screens.
- ***Invest in Main Street America.*** Get trillions of dollars in available capital off the sidelines and more productively invested in business growth. Reverse the long-time trends that have encouraged flows of credit to fuel unsustainable consumer debt.
- ***Share the knowledge, innovate the jobs.*** Empower small businesses with big data. Empower frontline employees with the capabilities of mobile technologies connected to networks of information. As innovated jobs add value in redesigned businesses, employers should want to invest in their workforce, and employees will see more valued career pathways.
- ***Better made, in America.*** Global trends invite more local and customized commerce; they also reward complex, high-value work. Americans can build up strong communities of American producers, connected on high-quality networks, to create good jobs and spin off more for all.

For personal development and more valued career paths:

- ***Match Americans to opportunities.*** With more useful credentials and interactive matching, build a labor market that functions at the speed and with the interactive capabilities of a network, a market giving up-to-date information every American can use.

• *Prepare for the life you want.* Use new educational designs—modular, lifelong, blending the personal touch with online capabilities—to redesign the way Americans teach, making needed knowledge available to anyone, anytime, anywhere, and at any point in their life.

These six strategies for action are meant to enable Americans who are eager to look forward and find new solutions.

Such Americans are not hard to find. Many of these leaders are at work in local communities, looking at what they have, imagining innovative possibilities. They are already out doing what they can, in ways that rarely make the news headlines.

Every country in the world is dealing with many of the same challenges Americans are facing. That includes factory-dense China and export champions like Germany and Japan. The economic revolution is hitting them too.

Compared with other countries, the United States has a range of advantages and tools. It sits at the heart of a continent, North America, with great human and natural resources. It has a deep bench for creativity and research. It has enviable access to private capital.

The essence of this economic revolution is its capacity to unlock individual potential. There are plenty of Americans who are ready to look forward.

Robert Kennedy once put it this way: "Few will have the greatness to bend history itself, but each of us can work to change a small portion of events, and in the total of all those acts will be written the history of this generation."[27]

Chapter 2

Fresh Chances
in a Networked World

Matthew and Tanya

Matthew Burnett, an African American who grew up in Detroit, picked up an interest in craft work from his grandfather, an assembly-line worker who had started out making five dollars a day at Ford's manufacturing plant. Matthew's dream was to become someone who designs and makes things.

Matthew followed his dream to the Pratt Institute in New York City. There he studied industrial design. Soon he was designing watches for brands like Marc Jacobs, DKNY, and Fossil. He then launched his own, Brooklyn-based brand of designer watches, Steel Cake, in 2007.

Matthew learned firsthand at Fossil that big buyers get high-quality attention from offshore manufacturers. After opening his own small business, he learned firsthand that small buyers are not so fortunate. They have nightmares trying to manufacture overseas. "Import taxes and shipping costs were expensive, and the time difference meant calls with overseas suppliers at 2 or 3 a.m."[1] Matthew sourced parts overseas in Asia, but it was difficult to find a manufacturer that he could trust and that would not demand a cost-prohibitive minimum order of a thousand or more pieces.[2]

After manufacturing errors and overseas shipping cost him $40,000, Matthew tried a new business in leather accessories made in America and using American-made supplies. He began searching for domestic suppliers.

The new accessories business was a success. Its merchandise was sold in scores of boutiques and larger retailers, including Nordstrom. Matthew brought in a business partner, Tanya Menendez, who quit her job as an analyst at Goldman Sachs.

Tanya told a journalist that the turning point for her in deciding to quit her job and jump into being a producer was when she visited another accessories producer in the clothing business. She found it "mind-blowing that products were being made in New York City, and that you could get the materials, have the assembly done here, sell it, and actually make a profit off it, actually make your own money."[3]

Then came the next frustration. The search for suppliers in leather and other clothing components turned out to be amazingly difficult.

"It was such an outdated process to find an American manufacturer," Tanya explained. "We were literally going to trade shows and looking through print catalogs. Looking through print catalogs to find something feels so out of date, but all of the other product-based entrepreneurs we knew were doing it that way, too. The main way to find manufacturers was through word of mouth, these catalogs, or trade shows."

"The thing that was ridiculous, is that it was easier to find a manufacturer on the other side of the planet than it was to find one in your own country," Matthew added. He got to be good at it. But every time he turned to a new product idea, he felt he had to start from scratch in searching for American suppliers.[4]

Matthew reflected on his problem. He saw a lot of sides to it. "There are extremely limited resources for discovery, fragmented regional communities that are offline, and very little transparency."[5]

It wasn't only the regional communities of producers that were

Matthew Burnett and Tanya Menendez of Maker's Row.

fragmented, cut off from each other. Even within a community, potential allies were not working together.

Matthew decided to try and build a way to connect them, online. "When we provide clear channels of discovery amongst industries online, everyone" would benefit, right "down to the end consumer."[6]

So Matthew and Tanya's frustration led them to a new business venture, an online directory of America's top manufacturers. They call their platform Maker's Row. Maker's Row has been described as "a kind of proto-Alibaba for U.S. businesses" that, in Tanya's words, can "bring outsourced manufacturing back home, and . . . plant the seeds of the next generation of businesses that will be able to easily find American manufacturing partners." That way, according to Matthew, "a good idea can become a great product here in the United States."[7]

The company has a growing database of suppliers in everything from zippers to tooling. Users can write reviews of suppliers in a Yelp-like manner. Maker's Row has taken off. "In its first year, the site connected 26,000 buyers to 2,000 domestic manufacturers with its easy-to-access platform, [plugging] holes within a variety of manufacturing ecosystems." It has expanded to help businesses, students, and designers by developing a service that offers personal guidance in manufacturing, marketing, PR, production, and more.[8]

Revolutionary Opportunities

Technology and globalization are frequently viewed as taking away opportunity. That has often been true. But in this era we believe these forces are the very means Americans can use to create enormous opportunity—more than ever before.

Matthew and Tanya are a small example of what could become a really big swing in the pendulum of America's economic future. American producers may be coming back, in new forms. These producers are catering to an on-demand economy. In this economy buyers expect a timely speed to market. More Americans can become entrepreneurs. There is a growing demand for producing small-batch design-centric goods.

Matthew and Tanya also exemplify how some Americans are looking at the new tools that this era of American economic history is offering to them. They are seizing ways to use these tools—like platforms and new kinds of producer-consumer relationships—to build new businesses. When they look at this digital revolution and the networked economy, they see new opportunities.

This chapter describes four broad currents that Americans can run with:

- the character of this economic revolution;
- more powerful networks spanning the world;
- yet also more localization; and
- more individual empowerment.

It then closes with some comments on how our economic indicators, designed for an earlier age, are no longer well suited to the measurement of performance in this one.

The Revolution This Time

The third economic revolution has a number of elements. Only some of them are technological. Others are global changes in the world of international finance and investment, the end of the Cold War, and the full entry of China and India into the world economy. Those changes in the 1980s and 1990s coincided and interacted with very important developments occurring during these decades in the world of technology. And then all of these changes—technological, political, and economic—began to come together during the 1990s and 2000s, leading to the second-order consequences that are becoming really revolutionary in changing the whole character of economies and societies.

Just focusing on the technological ingredients, it helps to notice at least three different ones: computer power, sensor power, and network power. They are commonly lumped together as "information" or "communications" technologies. But each of these three ingredients plays a distinctive role, and then, when they are brought together, they are much more powerful than just being better ways of conveying information.

Computer power is the power to process data, with effect. It is a combination of hardware, like microprocessors using many transistors on a piece of silicon, with software, the programming that tells the hardware what tasks to perform. "The Innovators" who engineered this development are masterfully chronicled in Walter Isaacson's recent book.[9]

Personal computers and useful software came together for the general public for the first time during the 1980s. The development by IBM of the "personal computer" as a tool for individual knowledge workers instead of large centralized departments was immediately recognized as a major advance, so much so that for the first time in its history, *Time* magazine did not name a man of the year in 1982. The personal computer was the "machine of the year." Even then the software that empowered everyday users to wield the computing power was becoming at least as important as the machine that provided the processing power.

Earlier technologies focused on supplanting the physical power of muscles, human or animal. But the new computer power is not about brute force. It is about neural force, cognitive and processing. Instead of augmenting muscles, it augments brains.[10]

The unspoken assumption in most writing about computer power is that the processor gets its data from humans. Someone types in the data; someone sends it in.

Sensor power is the power of a machine to gather data for itself. It can do this by converting the phenomena of the physical world around it into a digital form. A fundamental innovation in sensor power came with the creation of what are called "charge-coupled devices." A photon of light could be sensed by a machine and then converted into digitized data, 1s and 0s. One of the first great uses was for digital imaging.

Once digitized, such data can be processed with computer power. By converting external phenomena into data, sensors join the microprocessors of computing power to microelectromechanical systems: tiny responsive accelerometers, gyroscopes, or inertial modules. These can be sensors of pressure or temperature or touch. A driverless car or a wristwatch that knows your temperature and heart rate uses sensor power.

If computing power augments the human ability to process data to effect, sensor power then vastly amplifies what humans and their machines can sense—what they can monitor or observe. Humans already communicate through an Internet. As the machines can sense their surroundings and transmit this data, they are now communicated through another kind of network, an emerging "Internet of Things."

Network power arises from the organization of communication, organizations enabled by computer power. The Internet and the web are networks. The networks use hardware like servers, switchers, and routers. Also very important are the standards—

the "protocols"—that enable interaction among the machines and their packets of data.

The rise of network power is the most recent of the major technological ingredients in the third economic revolution. In 1980 Walmart linked a new Universal Product Code—the "bar code" now on every retail product—to computing power, big data analysis, and advanced communications. This costly investment in network power helped make Walmart the largest company in the world.[11]

As this "retail revolution" was changing the face of communities across the United States, other global political and economic changes were clearing the way for creation of unprecedented global electronic networks. Both the Internet and the World Wide Web became generally available for public use for the first time in 1993.

The combination of these powers set the stage for revolution.

Take the case of a platform, like the transportation service called Uber. It does not exist without the processing power on those tiny chips. It relies on the sensor power breakthroughs so that the interrelated GPS functions work without everyone keying in their locations. And the networking ties it all together.

But the revolutions, past and present, are not merely technological. They do not happen unless or until wider organizational and institutional creations employ these tools in novel creations. The creations then change societies. That is why the time lags between inventions and revolutionary changes in society from them are often measured in decades. It is why there are so many variations between different countries or different regions in the character and velocity of change, until one or two models become so influential that the rest of the world is obliged to conform, or wishes to.

The creation of the Internet, for example, was not an automatic, predestined consequence of the technological possibility. And the challenges in building and sustaining it were not merely, or perhaps even mainly, technological.

The early Internet was open. It had no gatekeepers. It was

decentralized. Functionality was intentionally pushed to the edges of the network. There innovative applications could be offered without the permission of network operators.[12] Network operators, like the telephone companies, could not control the equipment connected to the network. Nor had they any responsibility for the content they carried.

The early Internet was nondiscriminatory. Any item of data was as accessible as any other item of data. All points on the network were equally accessible from every other point. The Internet was user-controlled to a far greater degree than other media. Internet users had the power to choose where they would go online and what they would see or hear.

By and large, the broadband Internet shares these characteristics of the early Internet. But they are under challenge.

The Internet's enabling framework is a subtle mix of regulation and self-government. For example, even though the U.S. government funded the Internet's early development, it made no effort to control the technological design of the network. Even though the Internet was born under the auspices of the Pentagon, the U.S. government never mandated its core technologies. Instead, the technology of the Internet has been largely left to voluntary, consensus-based standards bodies such as the Internet Engineering Task Force.

The initial architects of the Internet used this freedom to create standards that promoted flexibility and interoperability. Vint Cerf, one of those creators, is fond of the phrase "IP on everything and everything on IP." By that he means that the Internet protocol can operate over any medium—including the copper wire of the traditional telephone network, the coaxial cable of the cable network, the airwaves, and even power lines—while at the same time every form of content (voice, data, and video) can be carried on IP. As a result, the Internet is uniquely versatile, open to innovation.[13]

The present digital revolution is still in its early stages. Most

Americans could tell that the computer age seemed like a big deal during the 1980s and 1990s, as some of the inventions could be applied widely in personal computers and networks. They had arrived. They started changing everyone's business and social life.[14] But the real revolution is not just about technological innovation, and it is only beginning to get fully underway.

Economic revolutions are not like political revolutions; they do not occur with a big bang. The revolutions unfold slowly. The initial innovations themselves become tools to create newer things—a factory allows you to make copper wire, which then allows the creation of a telegraph. When the initial innovations become "general-purpose technologies," the economic revolution really takes off.[15]

For example, the invention of the steam engine is commonly dated to about 1760. Steam engines were already very important by the 1820s, used in steamships and factories. But the takeoff, the most flexible uses of steam engines in factories in the United States, did not arrive until the period between 1870 and 1900, with engines using the Corliss design. That was more than a century after steam engines first came into use. When that happened, more and more factories could move away from rural, water-powered mills. They could relocate into cities. This transition then accelerated the growth of cities, reshaping the whole face of America.[16]

For another example, consider the case of electricity. For a long time electricity was just a scientific curiosity. It gained sensational public attention when it was used to communicate through an actual telegraph line (1844). More decades passed before Thomas Edison built his first electric power station (1882).

Still, even after wide adoption of electricity as a source of light, steam engines remained the main power source in factories. It was only more decades later, especially during the 1920s and 1930s, that the largest takeoff occurred, when industry itself was revolutionized by electricity. That is when factories were transformed once more in order to equip workers with electric engines—a drill, a circular saw—at a workbench or on an assembly line. There can be long time lags until industries sort matters out.[17]

But once the businesses did change, the results were astonishing. The electrification of industry during the 1920s and 1930s helped yield the greatest sustained productivity gains from innovation witnessed in any period in American history during the 20th century. Despite the afflictions of the Great Depression, electrification of industry and other innovations that finally achieved the potential of other older inventions, like the internal combustion engine (which had been around for more than thirty years), primed American industry for tremendous gains in productivity.[18]

This great surge of productivity during the 1930s occurred because the ideas, the solutions, created new demands. Innovation spurred demand, not the other way around.

For instance, scientists in the laboratories of a chemical company, DuPont, kept playing with polymers for about ten years, throughout the 1930s, and finally came up with a substance they called nylon. Sixty-eight million nylon stockings were sold in their first year on the market (1940).

As a revolution develops, teams of innovators combine different ingredients to create new fusions. The mapping application on your smartphone is an example of a fusion: computer power, sensor power, and network power.

Chemical engineering involved the invention of a new way of working and producing: a fusion of chemistry with another discipline, mechanical engineering. "The essential point to understand here is that chemical engineering is not applied chemistry." Chemical engineering has methods and processes all its own.[19]

For the digital revolution, that kind of takeoff appears to be getting underway. We may look back on the 2000s and 2010s as the period when all these different innovations in the third economic revolution really started to combine. For example, using digital innovations as the tools, another new way of working and producing—biological engineering—is only now begining to come into its own. This kind of engineering can involve genetic sequencing and manipulation of biological materials in synthetic biology to create new substances. If this seems strange, so too did it seem strange when chemical engineers began doing the same thing during the 1880s.

A steady flow of digital innovations runs from smartphones and tablets to novel robots for factories and warehouses to self-driving cars and *Jeopardy!* champion supercomputers. These are not gimmicks or toys. They demonstrate a fundamental improvement in machine capabilities and are being deployed to business benefit. For the first time in history, computers have learned to understand and produce human speech, accurately answer questions by combing through a large base of unstructured information, recognize objects, and map the contours and contents of a room. All of these are valuable skills, and all will be put to good use. None of the advances was possible even a decade ago.

Just like those in earlier revolutions, the ideas and new tools that accompany this revolution will invite countless complementary innovations in skills, business processes, organizations, laws, and governing institutions. These co-inventions, some large, some small, may take decades to unfold.

More Powerful Networks

The second industrial revolution was very much about organizations, like the creation of large corporations for mass production. In the 20th-century world economy, railroads and highways brought supplies to factories and took the products away, sometimes to a handful of key ports. The cities grew up around the ports, railroads, and highways.

The centralized approach extended to common public conceptions of how to manage an economy. Central government sprinklers—

fiscal and monetary—were to be turned up or down in order to manipulate the scale of consumer demand. The political parties mainly just differed about which sprinkler to use, and when.

The second economic revolution spawned big companies and big government institutions. Society became much more centralized, with more complex hierarchies.

But the essence of a networked design is different from the essence of a centralized design. This third economic revolution, using network power, pushes toward decentralization and flatter structures.[20]

HIERARCHY

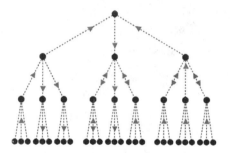

NETWORK

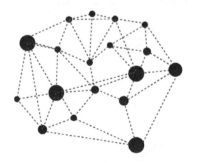

A networked design offers more flexible structures for participation. There are more openings to choose how, when, and where education happens or work gets done. That is why, even back in 1987, a farsighted group of scholars could already declare, "If our predictions are correct, we should not expect the electronically interconnected world of tomorrow to be simply a faster and more efficient version of the world we know today." Instead, in a more networked world, "[w]e should expect fundamental changes in how firms and markets organize the flow of goods and services in our economy."[21]

The Emergence of Digital Platforms. Digital platforms date back to the early days of the web. Some sites chose traditional resale, while others, like eBay, became platforms to connect buyers and sellers. Earlier systems were just better ways to do two-way communication. Today many platform-based organizations operate in a new way.

The Harvard Business School researcher Andrei Hagiu highlights the difference between a *reseller* and a *multisided platform*. A reseller is a commercial entity that simply buys products from a supplier, adds value in some way, and then resells these products at a markup. A true multisided platform creates a completely new marketplace for buyers, sellers, and even third parties (e.g., advertisers) to connect and transact.[22]

Airbnb, for example, coordinates the allocation of tens of thousands of rooms and apartments across people in need of somewhere to stay. Uber, Lyft, Sidecar, and RelayRides have all emerged as coordination systems to connect vehicles with people in need of transport.

Our emphasis in this chapter, though, is on how the rising use of platforms can help Americans overcome the mismatches that now limit their mobility to join, start, or grow a business.

Aaron Levie, founder and CEO of Box, a cloud data storage company (and itself a disruptive new business), has put it well: "Uber is a $3.5 billion lesson in building for how the world *should* work instead of optimizing for how the world *does* work." Since Levie wrote that in August 2013, the lesson has grown in value; the most recent investment in Uber (by Goldman Sachs) valued Uber at more than $40 billion.[23]

In most cities it is difficult, if not impossible, to call a cab or feel confident about when it will arrive. What the new smartphone-enabled car dispatch services realized was that when both drivers and passengers are equipped with GPS-enabled phones, it is possible to give potential passengers an easy way to summon a car on demand and give them a precise estimate of how long it will be until their car arrives. Not only that, the applications identify both the driver and the passenger to each other, with name, photo, and a picture of the car and its license plate, and give them a way to communicate in real time by phone or text message. Automatic tracking of distance and time traveled, and stored payment credentials, allow the passenger simply to get out when she or he gets to the destination, because billing happens automatically.

This deep reenvisioning of on-demand transportation has led to inevitable protests by existing taxi businesses, decrying the incursion of new supply into a tightly regulated marketplace. There are indeed serious questions of how this industry ought to be regulated (which we discuss in chapter 9). But there is no question that these services have already transformed and expanded the transportation business as the World Wide Web upended the media and entertainment business.

According to a recent study based on data released by Uber, the number of drivers "has more than doubled every six months for the last two years." Fewer than 1,000 new driver-partners started in January 2013. A total of 162,037 drivers completed four or more trips during December 2014. This number begins to equal the approximately 212,000 licensed taxi and limousine drivers in the country at the end of 2012 (BLS data).[24]

And Uber is still operating in only a small number of markets. For example, it has more than 10,000 drivers available in Boston, versus 1,825 licensed taxis. A larger proportion of the Uber drivers are part-time than is the case for taxi drivers. Still, the numbers are telling. In a related report, Uber's CEO claimed that during 2014 the total value of Uber rides in San Francisco was $500 million, versus the $140 million attributed to the licensed taxi industry.[25] Increased supply has led to increased demand.

From the workers' point of view, one of the great attractions of the platform is the increased control over working hours it affords. Jonathan Hall and Alan Krueger found that most "driver-partners" turn to Uber not out of desperation "but rather because the nature of the work, the flexibility, and the compensation appeals to them." These responses echo a growing demand in American society "for workplace flexibility that favors alternative work schedules, family-oriented leave policies, flextime, and telecommuting arrangements over the standard nine-to-five work schedule in order to support a more family-friendly lifestyle."[26]

Information empowerment also changes the barriers to entry. "Uber's driver-partners are more similar in terms of their age and education to the general workforce than to taxi drivers and chauffeurs." The proportion of women drivers is significantly higher, as is the proportion of drivers who are veterans.[27]

The platforms are already becoming a principal way millions of people look for work. Professionals often use LinkedIn. Mechanical Turk, part of Amazon's Web Services division, is a marketplace in which people can post small jobs, ranging from translating text to transcribing online information to participating in market research studies. Similarly, Elance-oDesk provides a marketplace for more-structured work assignments, resembling work that historically might have gone out through temporary agencies, but cutting the transaction costs.

New platforms can aid small firms looking to connect with outside experts and human resources they would be unable to retain as full staff. There are currently about 10 million freelancers worldwide registered on Elance-oDesk, and the company completed nearly $1 billion in transactions in 2013.[28] These talent marketplaces help both business owners and job seekers.

More Americans are turning toward self-employment. Many small businesses are sole-proprietor firms, and more Americans are looking to digitally enabled freelancing opportunities.[29]

Platforms also help businesses find suppliers. We recounted the story of Matthew and Tanya. The business they created, Maker's Row, is a platform specifically designed to help small producers find the suppliers they need.

IBM and several other large corporations in 2011 launched Supplier Connection, a website where small companies can connect with bigger ones and also compete for large contracts. John Deere, Dell, Facebook, several large banks, and hundreds of big companies have already gotten on board. As of March 2012, nearly a thousand small companies had joined as well. Since its inception, the corporate Buying Members have spent over $2.5 billion with the small businesses that have joined Supplier Connection.

Digital platforms do not eliminate the need for real estate. There are real human beings who need real places to work and interact with colleagues. What the platforms do is enable millions to work from the real estate they already have (like their home or apartment). Others take the concept of a platform and create a physical version of it, an interactive co-working space.

As we look around at all these kinds of platforms, what strikes us above all is their flexibility. They are set up to serve the needs of individual participants.

In the era of mass production, the towering hierarchical structures were the hubs. People worked hard, dressed right, conformed, so they could fit in.

In contrast, the essence of platform power is the openness of the structures, available on demand. The structures work hard, get user-friendly, customize, so they can fit you.

This is an American future that could be less centered on hierarchical institutions, more centered on participatory networks. There are echoes here of an earlier American ideal, from the period of American history that we discussed in chapter 1, before the Civil War, when the ideal was the "self-made" person. That was the model exemplified by people like Abraham Lincoln and Frederick Douglass.

Some of that ethos can return in a 21st-century form. We hope Americans will embrace the culture of the "makers" and the "new artisans." They are using digital tools in creative, complex ways—whether in craft work, specialized manufacturing, or even as medical assistants.

Networks and Platforms Spanning the World. All three economic revolutions have had at least one point in common: they connected people.

- During the first, steamships and railroads connected communities and regions in ways, and at a speed, that had never before been possible.

• The second economic revolution cabled the world together with the telegraph, telephone, radio, and television. Better means of transport built huge supply chains that linked industrial centers with the raw material producers that supplied them and the consumers to whom they sent their finished goods.

• The Internet and web-supported networks of the third economic revolution are now moving information and commerce in still newer ways, connecting buyers and sellers not just in brick-and-mortar stores but also through web-based platforms.

Today's revolution is more borderless than any other. Networked digital commerce may change everyday interactions with other societies on a scale Americans are only beginning to grasp.

Networked Ways to Innovate. Quirky is a design firm, based in New York City and founded by Ben Kaufman, with an online platform that allows many people to collaborate on product designs. It has more than a million people in a design community working on many kinds of consumer products, from vacuum cleaners to snow shovels. The community offers ideas and also helps vet them.

Quirky quickly brings the more promising ideas to market, sold online and through major retailers. Thousands of new ideas come in every week, and the list gets culled down to the dozens that go into production. Inventors whose products are developed get compensated, cash payments totaling about 10 percent of the revenue. Five years in, that revenue is on track to exceed $100 million in 2014.[30]

Major firms see the potential to boost their own in-house inventive talent. As its crowdsourced designs began to reach mainstream commercial success, Quirky partnered with GE, which sees a way to use Quirky's network of innovators to improve its own products.[31]

For example, in November 2014 Quirky, partnering with GE,

announced a product line to demystify a "smart" home and put the costs in reach of everyone. There are inexpensive sensors to detect water leakage, monitor home energy use and room temperatures, and more. All of them are connected through an app, Wink, which is being nationally marketed as a friendly alternative to creepy robot butlers. Quirky also announced that the partners would build a new microfactory in San Francisco to produce low-priced and customized home sensor kits.

In software production, application programming interfaces (APIs) allow one software program to use another so that complex solutions can be built up, like Lego blocks, from simple parts. APIs are important in building up a new Internet of Things (IoT), in which the products themselves will be networked with each other and their environments. As consumer goods like the Nest thermostat system, wearables to check a user's health, and smart vehicles begin to connect and communicate with one another, the world of networked, combined innovations seems likely to grow.

In the digital production of physical objects, made by machines like a 3-D printer, the digital production specifications are so shareable that this too encourages the same kind of openness that is often found across the software development community. The software cooperative GitHub has begun hosting digital designs produced by users interested in sharing.[32]

Google's chief economist, Hal Varian, calls this "combinatorial innovation." As always, new innovations combine components that were older innovations. But when the innovations are digital, and can be recombined at network speed, tens of thousands of smaller individual innovations can combine to build a single smartphone.[33]

Over time, as layer after layer of new innovations recombine with one another, intellectual property becomes increasingly entangled as the number of possible new innovations expands exponentially. Therefore, some cutting-edge producers are wondering whether the existing intellectual property system, based on the patent system founded in the early 1800s for the age of markets and manufactures, is now an aid to innovation or, on balance, a hindrance.

The electric vehicle manufacturer Tesla surprised many when, in mid-2014, its CEO, Elon Musk, dramatically declared that the company would convert all of its many patents to open-source. Tesla and other organizations have begun to recognize that more open innovation can be a powerful tool leading to better outcomes for all of the players in a space. This logic holds true even in some more established industries. Smartphone manufacturers have recently moved toward a moratorium on the messy intellectual property lawsuits that had become such a big part of the industry.[34]

New standards of openness are taking shape. The journal *Pharmaceutical Research* editorialized that this industry-wide shift toward openness could "represent the further crumbling of a 150-year-old-plus paradigm of the large company being the predominant source for developing therapeutics for profit."[35] In addition to data sharing, large firms like Eli Lilly, GSK, Merck, and Pfizer have all begun to apply crowdsourcing concepts to early drug discovery and development.

An ambitious recent study, conducted by McKinsey, tried to estimate just how much economic value could be gained from open data, if combined with advanced analytics. The team came up with remarkable totals: $3.2 trillion to $5.4 trillion *per year.* These large estimated potential gains are based on a study of possible applications of open data in seven sectors: education, transportation, consumer products, electricity, oil and gas, health care, and consumer finance.[36] While estimates like these can only be suggestive, they suggest a lot.

More Localization

Reaching the Limits of Outsourcing for Complex Production. Toward the end of the 20th century, firms embraced the fad of using more and more complex global chains to make products in schemes for clever cost cutting. They tended to underestimate what was involved in the physical assembly of objects and did not grasp some of the differences between some low-skill mass production processes and other kinds of more specialized production. Nor did they fully understand the intimate relationship between R&D and the production process.

"For years," Charles Fishman has explained, "too many American companies have treated the actual manufacturing of their products as incidental—a generic, interchangeable, relatively low-value part of their business. If you spec'd the item closely enough—if you created a good design, and your drawings had precision; if you hired a cheap factory and inspected for quality—who cared what language the factory workers spoke?"[37]

Fishman then recounted the experience that GE had when it insourced an innovative water heater, the GeoSpring, from China. As GE got ready to make the GeoSpring at a plant in Kentucky, the company discovered numerous problems with the way the older version of the water heater had been assembled. GE decided that, to remake the machine, it had to redesign it.

The rework process for the GeoSpring brought in staff from marketing and sales. Their input turned out to be important in getting a good design. The rework also included line workers who would have to build the thing.

The process worked. It ended up not only improving the quality of the Kentucky-made product; it even brought down the retail price by nearly 20 percent. GE made similar discoveries and innovations when it in-sourced other appliances, like refrigerators.

Innovation consists mainly of incremental problem solving by the people living with the problems. GE rediscovered, as its head of appliance design put it, that when the actual manufacturing part went away, "your whole business goes with the outsourcing." Or listen to the longtime leader of a remarkably durable and successful American steel company, Nucor, Dan DiMicco, who learned that "if the United States doesn't make what it innovates, soon enough we'll lose our ability to innovate too."[38]

What Nucor knows and GE rediscovered are lessons that other American producers have also rediscovered, including significant new companies like American Giant, based in San Francisco and producing well-made clothes in the Carolinas; or Cree, based in Durham, North Carolina, and becoming the leading consumer brand for LED bulbs; or Warby Parker, based in New York City and a growing force in the marketplace for eyewear. They are rediscovering that the best complex production efforts need a very strong core, and that large benefits flow from centering that core in the United States.[39]

So far, American Giant sells only online. Its clothes routinely sell out, and its sales have reportedly tripled each year since the company was launched, in 2012. On the surface the reason is simple: people like the quality and the price. Although it is assumed that making clothes is low-quality work, American Giant's chief executive, Bayard Winthrop, found that when he tried to mass-produce to their careful design specifications overseas, the company's "ability to control the quality was really crappy."[40]

Putting that point a bit differently, an economist, Michael Kremer, wrote decades ago about an O-ring theory. His O-ring metaphor refers to the tragic 1986 loss of the space shuttle *Challenger* with its crew of astronauts. The accident happened because one tiny component failed among thousands, a component known as an O-ring.

Kremer's point was that in a complex production process, quality and skills are intertwined in ways not captured by simple unit labor cost analysis. One small mistake can ruin the value of everything else.

The model does not just mean that investing in skills can yield valuable returns (though it can mean that). The deeper point is that if a company is producing a complex product, it needs to concentrate and maintain reliably high skills across a tightly connected team of many role players.[41]

Stories like that of GE's water heater are little illustrations of Kremer's O-ring theory. The Boeing Company learned the lesson on a much larger scale.

In the early 2000s Boeing developed a visionary design for a new kind of commercial aircraft: the 787 Dreamliner. The aircraft incorporated many innovations, including the wide use of carbon fiber and other novel materials. Not long after this design was announced in 2003, the potential of such a remarkable new aircraft attracted a long order list of buyers. But the aircraft still had to be built.

Boeing combined its innovative design with an unconventional global value chain to produce it. A typical Boeing production pattern, as with the 737, outsourced 35–50 percent. The 787 production plan would outsource 70 percent. Rather than a central hub-and-spoke supply chain for assembly near Seattle, Boeing created about 50 production hubs, "tier-1 strategic partners," responsible for various portions of the assembly (wing, engine, etc.); only the final assembly would occur near Seattle. Boeing announced that this process would cut production time and cut production cost.

In 2001 one of Boeing's top engineers, John Hart-Smith, wrote a prescient internal paper, warning that Boeing would outsource the profits along with the production and risked grave cost overruns and quality breakdowns. Citing the history of why the once-renowned Douglas Aircraft Company (for which he had worked) had collapsed, and without commenting directly on the 787 project, Hart-Smith pointed out that highly complex production processes needed very strong core organization to make constant and well-coordinated production adjustments.

Hart-Smith added that there were longer-term capabilities that needed to be maintained in the core: not only research, but also the ability to provide knowledgeable product services that would be a major long-term source of profits for the company. Toward the end of his paper, he tartly told the company, "[L]isten *more* to your own employees about how to save cost than to any outside business consultants who have never run a factory producing your kind of product."

Hart-Smith also warned that if, for a time, there was not enough work to maintain the core capabilities, the company should "find work to fill excess capacity; . . . not close it down or sell it off to boost RONA [return on net assets, a standard criterion for port-folio investors]. . . . Otherwise, irreplaceable critical skills will be lost and it will not be possible to deliver even core products." That was written in 2001.

By 2007 Boeing had begun encountering its first major delays and quality issues with the 787 project. The plane did not take off on schedule. Its unionized and highly skilled workforce, furious that it had not been consulted on the 787 plan, went on strike in 2008, creating further delays and costs.

The hoped-for cost savings disappeared. Then the situation got worse. No time was saved. The production cost a colossal $12 to $18 billion more than expected. Quality issues dogged the bril-liant design for years.

All the top Boeing executives involved in the original 787 pro-duction choices were gone by the time the plane finally flew. Nor could investors have been pleased: Boeing's stock value sank, and it took six years for the stock to recover the nominal share price it had in 2007.

It was a hard lesson, but Boeing's new leadership learned it. In 2013 Boeing announced its plans for the next version of its 777 airliner, the 777X. There had been particular problems with the Japanese-made wings in the 787. For the 777X all that construc-tion was moved to Washington State. Many other shifts had been made in the way the aircraft was being produced.

Boeing worked closely with the union in devising the plans to produce the 777X. It invested in a new factory and new worker training, preparing Boeing workers to deal with the new kinds of advanced composites being used. The CEO of Boeing Com-mercial Airplanes talked of putting "our workforce on the cutting edge of composite technology." The union president spoke of the Pacific Northwest's becoming a "home to the jobs and technology of tomorrow."

Perhaps most interesting of all, the foreign buyers also had something to say. They said, We want to buy this airplane! Reassured and pleased with the Boeing plans, they lined up to buy the 777X. Huge orders have been placed for the aircraft, while large orders for Airbus planes—plagued with quality issues of their own—were canceled.

The CEO of Boeing Commercial Airplanes previewed the company's new outlook in a 2011 speech to a packed auditorium. Reflecting on the 787 experience, he said, "We spent a lot more money in trying to recover than we ever would have spent if we'd tried to keep the key technologies closer to home." The company still believed in networked production. But Boeing had learned its lesson: "We need to bring it back to a more prudent level."[42]

The Boeing example is not an isolated one. American companies that try to combine complex production with innovation more and more keep R&D integrated with production in their core operations.[43]

Dow Chemical is a very global company. Most of its sales are to foreign buyers. It uses complex global value chains. Its CEO, Andrew Liveris, is an Australian immigrant to America. He and his company are based in Midland, Michigan.

Liveris stresses that American firms are well positioned to support growing global demands for advanced products. Firms like his are taking advantage of huge price advantages in key inputs like shale-produced natural gas.

To Liveris, centering production in the United States also centers innovation in America. Dow recently brought a significant part of its production of lithium-ion batteries back to Michigan, resetting roles in a joint production arrangement with French and South Korean partners.

But Liveris worries. He worries about the outdated cultural image that got Americans "used to thinking about manufacturing jobs as a caricature of what [they were] decades ago: jobs that required relatively little skill and even less critical thinking."

He also worries about support for R&D in the United States,

especially among private investors cutting up companies for short-term gain. Although the company was doing well, Dow narrowly escaped being broken up in 2006 in a proposed sale to private equity investors. Pressure from investors during the financial crisis also nearly derailed a critical purchase of another chemicals firm, Rohm and Haas.

Liveris is optimistic about the American people. "We are recognizing that joblessness is a crisis. If we ring the alarm bell, we can move to the solution stage."[44]

One effect of the digital revolution is that production networks are becoming more advanced. Our argument is that as Americans seek to hold and enlarge their position as a leader in complex high-value products, this trend can reward more localized production centered in America.

The United States also has another fundamental asset. Not only is it the world's largest market; it is the core of an increasingly integrated market for all of North America. This is a continent-size base for global competition.

Less Tethered to Faraway Resources. As Dow Chemical's chief noted, American producers now have greater advantages in their access to resources, like the natural gas his company uses as a feedstock. The inhabitants of the United States have long been accustomed to abundant resources.

Yet the country's natural geological endowments are not especially superior to those that could be found in other large countries or regions. What the United States did master, perhaps better than any other country, was the application of capital-intensive techniques to the exploitation of its available resources. This American abundance was not really "natural." It was engineered.

Historically, this engineered abundance has been a story of the kind of private-public alliances we emphasized in chapter 1.

- Few Americans have heard of the U.S. Geological Survey, an agency established in 1879. This agency was vital, the principal scout that located mineral deposits for private exploitation.

• In the petroleum industry, the federal government's breakup of the Standard Oil trust opened the way to about twenty large, vertically integrated firms surrounded by hundreds of niche operators. The leading firms worked closely with one another, the U.S. government, and the Texas state government to manage production, prices, and markets. After New Deal attempts to manage oil production and pricing at the federal level were overturned by the Supreme Court, American petroleum producers used a complex system of private-public coordination that relied on state regulators, like those in Texas, and looked to the federal government to help facilitate international partnerships.[45]

Private capital also played an enormous role in the past age of American resource abundance. The capital did not come in because the resources were easy to get. In railroads, then mining, American firms leveraged their own and foreign (often British) capital in technology-intensive efforts to extract resources from nearly inaccessible wilderness, much of it in the American West. Rather than cheap resources being a disincentive for technical investment, the investment created the cheap resources.

As a result of such efforts, by the beginning of the 20th century the United States had become the world's preeminent industrial power. This rise rested on minerals like copper, coal, zinc, iron ore, and lead. Less important than having a lot of one or two of these minerals was the value of having ready and affordable access to so many of them. Later in the 20th century petroleum and natural gas joined the list of America's growing resources, after historic new discoveries and exploitations of these resources in Texas, California, and Oklahoma.[46]

But these earlier foundations of American industrial success began eroding during the middle of the 20th century. One mineral after another passed into the net import column. In the early 1970s the United States began relying on net imports of oil. Severe jolts in energy prices started during the 1970s and continue to the present.

There is not much doubt about the role that this engineered abundance of natural resources played in the golden age of American industrial success. Nor is there much doubt that, in energy alone, the era of net imports imposed significant cost shocks on the American economy. For decades these costs have been perhaps the single largest contributor to America's current account deficit in world trade. Those deficits, in turn, helped build up the destabilizing imbalances in global capital markets that were such a key factor in causing the great global recession that began in 2007.

Americans want to be less dependent on faraway raw materials. They would like cheap energy close to home and to high-energy industries, like chemicals and agriculture. They would like their resources, including food, produced in an ecologically sustainable way.

The trend that favors Americans today is a swing back toward more of this kind of autonomy. The United States is already becoming self-sufficient in energy. Inexpensive natural gas is providing a valuable advantage in many industries. If the United States can join forces effectively with Mexico and Canada, North America could become a continental energy powerhouse.[47]

The production of energy is also becoming more networked, enlisting many individual producers who may be contributing to a larger grid from the solar panel on their roof. Natural gas may be produced by new kinds of local fuel cells. Consider the figure below, from a February 2014 publication of General Electric, contrasting the preindustrial world of electricity production with the centralized industrial approach that dominated in the 20th century and with the more networked and distributed potential emerging now.

Phases in Energy Production

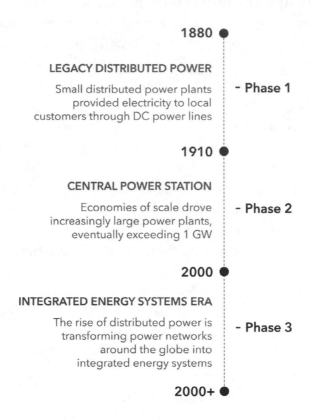

1880 ●

LEGACY DISTRIBUTED POWER

Small distributed power plants
provided electricity to local
customers through DC power lines

— Phase 1

1910 ●

CENTRAL POWER STATION

Economies of scale drove
increasingly large power plants,
eventually exceeding 1 GW

— Phase 2

2000 ●

INTEGRATED ENERGY SYSTEMS ERA

The rise of distributed power is
transforming power networks
around the globe into
integrated energy systems

— Phase 3

2000+ ●

Today's networks of "distributed" energy production are actually approaching cost parity with more traditional, centralized models. This could become the dominant model of energy production over the next couple of decades.[48]

Big data, ubiquitous sensors, and improved analytics are creating a new paradigm of resource sustainability. "[N]etworks can help to transform the productivity of resource systems, creating smarter electricity grids, supporting more intelligent building, and enabling 3D and 4D seismic technology for energy exploration," a McKinsey team concluded. The impact could be decisive: productivity improvements using available technology could "address more than 80 percent of expected growth in demand for energy, 60 percent of anticipated growth in demand for water"—a total value of at least about $3 trillion.[49] Some scholars go further, believing that resource productivity breakthroughs could drive a broad long-term economic growth cycle.

One of the members of our initiative to rework America is Mike McCloskey, chairman of Fair Oaks Farms and co-founder and CEO of Select Milk Producers, one of the largest milk cooperatives in the country. Based in northwest Indiana, he has already demonstrated, at scale in a large dairy and pork farming co-op operation, the possibility for deep changes in sustainable energy productivity in one sector—agriculture. His dairy cows produce the natural gas that power his trucks and the fertilizer that grows much of their feed. His operation is ecologically sustainable and uses many well-paid skilled employees.

The rise of such a "circular economy," another McKinsey team explained, is also providing "an alternative to the 'take-make-dispose' business model for the use of materials in manufacturing."

Mike McCloskey at his farm in Fair Oaks, Indiana.

The team called attention to rising opportunities for recycling, or "refurbishment," in products made from steel.[50]

An entirely new generation of materials may be emerging. Some of them, like carbon fiber or even more-advanced nano-materials like graphene, may take some of the place of materials like steel or silicon, respectively. Other materials may be synthesized biologically, taking advantage of developments in biotechnology.[51]

All of these developments can help local communities become more autonomous in their relationships to natural resources. This can happen even as the communities are becoming even more networked in their commerce.

Growing Local—More Producers in America. Most people intuitively accept the reality that commerce is getting more global. What they may not see so clearly, though, are the broad forces that, at the same time, are also making commerce more *local*.

Customers want products to be more customized to their needs. Machines and humans can complement each other in novel ways. Together they can actually lead a renaissance: of artisanal culture, tailored products, and personalized service. Once a luxury available only to the wealthy, this level of service can become the new average. And it definitely could be labor-intensive, with millions employed at a different level of customer service.

Liam Casey built a business on outsourcing; now his firm, PCH International, is incubating hardware start-ups in America. For contemporary high-value products, low-cost labor is not the key factor. "It's more important," Casey explained, "that producer and customer are close to each other."[52]

Industries see evidence of all this customization in the creation of many more products. A distinct product usually has its own stock-keeping unit, or SKU, shown on its bar code. The number of products is multiplying so fast that "the proliferation of retail SKUs . . . has challenged suppliers in advanced economies and is spreading to emerging markets as consumer preferences evolve."[53]

There are more niche products. There are products from every corner of the world.

Think about this problem from industry's perspective. Rather than maintain colossal inventories of hundreds of different products or models centrally, there are now very large incentives for companies to push as much of the production process as they can outward, toward the market.

The growing size of the world economy has also put older forms of transportation, like shipping, under strain. Costs and bottlenecks in traditional transportation are increasing the incentives to bring production closer to the end market. Major producers like IKEA and Emerson have been moving to regional manufacturing solutions to solve transportation problems.[54]

The major producers will be pressured to do even more of this if smaller producers can get the know-how and capital they need to take advantage of the lower barriers to entry. We discuss these opportunities in other chapters. If smaller-scale producers can acquire the people, know-how, and capital to take advantage of the lower barriers to starting up a business, they will be able to become more vigorous competitors in offering locally produced and customized products or services.

More Individual Empowerment

Big Data and Tools to Use It. The networked economy and the digital revolution add brain power, not brute power. We can sense more things about our environment. We can convert all this new input to a digital form. It becomes data.

In the 21st century data has become a central resource. It is the energy of the digital revolution. As with "natural" resources, access to data is also engineered.

Everyone constantly produces data. It flows from and informs the applications we use. It personalizes our Internet experience. It connects us to others. Soon many of the objects around us will be producing data too. One estimate projects that by 2020 there will be about 26 billion connected devices—an average of 3.3 devices for every person on the planet.[55]

In the overwhelming majority of the U.S. economy's sectors, a company with more than 1,000 employees stores, on average, 235 terabytes of data (more than is stored in the texts of all the books in the Library of Congress).[56] "Big data" is defined primarily by its volume, complexity, and diversity. It is generally produced faster than it can be analyzed. It requires significant computing resources to store and process it.

Open data is that part of big data that is being distributed beyond the usual proprietary walls of the data collectors. Government data, science data, and shared corporate data are three of the most important types. It is "publicly available data that can be universally and readily accessed, used, and redistributed free of charge."[57]

Over one million datasets appear to have been made open.[58] The United States has been a leader in the open data movement. Following a 2009 initiative of President Obama, data.gov, the central open data hub for the U.S. government, houses some 100,000 datasets, downloadable in various formats. Many government-led open data initiatives have become more important following the signing of the G8 Open Data Charter in 2013, which outlined principles of open data programs to be adopted by member (and potentially other) countries.[59]

A sea of what might have once been considered meaningless information is yielding new insights and a better understanding of our world. As the *Economist* recently put it, open data is a potential "gold mine."[60]

Entrepreneurs are using this resource to build new businesses. For example, Zillow combines data from sources like the Bureau of Labor Statistics, the Federal Housing Finance Agency, and the Census Bureau to display neighborhood home and rental values to help consumers make better decisions on housing. Commuter apps like NextBus use metropolitan transportation data to tell commuters when they can expect the next bus to arrive.

Scholarly research data is also opening up, with a bit of prodding from government funders and activists. In fields like genomics and neuroscience, researchers have started sharing science data through the use of cloud applications (such as the Open Science Data Cloud, the Open Science Grid, Amazon's public cloud, and the Internet Archive).[61] One of the biggest initiatives underway is the Global Alliance for Genomics and Health—"an international coalition of over 140 member organizations dedicated to improving human health by maximizing the potential of genomic medicine" by accelerating the sharing of genomic and clinical data. It is supported by the Broad Institute of Harvard and MIT.[62]

Almost every sector of the economy is being transformed by the use of complex algorithms to apply these data resources.

Just what is an algorithm? Basically an algorithm is a set of step-by-step instructions. It is a recipe "that leads its user to a particular answer or output based on the information at hand."[63] Applying its recipe, an algorithm can take input data and categorize it to produce a prediction, a characterization, or an inferred attribute. Computers are able to go through very complex algorithms and huge inputs in microseconds. The Watson computer that won *Jeopardy!* used more than 100 algorithms with a total of over 6 million logic rules.[64]

Some of the most exciting, state-of-the-art algorithms can "learn" from data rather than just follow preordained instructions. Machine-learning algorithms ingest training data— datasets of past events with known outcomes—to refine their recipes.

An algorithm can unwittingly reflect discrimination, bias, and unfairness. Algorithms have become standard tools in making decisions about hiring, insurance, and credit—three key economic opportunities.[65]

Yet big data and the analytic capabilities that have accompanied it offer huge benefits to consumer-facing businesses. They can reduce fraud and protect consumers.[66] The design of the algorithms can also open opportunities to people who might not otherwise have them and counteract bias.

Apple and Humana recently partnered to allow the insurance company to access health data stored in HealthKit, Apple's clearinghouse for data from health apps on Apple devices.[67] Humana is planning to offer discounts to members who can show healthy lifestyle patterns on the basis of data obtained through the arrangement. The data may also help the insurance company refine its algorithms, yielding further insights that could point consumers to healthier habits.

Apple has carefully built a high level of transparency into the HealthKit system, providing users with very granular controls over their health information. Users have to specifically give each app permission to access each sensitive data element, and Apple prohibits app developers from redisclosing the data. In the world of big data analytics, these features give consumers transparency into, and control over, a critical ingredient—the collection and compilation of the data that feeds the process.

The Apple example, and experience with laws to govern credit reporting, yields a powerful principle for policy: transparency. In the Apple case the individual is voluntarily contributing data to an assessment process. The principle is to make sure the contribution is knowing, as well as voluntary.

As algorithms are used to make more and more decisions that affect human beings, as humanity is distilled into inputs for the algorithms, governments will face another new task: to set standards for judging the algorithms.

Digital Production. Another reason this historical moment is so pivotal is that it is getting much easier to decentralize and distribute the production process, as that process becomes more digitized. Computer-aided design (CAD) software, for example, can drive the design process. CNC (for computer numerical control) has been integrated into a vast spectrum of intermediary cutting, drilling, and machining processes, greatly increasing precision and overall efficiency.

At the frontiers of digital production, the emergence of early 3-D printing (a more technical term is "additive manufacturing") allows a user to simply upload the digital specifications for an object to be rendered in physical form. The producers can analyze the design and specs before the item is physically created. Much of the expensive trial and error can be eliminated. Armchair hackers and open-source creators can get involved in manufacturing too.

No supply chain is tougher to solve than that involved in getting replacement parts for your vehicle—if it happens to be in outer space. It is hard to keep everything needed in inventory out there. And it is even harder to build a parts factory in outer space.

At least it was even harder until Aaron Kemmer, Jason Dunn, and Mike Chen co-founded a small firm, Made In Space, that has built 3-D printers for zero-gravity production of parts in outer space. One of its printers has already been placed in orbit on the International Space Station.

One of the printer's interesting design problems was that the machine had to filter out the minute amounts of toxic gasses emitted in the production process, amounts that would have been safely ignored on earth. To solve that problem, the company developed a filter so efficient that it can also, by itself, purify a room on earth. "We're actually in talks with other manufacturers about spinning that off," one of the engineers commented, "doing crazy things that even if you fail to meet your goal, you could revolutionize another industry."[68]

Here on earth, Shapeways is an online marketplace for goods that initially exist only in digital form. The site allows users to browse thousands of software files for everything from jewelry to specialized hardware. It manufactures, or "prints," and ships items after they have been ordered. Objects are printed in a variety of materials including porcelain. Since its foundation in 2007, Shapeways has sold millions of customized designer-created items.[69]

The cost of production using 3-D printing technologies does not necessarily rise with complexity. Many of the most popular items in Shapeways' online store would be impossible to produce at all with more traditional manufacturing methods.

Another firm, Bespoke Innovations, based in San Francisco, produces—"prints"—personalized prosthetics for people who have lost limbs. Many of its clients are injured combat veterans. Through 3-D design innovation, the company enhances the prosthetic with patterns and materials so that it looks like a real limb, including the look that a prosthetic wearer wants, customized with leather, chrome, and even tattoos.

At the research level promising work is underway in the use of 3-D printing to produce custom pharmaceuticals,[70] and even printing of working organs for the human body, using stem cells. On a much larger scale, there are innovations like the Kamer-Maker, a 20-foot-tall 3-D printer, which was developed by a Dutch architecture firm to fabricate rooms that can be assembled to form an entire house.[71] As an industry that has been shielded from some of the mindset of the mass production era, the construction trades may be a particularly promising sector to explore new ways to produce the customized products people may want.

In America the "maker movement" has been gaining momentum for several years. Matthew and Tanya are a part of it. There are more "hackerspaces" and "makerspaces," community-run spots for people that broaden participation in physical and digital production.

America is shifting toward customization of consumer products. "The scales haven't tipped yet," John Hagel, John Seely Brown, and Duleesha Kulasooriya observe. "While alternatives exist to almost any mass-produced item, most US consumers haven't yet explored the full range of possibilities." Some observers find it tempting to "dismiss the maker trend as a fad" since many at large firms "are mostly unaware of the platforms and tools makers are using."

But Hagel, Brown, and Kulasooriya conclude that this trend does foreshadow "the economic landscape to come." Soon, they believe, "multitudes of niche products collectively [will] take market share away from generic incumbent products. . . . Some areas will fragment into smaller and smaller entities, while other areas will consolidate, and only a few, large-scale entities will survive."[72]

Like the cultural movements promoting "local" and "slow," the maker movement celebrates the culture of production. It sees that culture as part of a broader community spirit. That spirit is alive in communities all over America.

The Out-of-Date "Leading Indicators" of the American Economy

When Americans wonder how their economy is doing, when people in every nation in the world wonder how their economy is doing, the first number they usually turn to is a measure of gross domestic product, GDP. It is the standard measure of economic growth, the standard telltale of a recession.

The whole notion that there is a thing called an "economy" whose performance can be measured in this way is a relatively new idea. The idea grew logically out of the era of mass production. GDP is a measurement devised during the late 1930s and 1940s, significantly refined and made an international standard during the 1950s and 1960s.

A principal inventor of the modern form of such statistics was an American economist named Simon Kuznets, who had grown up in the Russian empire, survived the revolution and civil war, and come to America as a young man. In less than five years he earned a PhD at Columbia and began working on the systematic collection of economic data at a then new and obscure private nonprofit, the National Bureau of Economic Research. A progressive U.S. senator noticed this work. The legislation he sponsored required the U.S. government's Commerce Department to prepare regular estimates of national income.[73]

The calculation of GDP is very complex. Its assumptions are opaque to all but a few professionals. But, at its core, it measures outputs and inputs. Outputs: How many things did you make, worth how much (usually on the basis of their market price)? This is measured by total money spent, counted by, for instance, asking companies about their car sales.

The total spending is then roughly equated with the amount that was produced. In the case of government, it is basically treated as a big consumer buying goods and services, which are valued at what the government spent for them. Then the statisticians examine how much it appears to have cost in order to produce this output.

If there is more spending—quantity + value = output—that is more growth. If it costs less to produce it, that is more productivity.

This metric is a great fit for the mass production paradigm of an economy. A hundred cars rolling off the line priced at $10,000 apiece = a million dollars of output. Cut production costs for the million dollars of output = productivity grows. More consumer demand for cars = more output = more growth.

This measure was an advance on what came before, which was little accurate measurement at all. The measures have always had some significant limitations, as their designers knew. A recent chronicler explains, "Kuznets and his cohort understood full well . . . that it was imperative that anyone using these numbers recognize the limitations. But as the numbers became touchstones of public policy and media reference points, those subtleties were lost."[74]

The lost subtleties are no longer subtle. The shift from the mass production era to a different economic system is making the dominant indicators not only obsolescent but actually misleading. A few examples follow.

The "Free" Problem. In standard national accounting, what is free has no economic weight. Consumers now have access to millions of free goods and services on the Internet, from apps to videos. But goods with zero price contribute zero to the GDP statistics.[75] Productivity statistics are calculated directly from the GDP numbers, so if we undercount in the latter, we will underestimate in the former number as well.

The "Digital" Problem. When music moved from CDs and records into digital rentals, more people were listening to more music. Yet it seemed to disappear from the economy. "Music is hiding itself from our traditional economic statistics."[76] Many intangibles in digital commerce defy traditional measurement. "A measure of the national economy designed for tangible, physical products only is not really a good measure of an increasingly weightless economy."[77]

The "Services" Problem. The original accounts always had trouble measuring services. For example, from the start the system excluded housework as unquantifiable. If you receive a service like education, it is only valued at the salary of the teacher or a tuition bill, if there is one. Commercial services are valued at market price; public services are valued at cost; unpaid services are not valued at all. The only rationale for this was "practical convenience."[78]

If more excellent education was free, the accounts would show an economic decline. Financial services on the other hand, seem like a huge contributor to the economy if much money appears to be spent on them. But what if, as in the Great Recession, some financial services are literally counterproductive, even ruinous—should they be counted as a cost or as a net drag?

Such problems in measuring services could be met with a shrug when most of the economy was in goods. Now most of the economy is in services.

The "Quality" Problem. If your house gets electricity, and you replace expensive, smoky tallow candles with light bulbs, you light up your life and save money. In the accounts the economy shows a decline.[79] If computing power is a hundred times faster at half the cost, the standard accounts show an economic decline. This problem has become so glaring that "hedonic values" were invented for GDP calculations in order to doctor the nominal prices of some products, although this construct cannot keep up.

The "Import/Export" Problem. For accounting, the iPhone has to be classified either as an import or as an export. Because the final assembly occurs in China, it is classified as an import from China, and the import is valued at the total market price. On the other hand, Walmart counts televisions manufactured by Element Electronics as "Made in the USA" for marketing purposes. Yet the only U.S. content in these televisions is a quality inspection and a memory card.

The words like "import" and "export" fit how the old mass production system imagined "trade." But both the iPhone and the Element TV were made by a networked system, not a national producer.

Only a small percent of the manufacturing value of the iPhone was contributed by China. The principal value contributors to the supply chain are countries like Japan, Germany, and South Korea, followed by many others, including American suppliers. Then there are the issues of how to value design and software, each with multinational supply chains of their own. The U.S. government and our culture have neither the right measurement tools nor the right language for the emerging new global economy.

The existing accounting systems—codified mainly in the 1950s—frame the view we described earlier in this chapter, the macroeconomic filter that affects so much of what Americans hear about their economy, about the supposed regular cycles in its progress, and its current dismal prospects. Frame the problem as mass output. Measure it in mass consumption. The agenda will become an agenda of juicing up "aggregate consumer demand."

The mass production mindset extends well beyond macroeconomics. Take universities: like the GDP metrics, the well-known *U.S. News and World Report* rankings give great weight to total spending, per student. Universities that educate more, but spend less, are therefore *penalized* by the rankings. They are strongly incentivized *not* to do this.

Or consider health care. The mass production paradigm concentrates on output: services rendered, money spent. If a hospital wants more Medicare money, it needs to perform more medical procedures or treat more patients, and cut its own costs to do it. It is the mass production paradigm. It would not, for instance, necessarily encourage hospitals to invest in the skills of nurses or paraprofessionals, empowering them with more technology, unless that produced more billable procedures.

Measurement is required to manage. Conventional GDP measures do not capture a large part of the digital economy. Many experts, like those in the Commerce Department's Bureau of Economic Analysis, are all too familiar with these weaknesses. Congress should provide both the funding and the mandate to fix them, organizing a major effort to reevaluate the leading indicators of economic performance in this 21st-century world. One of the options for improvement would be to use new synthetic means to measure employment, trade, and other parts of the economy by using real-time event and transaction data from the underlying Internet-based high-scale platforms.

Seeing how much of the old system is an artifact of an age that is passing makes it easier to see ways to design anew. Then we can do what Americans of past generations did so well. We can set the table for a conversation about how Americans can get their country back on track for a promising future.

Chapter 3

Connect to a World of Buyers

Imagine a town in the countryside. It used to be home to a polluting food processing plant. That is over now. Instead, today more than half of the 3,000 residents make their living in online retailing. Most of them sell clothes made in nearby factories, generating millions of dollars of revenues.

The local government helps. It offers free wireless Internet to residents. It gives the residents space to store their inventories. It has opened a school to teach the art of online selling.

The story is true. The town is in China, in southern Guangdong Province. There are reported to be already twenty more towns like it. They are called Taobao villages, after the name of the giant online retailer that millions of Chinese now rely on for much of their shopping.[1]

Driven by necessity, China is using digital commerce to connect its citizens to their vast market.

Driven by opportunity, Americans can do the same. But Americans should aim at connecting their citizens to an even larger market: the whole world.

Conditioned by the experience of the last 40 years, Americans tend to have negative reactions to terms like "globalization."

They equate it to "jobs going out." This equation has some basis in reality. Too many workers and their families have experienced pressures, not prosperity, as the world economy has expanded and connected.

But past need not be prologue. We see a different world ahead. It is not a guaranteed future. But it is attainable. More Americans may be able to find good work by connecting to a dynamic global economy.

A surge of upwardly mobile consumers around the world will want things that American producers are well positioned to provide. There will still be plenty of competition from foreign workers. But those foreign workers could more and more become consumers of the kind of products and services that Americans can provide.

The U.S. National Intelligence Council forecasted that, by 2030, "[t]he growth of the global middle class constitutes a tectonic shift: for the first time, a majority of the world's population will not be impoverished, and the middle classes will be the most important social and economic sector in the vast majority of countries around the world."

The potential marketplace is so large that it is difficult to grasp or measure. Assume that about a billion people today have middle-class buying power, a purchasing power equivalent to what an American could buy with at least the ability to spend $10–$50 per day. Even the most conservative estimates see that number at least doubling by 2030, if not tripling. The spending power of middle-class consumers in emerging markets is forecast to rise by $20 trillion over the next decade.

In other words, this is a projected rise in global spending power on a scale significantly larger than the entire present economy of the United States. According to the U.S. Department of Commerce, 95 percent of the potential customers for U.S. goods and services live outside of the United States. Even trade measured in the conventional manner is likely to more than triple by 2030.[2]

To rework America, we must have a strategy that brings this world of buyers right to America's desktops and to its tablets.

- First, given global trends, this global engagement is mandatory. To create more good jobs, Americans should welcome chances to produce for the world's buyers.
- Second, the significance of a *networked* global economy is that terms like "imports" and "exports" can be misleading. Americans have roles to play in global value chains. That can mean more ways to contribute value.
- Third, digital commerce is creating new advantages for all American firms, including smaller ones, even individuals, in selling directly to customers across the world. They can become "micro-multinationals."[3]
- Fourth, online sales of online *services*, in particular, could bring billions of potential new buyers to Americans, including in sectors that people previously thought of as local services.

Welcoming the World's Buyers

Of the ten million jobs created in the slowly reviving American economy during the past five years, about one-third were created by sales to other countries. This occurred mainly from private initiative. There have been no major breakthroughs in trade agreements or other government-sponsored policies to promote trade.

The figure below illustrates another basic fact. In the future, if American producers of goods or services or blends of both are aiming at middle-class buyers, they will have to aim more and more at the rest of the world.[4]

There is good news, though. A networked world may give Americans unprecedented capabilities to reach these global buyers, without either side having to leave their homes.

Shares of Global Middle-Class Consumption

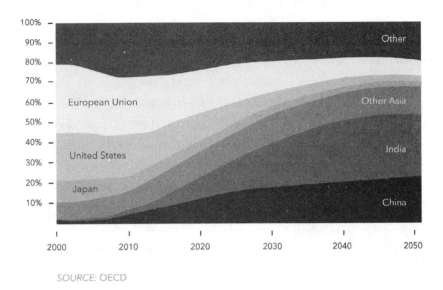

SOURCE: OECD

The Rising Promise of America's Micro-multinationals

Empowered by emerging platforms, small and medium-size companies, even individuals at home, can operate as micro-multinationals. Global engagement is no longer the privilege of large corporations.[5]

In 2012, the year with the most recent data, the United States used online commerce for international deals worth nearly a trillion dollars in sales—more than 6 percent of the entire U.S. GDP. And these sales have been increasing at double-digit annual rates in almost every category. Online international transactions are expected to triple just within the next five years.[6]

Americans are buying in online commerce, not just selling. But the online sales were more than $935 billion and the online purchases only $422 billion. In other words, although the connectivity runs both ways, Americans currently bring in nearly half a trillion dollars more in revenue than they spend outward. This is a very positive balance. So online commerce seems to be an area where, at this time anyway, American firms seem to enjoy a very strong global position as they think about the future.[7]

Large firms play a major role in this commerce right now. But thousands of small and medium-size enterprises are fishing in these waters. Even individual sellers are stepping in.

Sellers on eBay are already testing the possibilities. Practically all commercial sellers on the site, those selling at least $10,000 worth of merchandise a year, sell to buyers around the world as well as in their home country. Among such sellers, the proportion that sell to foreign buyers is an incredible 97 percent.

By contrast, ordinary merchants, not selling through a platform, rarely sell outside their home country. The proportion of ordinary merchants selling internationally is about 5 percent.

With use of the platform, many of the usual costs and burdens vanish.[8] eBay provides the figure reproduced below.[9]

Platforms like eBay, Alibaba, and Amazon are building up

Traditional Trade versus Tech-Enabled Trade

TRADITIONAL	TECH-ENABLED
Sell through a middleman to the customer	**Sell directly to the customer**
3–4 Countries	**19 Countries**
Average size of export market network	Average size of export market network
>5% of Businesses	**90–100% of Businesses**
Using a traditional model exported their products	Use the online marketplace to export commercially
20%–30%	**50%–80%**
New businesses survive the first year	New businesses survive the first year

SOURCE: Data from U.S. sellers who generate annual sales of $10,000

their capabilities as transnational intermediaries. They are making progress on issues like payment systems and ways to connect buyers and sellers.

To date Amazon and eBay have competed in many national markets, especially the United States, but also in a number of other large national markets. During the early 2000s Alibaba and eBay struggled over e-commerce dominance in the Chinese market and Alibaba eventually prevailed. Alibaba's dominance in e-commerce inside China, which is a huge and growing e-commerce market, has now made it one of the largest retail platforms in the world, publicly held in the United States, with a market capitalization of about $250 billion. It now rivals Walmart as one of the two largest retail industry companies in the world.

The e-commerce innovators have still sold mainly within countries. They are taking early steps into transnational e-commerce. In the initial stages the platforms are, in essence, shopping malls for the local affiliates of a foreign firm. Disney might sell its products on Alibaba, for example, just as it would market its products at a Disney Store in a shopping center.

American businesses using e-commerce to sell in China are still, therefore, mainly the firms that know how to set up the local affiliates. One of our recommendations at the end of this chapter will be to build up platforms as effective global intermediaries, so that any American firm can use them as their "foreign affiliate."

A Possible Breakthrough: Intensifying Global Digital Commerce in Services

We start by recalling the following three really large facts about the U.S. economy:

1. Most of the U.S. economy consists of commerce in what are classified as "services."
2. Most services are routinely regarded as local. The usual assumption is that about 63 percent or so of services cannot serve customers in other countries. These are services

traditionally delivered in person, like food service or a haircut.

3. The United States is a producer of high-quality services. That is why, to the extent services have been traded, it routinely runs large surpluses in such trade.

Producers of services that involve communications will find it easier to offer services to anyone, anywhere. A biology teacher in Richmond can offer a class to students in New Delhi. A group of electricians in Nashville might help solve a fire safety problem in a Guangzhou building project. An architect in Minneapolis can manipulate plans on a screen with draftsmen and clients in Guangzhou. These possibilities are so large, but so novel, that they may be hard to grasp.

There were a billion Internet users in 2006; now there are three billion and growing. In 2013, mobile users downloaded an estimated 70 billion apps.

Developed economies like those in the United States and Europe are increasingly dominated by the provision of services. Services do not require costly manufacturing, warehousing, or transport. They are highly customizable. Smartphones can serve as conduits for service provision. Web-based payment systems are getting better at handling international financial transactions. Online platforms, like the ones we just described for selling goods, might also arise to match supply and demand for services in foreign markets.

The portion of digital trade that both originates from an online connection and is *delivered* online was about $300 billion a year in the International Trade Commission study. This was dominated by the early entrants: record companies selling music digitally; software companies; and banks and financial services all sending information online. These are often not face-to-face services that use video links.

The next stage could come as the video links, the telepresence, become more sophisticated and more commonplace. To consider the possibilities, think of engineering as an example of a multinational service. Engineering is big business in the United States, employing almost a million workers in 2007 (well over a million when combined with architectural services and other closely related industries). With average annual wages of about $74,000, engineering service firms pay well.

U.S. engineering and construction companies have valuable expertise that could be more widely exported to developing countries in the building of water and sewage treatment systems, roads, bridges, airports, seaports, railroads, and other types of projects. Two architectural firms, one in St. Louis and another in Baltimore, have been planning a $10 billion city project in India, near Mumbai. It is called Lavasa. They are building a beautiful lakeside, environmentally conscious city from scratch, a city that is expected to have a population of about 200,000 residents. As the first residents move in, the city looks, one observer wrote, as if it had been transplanted from the Italian Riviera. Everything about the design was adapted to the local landscape and climate.[10] The U.S. firms are providing advanced architectural, engineering, and green designs—including the overall master plan—drawing on practices perfected in the United States and being developed now with offices and clients around the world.

Projects on this multibillion-dollar scale are not unusual in Asia. The Songdo International Business District near Seoul, in South Korea, is a $35 billion effort on 1,500 acres of reclaimed waterfront. China's urban population will likely require millions of additional buildings, the equivalent of constructing at least ten New York Cities.[11]

Imagine that these existing undertakings are enhanced by a growing ability to reach clients directly through high-quality video links. In some cases, language barriers may be a problem, although some video can use the universal language of drawing diagrams or showing calculations. Machine translation is already advancing rapidly, and remarkable new translation software and applications are in the pipeline. In millions of other instances, though, video material is already overcoming barriers.

Teachers in America are already reaching hundreds of thousands of pupils across all of Asia, for example, through courses (most of them free of charge) on platforms like Khan Academy, edX, and Coursera. The Berlitz company now offers language education over global networks. Berlitz uses virtual classrooms and teachers coaching students online. It does this 24/7, reaching students in over 70 countries.

Even under existing constraints, many services that can be provided in an office, without physical contact, can be provided in a virtual office. Demonstrating a prototype of a new augmented reality device, the Microsoft HoloLens, a reporter used Skype to make a video call. Then, using the device, he called an electrician who showed him how to install an electric light switch. "I could see the electrician superimposed in my field of view as I worked on the switch; he saw what I saw because of the camera on my HoloLens, and he could draw diagrams in my view that helped guide me along."[12]

Telemedicine and telehealth services are already widely used in the United States, with more than 200 telemedicine networks and 3,500 service sites. The majority of U.S. hospitals now have this capability in some form. According to an industry analyst, Roeen Roashan, the technological barriers are dropping very quickly. The remaining obstacles are more in how to link such services to payment systems, including insurance, and handle the legal issues. Roashan adds, "[W]e're seeing change, a lot of doctors are ambassadors for virtual healthcare, and so patients will adopt."[13]

As an example of how to extend these services to reach the rest of the world, a company called HealthTap allows patients to seek care from tens of thousands of participating U.S. doctors who, collectively, can help in 106 languages. Patients store their medical records with HealthTap, ask questions on an expert network, and arrange consultations. Combined with new medical sensors and remote monitoring services, doctors, nurses, and other medical professionals can get up-to-date information on some aspects of a patient's condition. A new FDA-approved device from AliveCor is a smartphone-enabled heart monitor. A single-lead EKG reader attaches to the back of a smartphone and displays heart rate via an app. Many more such devices are on the way.[14]

Medical equipment and telehealth technologies are already being used to enable robotic surgeries where, in some cases, physicians do not even need to be in the operating room with a patient when the surgery is performed, allowing surgeons to operate out of their "home base." Wearable and digestible sensors, remote monitoring devices, and diagnostic software are transforming the ability to provide care to people in their own homes or thousands of miles away with connectivity and access enabled by the network and mobile devices.

The job creation potential of advances like these can be broad. Such services can involve many kinds of coaches, advisers, tutors, experts, assistants, drafters, artists, and others. In effect, America can look for new ways to engage one of the best and most well-developed service sectors in the world—for the world.

The total impact on job creation is difficult to estimate. But it could be very large. If the global market for digital services expanded even to a modest extent, the numbers of affected jobs could be great.

The potential is especially large in areas like health care and business-to-business services. If just the tradable business services sector alone attained the same foreign sales ratios as are now experienced in manufactured goods (about 20 percent), the resulting addition of $800 billion in sales "would represent about 3 million jobs." These are crude estimates, but enough to hint at the possible scale of opportunity.[15]

The First Obstacle: Mindset

Americans need better bridges to foreign markets. To create many more American jobs, Americans will have to sell more goods and services to foreigners. Yet, for almost all American firms, selling to foreigners still seems hard.

Long content to sell to the large American marketplace, most Americans are not used to looking beyond America for their buyers. That is one reason why exports make up just 14 percent of U.S. GDP. In countries like Great Britain and Germany, the export shares are 32 percent and 50 percent, respectively.[16]

Why do Americans find foreign sales so hard? Nearly half of small-business owners admit that they don't know where to start. When they look harder at it, three complaints usually come up:

- too much regulation and paperwork;
- problems in managing the finances, including shipping costs and transferring payments; and
- the challenge of figuring out how to market to unfamiliar places using languages the firms do not understand.[17]

Some of the challenge is not structural. It involves mindset and habit. American farmers and manufacturers have long been used to watching foreign markets. Unfortunately they are more the exception than the rule. Among smaller firms, 25 percent of manufacturers export, but only 5 percent of high-skilled services firms do.[18]

Most Americans do not grow up watching foreign trade opportunities the way young people do if they grow up in naturally networked countries like the Netherlands, Dubai, Singapore, or Hong Kong. Their geography oriented those citizens toward the world.

But now virtual geography—online networks—are affecting the way Americans see the world. They follow foreign pop singers, funny YouTube videos, and commercial opportunities.

Yet even if mindset does adjust, the issues of regulations, finances, and marketing across the gaps of culture and language will remain. We have two main recommendations for action. Both are designed to build bridges and lower barriers: build global inter-mediaries, especially for digital commerce in services; and ensure the freedom and security of these new kinds of global commercial networks.

Platforms as Intermediaries

In the 18th and 19th centuries, foreign firms doing business in Asia would usually form relationships with local merchants, a "comprador" (the word's origins are Portuguese) to act as their agent, decode local customs, and sometimes manage the business. In the 20th century the larger international firms developed foreign partners or affiliates, or set up branches with their own trained managers, in order to solve problems like these.

Of course, few American firms have these options, which are complicated and costly. So it is no surprise that, traditionally, most American firms did not engage.

Platforms can become the intermediaries. They can network capabilities to manage paperwork issues, simplify shipping costs and payment problems, bridge language and culture differences, and help connect buyers with sellers.

That is why we believe this area of growth can take off as intermediaries arise on either side of the oceans to do a better job of bridging the different societies. These will be firms and platforms that provide actual translation and more, the effective "translation" of foreign demands to American supply. Some financial institutions are already becoming accustomed to this role. But it can go much further.

eBay has created a global shipping program. It is a platform specifically designed to make it easy for an American seller to handle the process of selling to a foreign buyer. eBay takes care of arranging the shipping, and it handles the customs issues, as well as arranging quick and secure payment transactions through Pay-Pal. Thus eBay opens up markets to smaller sellers. In traditional trade the largest 5 percent of the companies handle 90 percent of the exports. The largest sellers on eBay take only 20 percent of the business. From Valley, Nebraska, Tracey Johnson is selling jewelry and hair care products to dozens of countries, ranging from China to little island states like Malta. As one of eBay's analysts explained in congressional testimony, "Businesses of all sizes are competing and winning online; their growth is coming from overseas buyers."[19]

A platform developed by Overstock simplifies transactions with the world through programs like Worldstock. This links American buyers directly to artisans around the world, also simplifying the shipping, customs, and payment concerns.

Welocalize.com, based in Maryland, started in 1997 just as a business translation service. It now employs more than 600 people with offices in the United States, Britain, Germany, Ireland, Japan, and China. Its rapidly growing business helps companies adapt to a local environment, helps find suppliers, gives translation help, facilitates legal advice, and assists with staffing or marketing goals.

The experience of one platform aimed directly at connecting American businesses to the Chinese market has been revealing. The platform is called Export Now and was founded by Frank Lavin, a former U.S. official who had worked extensively in Asia. The platform directly tackled the "soft" barriers to business—such as finding a warehouse, hiring staff, and incorporating. At first, though, American firms were slow to take up these opportunities. Lavin explained, "Alibaba tells us we have the only company in the world that does this service [in China and] we're making the largest e-commerce market in the world, the fastest growing consumer market on the planet, accessible to anybody in the world from their desk." In the first years few American companies were interested in selling in China, at least in the electronic department store model Chinese consumers tend to use, on websites like Tmall. Fortunately, the situation is changing. Attitudes among Americans are evolving. They are designing new e-commerce models.

More of them realize that their products need to be customized for the Chinese market. Then platform marketplaces can help take them the rest of the way.[20]

The kinds of platforms that would help the most could have several elements:

> • They should have common functions that could benefit many firms, so each company would not have to build its own. It should help process payments, provide advertising, and enable communications among buyers and sellers. It should ideally be tailored to particular sectors or regions. If a government helps set up the platform, it must partner with private firms. The broadly focused platform ConnectAmericas.com was created by the Inter-American Development Bank. But it partners with Google, Visa, and DHL.
>
> • It should help the participating American sellers obtain better access to information about their market. But it should also give the buyers access to more information about the sellers, to build trust over time. Building trust both ways might be aided by methods to rate the service. Europe has a "Trusted Shops" program that awards an online label to those businesses that show they have standards for consumer protection and security for the customer's data.
>
> • Ideally the platform might also include links that can help sellers get access to loans. Although ConnectAmericas.com was created by a development bank, its financial service currently just provides information on credit providers. It does not use the platform as an intermediary to access the bank's own credit lines.[21]

Fortunately, the United States has some natural advantages in creating superior global intermediary platforms:

• The United States is the largest single national market. So it has a strong base of producers, including in digital services, and great experience in the ability to research and explore new markets.

• Another fundamental American advantage for intensified transnational e-commerce is the diversity of the population. Go to Houston, Los Angeles, or New York, and you will find citizens who can speak every language in the world. There are language capabilities and local knowledge that companies may only have started to tap.

These platforms need to be able to connect established sales and marketing channels on all sides. They can help provide links to information about possible markets. They can help forge foreign alliances to better tailor services, or goods, to the needs of foreign buyers.

A Networked World Economy

Our argument looks beyond "trade" in the traditional way that term has been understood. It is about how networks make us part of the world economy and how, if needed, we can use that to our advantage.

Like most people, Americans hear about trade with the world in two categories. One is called "imports." The other is called "exports." These terms used to be very meaningful.

The world today still has plenty of that old-style trade. But the networked world economy of the 21st century is deeply different.

• The scales of global flows are now much larger. To the extent they could even be measured, they were about $3 trillion in 1980. That then amounted to 24 percent of global GDP. By 2012 the flows had increased to $26 trillion, or 36 percent of global GDP. By 2025 the flows could approach half of all global GDP.[22]

• More of the trade is now digital. There is no cargo at all; the packets are digitized. Movies, financial services, the production specs to program digitized production of an engine part, and many other items are being transmitted, not shipped.

• And much of the commerce is neither in raw resources nor in finished goods. It is about the exchange of ingredients within a group of producers. It includes the added services that go with the goods. These producer communities have no clear national label at all.

To illustrate what we mean, think of the old economy. An Arkansas plantation might sell its cotton to buyers in Great Britain. Factories in Britain would make shirts, which could be sold anywhere, including back to the plantation owner in Arkansas. Easy to categorize that: export U.S. cotton; import British shirts.

Now think of today's economy. There is an American clothing company that runs a production network. A T-shirt and its supply chain to make it might all be designed and choreographed from New York City. Then cotton grown in Arkansas would be harvested and shipped. It would go to an advanced facility in Indonesia that turns the cotton into yarn. The yarn might then be sewn into the men's version of the shirt in Bangladesh. The woman's version of the shirt would be assembled in Colombia. Then the T-shirts from Bangladesh and Colombia might be shipped to Miami for further distribution to sellers around America and the world.[23]

The T-shirt we have just described would be classified as a foreign import, from Bangladesh or from Colombia. To the extent it is possible, the various inputs from the United States would be netted against the value of the T-shirt to determine the impact on the balance of trade. But the finished product would be classified as an "import," an "export," or "Made in the USA," in the absence of any easier way to do it, on the basis of the country where the final assembly occurred. This sort of production network can be called a "snake" because of the way it winds around the world.

The T-shirt story with its production snake seems simple when compared with a product like the iPhone. That is not a snake story, although it ends with assembly in Shenzhen, China. The iPhone is more of a "spider" story.

Starting with American-based design and choreography of an almost incomprehensibly complex network, suppliers from all over the world contribute specific components. All of these production legs converge for final assembly in China. But little of the phone's underlying production value may actually come from that final assembly in China. Much more of the value comes from component suppliers based around the world, in Germany, France, Japan, South Korea, Singapore, Taiwan, and the United States.

The story gets more complicated. A Japanese or American supplier might be "fabless." That means that the Japanese supplier of one component actually did not do its own fabrication of the component. The Japanese supplier has used another production network, just for that component. In that Japanese-centered network the actual fabrication of that particular component might occur in China or Taiwan or the Philippines.

Take the Gorilla Glass on the outside of the iPhone. It was designed by an American company, Corning, which is based in New York. To make the Gorilla Glass, Corning uses fabrication facilities in another part of the United States (in Kentucky), or in Japan, or in Taiwan.

When companies design these production networks, labor cost may not be the key factor driving where work is done. Much more important is the character and quality of the component, or the capacity to produce it in a given period of time and a given quantity, or the reliability of the supplier, or other cost factors, which might include labor but might also take into account the raw materials used and the price to transport the component to the next stop in the network, until it all converges for final assembly.

The iPhone, like so many modern products, comes out of a spidery production network, or actually layers of spidery networks. So even more than with snakes, such networks seem to defy classification as either an import or an export.

Production labeled as exports from the United States is supposed to have supported about 11 million jobs in 2013. About two-thirds of this was in trade of goods. The rest was in trade of services. Today trade in services means mainly that a foreigner came to the United States and used a service, like going to Disney World or attending a university.

But these traditional measures not only do not work very well in the effort to understand the global production of goods. They work even less well in labeling products like "information" or services.

The *Lord of the Rings* movies are filmed in New Zealand. That country now also has developed supplier networks for many of the objects used in the movies. But almost everything else about the movies defies easy national labels.

Suppose the director, Peter Jackson, has a Skype online conference with an American expert and a British actor, one of whom has a fee sent to Switzerland and the other has a fee sent to the Cayman Islands. The American lawyer participating in the call from Los Angeles is actually assigned to a branch of his American-based firm that is incorporated and based in London. So his fee might go to a London account.

It is not easy to see how much of this even gets tracked in the way that trade data is collected, much less categorized as imports and exports. The production network might not even be a snake or a spider if all the cooperation is occurring in a digital "cloud."[24]

How to escape this confusion? One way is to get away from the old labels. Go back to thinking about people and how they contribute. Americans participate in many networked communities of producers and can become links in these complex global value chains.

Instead of calculating imports and exports, a team of European scholars based in the Netherlands worked on how to "slice up" contributions to global value chains coming from different countries. They noticed, for instance, that in 1995 four-fifths of the value of a German car assembled in Germany came from Germans. But by 2008 the Germans were providing only two-thirds of the value that went into a German car assembled in Germany.[25]

There are growing opportunities for Americans to join these global value chains. They can be hubs, links, and the heart of a continental base.

- First, as we pointed out in chapter 2, if the production is complex and innovative, Americans are rediscovering why they should center the production firmly at home, as Boeing, Nucor, GE, American Giant, Cree, Warby Parker, and many other companies have learned.

- Second, particular communities may find other niches in the global network. A rural community in central Washington State had natural resources—access to Columbia River hydropower. A German car company, BMW, had a problem: how to build cars made from carbon fiber and be able to mass-produce carbon fiber, which requires a lot of electricity. So the town of Moses Lake, using its Columbia River hydropower, has become the site for a $100 million factory to cook and produce carbon fibers. Moses Lake has made itself a role player in the network producing BMW's new i3 electric sedan. Meanwhile, American scientists in Tennessee, at the Oak Ridge National Laboratory, provide another possible link in this global value chain. They are doing some of the pathfinding work to bring down the cost of mass-producing carbon fiber.[26]

- Third, North America provides a strong collective base for America's production networks.

These supply chain networks in North America are already so elaborate that when scholars studied U.S. imports from Mexico, they found that fully 40 percent of the value of these Mexican imports had actually been produced in the United States. When they studied imports from Canada, they found that 25 percent of the value in those products came from the United States. Similarly, Mexico and Canada contributed value to products labeled as made in the USA. No other countries are so integrated into U.S. production. Therefore it is now possible to imagine producer networks across North America successfully selling to buyers around the world.[27]

Freedom and Security of the New Commercial Networks

Freedom of the Internet may be this century's version of freedom of the seas. As with the oceans, governments are making their claims. As with the oceans, pirates abound until the sea lanes are secured.

Foreign governments have concerns that are both political and economic. They may wish to limit access to data. They can sincerely, or not so sincerely, claim to be protecting interests of privacy or safeguarding consumers. They can insist that data about their citizens be maintained on servers physically based in the same country. In effect, these efforts could seek to break up the Internet as a global medium of information and attempt to create many national internets.

Imagine that a shoe could be custom-made by a 3-D printer, at a local shoe store in China, using a design created in America and transmitted digitally. That is exactly what one of the "new artisans," a young woman named Mary Huang, wants to do.

Mary, a graduate from a design school, has set up her Continuum fashion company, based in Brooklyn. She wants to design shoes personalized for the Chinese customer, produced digitally, no sweatshops required. "That [kind of local production] is not that far away," she comments. "So why aren't we doing it? It's incredibly efficient for business." But she wants to be sure the Chinese shoe shop will be allowed to buy her digital design.

The free flow of data has become the next frontier in battles over the free flow of commerce. As one cyberlaw expert commented, "The distinction between a good and a service vanishes with a smart watch" and its apps. The global trade regime "doesn't have the conceptual framework to deal with that."[28]

The potential effects of data protectionism on the global economy are only starting to be measured. But even more interesting would be the measures governments might need to adopt in order to enforce such national rules on data control.

The explosion in global trade following the advent of modern container shipping was bolstered by trade agreements and international cooperation—on the standardization of container sizes and on other mundane but necessary efforts. The defense of open data in global commerce will also rely increasingly on common understandings of shared interests and shared standards, at least among countries that see a global Internet as a realm of opportunity, more than one of threat. Since the G-8 countries adopted the Open Data Charter in 2013, there is some ground for hope for a cooperative approach.

An example of the kind of unglamorous global governance that goes on behind the headlines is the Open Geospatial Consortium. In this group, representatives from industry, nonprofits, and governments work on finding a global consensus to set the open standard specifications for geospatial software. Such agreements allow different platforms to share data about where something is, like a missing Malaysian airliner.[29]

Another promising sign is the November 2014 agreement between the United States and China to lower or eliminate tariffs on most trade in information technology. That will make it easier for the two countries to work together on the creation of shared networks. They still have much to discuss, however, on the topic of network security.

As more commerce becomes digital, companies—especially

smaller ones—worry more about the security of their data. A high percentage of cyberattacks are directed against small businesses. In one survey of British firms, 87 percent of small firms reported an online security breach in 2012. More global digital commerce may mean more reliance on cloud services. On the other hand, safe and efficient payment systems to enable digital commerce are evolving rapidly too, from companies like PayPal and Etsy, including digital wallets that can be accessed anywhere with mobile devices.[30]

If we are right, changes are coming to the world of global commerce on a scale so large that they are bound to bring with them plenty of problems, plenty of new issues. Our point is that, if Americans prepare themselves, these are trends that can open many more opportunities for Americans to participate, not just in their own economy, but in the dynamic and growing commerce of the whole world.

Actions Needed

- The future growth of the global economy will be very large, especially for firms selling to middle-class buyers around the world. Any agenda for America's economic future by any political leader must include a strategy that takes this into account.
- Commerce through online connections is large and growing fast. It creates excellent opportunities for firms of any size to become micro-multinationals. To attain this potential, American businesses of every size should develop a mindset that analyzes and reaches out to buyers anywhere in the world.
- Online businesses should develop platforms that combine features that help American sellers reach foreign buyers and build trust with them. These platforms need to facilitate this commerce, dealing with shipping, taxes, and customs.
- Also necessary will be government actions to keep Internet-based commerce open, with suitable standards.

Chapter 4

Invest in Main Street America

No serious vision for an economy can neglect the money that fuels it or the circulatory system that connects capital to investment. When Americans wanted to remake their country during the 19th century, to build railroads and new factories, they did not have enough money of their own. They relied heavily on foreign capital, especially from Britain. Fortunately, in the current era, Americans have plenty of capital of their own and easy access to foreign capital too.

The problem is not lack of capital. The problem is not high interest rates, for they are at historic lows.

The problem is that too much of America's money capital is parked. Not enough is being put to work to remake America once more. Less and less investment money is available for young, growth enterprises. The economy is more sluggish than it has been in generations.

Trying to read about finance issues can cause eyes to glaze over pretty quickly. They can seem dry stuff. Still, we Americans need to keep thinking about how these issues play out in the lives of the communities around us.

South Carolina was once a great center of textile production, going back to the days when cotton was king. Working conditions were not easy, but many families made a living. Now almost all those livings are gone. In South Carolina the last textile factory closed in 2007. Most mass production of textiles has moved out of the United States. For some families it can be heartbreaking to drive by the old factory buildings, rotting away now, holes in their rusting roofs.

Jack Collins, a lean man from Walhalla, South Carolina, gray hair speckling his beard, has declared, "If it wasn't for textiles, I wouldn't have anything." It was what he did to take care of his family. A friend comments that Jack had "no hard feelings about the Chinese or anybody about what happened to textiles." For years wages had been held down, as the plant supplied textiles for Walmart. The doors closed around 2000, and now his old plant was an empty shell.

So it is newsworthy, jaw-dropping even, for South Carolinians to hear about companies reopening textile factories in their state. In Lancaster County new textile factories are being constructed and are about to open their doors. One company has built a yarn production facility, an investment of over $200 million that will employ 140. The company plans to build three more plants that will employ hundreds more. A workforce program is gearing up to train electricians, technicians, sales reps, and others.

South Carolina cotton is still good and price competitive. Energy costs in America are relatively low. The American market is large. Labor costs in China have risen, and the textile company would want to use American cotton anyway for its yarn, so it saves on shipping, although the yarn may go right out of the port of Charleston to the next stop in the global production snake. These are some of the factors that we mentioned in chapter 2, some of the reasons trends are now running in favor of basing more production in the United States.

The most interesting part of the story is where all the money to do this is coming from.

The investment is coming from China, of all places. The company, Keer, is Chinese.

The Chinese know the textile business. They saw the opportunities. They saw that they could build on deep local knowledge about textile production. About one-third of the applicants to the training program are former textile workers.

One of the Americans helping open the new factory said, "It's exciting to see that the textile manufacturing business that was so prevalent here in the Carolinas is returning." Another had talked to his cousin, who was already working on the new project, and said "the benefits [for employees] after the Chinese purchased it were wonderful. A lot better than what they had."

A lot of Carolinians are talking about it. "This is a country, you know," one said, "we've always survived. And I've still got the belief that we're gonna flourish." Said another, "If you work together [with the Chinese], you'd learn more about each other, and that way you'd know each other's habits and you'd care about each other more."

Keer is not the only Chinese company to see this opportunity. To borrow a Chinese expression, Keer expects many other Chinese companies and investors to follow "the first one who dares to eat the crab."

One company already making the move is JN Fibers, which has taken over one of the empty shells in Richburg, South Carolina. It will build a plant to recycle plastic (polyethylene terephthalate) bottles into polyester fiber, employing more than three hundred people. Danny Christopher, a veteran of both the military and the textile industry, works in Richburg. He was the last guy left looking after the empty shell. Now he has joined the transition. "I think it's great," he said, "that jobs are coming back to the area and I think the new space is gonna welcome [them], just because it's been so empty for so many years. It's really brought hope to a lot of people that don't have jobs."[1]

We are glad to see Chinese companies making these moves.

It is a bit puzzling to us that American companies were not there first, seeing the opportunity.

It is not as if America doesn't have the capital. But Americans have, to a large extent, just gotten out of the business.

As a country, America has plenty of private capital and the ability to borrow much more on favorable terms. Yet indicators of forward-looking, longer-term business investment have been declining for decades. If one steps back to understand these large, long-term trends, a few observations stand out:

- The overall flow of credit has shifted significantly toward household and consumer credit.
- Among the larger businesses that have access to a lot of capital, investment perspectives have become more short-term and defensive.
- For young growth businesses, the flow of credit has diminished.

This chapter concentrates just on strategies to open up business investment. In chapter 6 we will widen the aperture to include the role of public co-investments that can attract more capital to the needs of the whole ecosystem of producers. But for now there is plenty to say about the blocked arteries near the heart of private capitalism.

The Scale of the Capital Mismatch

Even with interest rates practically at rock bottom, there is no absolute shortage of domestic funds. Nor, at present, would there seem to be any particular difficulty in attracting foreign funds for a suitable investment.

In 2012, with the economic recovery underway, a business writer and senior fellow of the Milken Institute, Joel Kurtzman, was invited to meet in Milpitas, California, with a group of chief financial officers. These were CFOs of good-sized high-tech companies in Silicon Valley. They were not the giants, but still companies with billions of dollars in annual revenue.

Kurtzman was a bit taken aback to hear that the CFOs worried, actually worried, that "*they had too much money sitting idly in the bank.*" Their boards, they complained, "would not allow them to put their money to work on anything but surefire investments." To illustrate this, one CFO said she had a year's worth of revenue sitting in the bank with no better place to put it.[2]

On a national level the scales of money are beyond our everyday intuitive ability to comprehend them. The sums are in the trillions of dollars. The money is sitting in corporate cash accounts. Or it is used by companies to buy back and accumulate more of their own stock. Or it is parked by banks in accounts at the Federal Reserve. Those seeking proof of the scale of U.S. financial capital accumulation can look at several ways of trying to tally it.

- One is the ratio of privately held capital to national income. This ratio was a little more than 3:1 at the end of the 1970s. It is now more than 4:1.[3]
- In 1980 mutual funds under management held $134 billion in assets. In 2007 that number was $12 trillion. At least another $2.4 trillion is lodged in alternative investments, such as hedge funds and private equity groups.[4]
- Since the 1970s capital in the U.S. economy has become more "financialized." That is, profits in the whole economy are going more to portfolio investors and less for reinvestment by corporations. It can be seen by comparing the flow of income received as interest, dividends, or capital gains and then contrasting that total with the share of income received from traditional sales and trade.[5]
- If one reckons the funds actually held by corporations, cash holdings or investment in stock buybacks

have grown much larger in the past ten years. Publicly available data indicate that the total amount of cash that businesses have on hand or in banks more than tripled between 2003 and 2013, to over $2.6 trillion.[6]

The accumulation of capital could—in theory—be great for the American economy. It could—in theory—be money well spent for all, if the accumulation was plowed back into the growth of American businesses.

Suppose that most of this capital were invested in business growth in America. Suppose, too, that those businesses used this capital for productive R&D or to buy capital goods, like machines, in order to grow their businesses. Or suppose that investors put the money into a larger or better labor force to grow their business or improve the value of its products. If almost all the capital were productively redeployed to these purposes, then the positive effects for the rest of the American economy would be very large. There would be a palpable sense of dynamism, innovation, and growth in both employment and wages.

Unfortunately, a *smaller* proportion of capital is being reinvested into business development.

A straightforward way to see whether capital is being put back to work, invested in American business, is to look at net U.S. domestic investment. As a ratio to national income, net domestic investment has been declining steadily since 1970. During the 1990s this ratio was lower than at any other time since the Great Depression. From that low point it then took a steep further fall during the 2000s, so that this ratio of net domestic investment to America's national income reached the lowest level in more than a hundred years, excepting (barely) the Depression decade of the 1930s.[7]

Net domestic investment is a broad measure. We should take housing out of the equation. The share of GDP devoted to nonresidential fixed investment also has been in gradual decline since 1980.

We could break it down some more, and look only at an interesting index of innovation, investment in IT-related equipment. There the pattern did show steady growth in the 1980s, a lift during the 1990s, but then stagnation from 2000 through 2011 (the latest year with available data).[8]

Still another critical index of innovation investment would be corporate spending on R&D. But even though the amount of money corporations have put into cash holdings and stock buybacks annually has doubled over the past ten years, levels of corporate R&D spending during this period have stayed flat.

Finally, most important, a large portion of capital goes to finance mortgages and other kinds of consumer debt. The most comprehensive study to date of the data concludes, "To a large extent the core business model of banks in advanced economies today resembles that of real estate funds: banks are borrowing (short) from the public and capital markets to invest (long) into assets linked to real estate. . . . The intermediation of household savings for productive investment in the business sector—the standard textbook role of the financial sector—constitutes only a minor share of the business of banking today, even though it was a central part of that business in the 19th and early 20th centuries."[9]

In Kurtzman's conversation with Silicon Valley CFOs, another CFO said his board had vetoed every plant expansion plan the CEO and others had offered. The board instead wanted to put the money into Silicon Valley commercial real estate—which seemed pretty safe. "'Isn't it a better use of the company's time and money to expand production or acquire a related business than to go into a real-estate business? Buying real estate makes no sense to me,' said one CFO with his head in his hands. The other CFOs nodded sympathetically."[10]

These are broad, long-term trends. The main arguments about the causes of these trends tend to fall into two families. One family argues that, because of other conditions in the economy, such as loss of skills, competitiveness, taxes, or regulations, the opportunities for investment in American business are not so tempting.

The other family argues that the short-termism in the ownership of U.S. companies discourages any spending on assets, like R&D, that do not yield a quick payoff. It notes that this short-termism is now embedded deeply in the standard formulas being used to make and evaluate investments.

Not enough good investment opportunities in America? Too much short-termism? Either way, both families are quarreling over the apportionment of a shrinking pie. As we have stressed, perhaps the largest trend is the declining share of funds devoted to business finance at all.

The Overall Shift toward Household and Consumer Credit

In the boom years in America after 1945, private capital accumulated rapidly. Back then, if people and firms had capital to invest, loans to businesses were a dominant form of credit. Until the 1970s and 1980s, capital controls and other legal obstacles hindered casual or short-term foreign investing.

Since the founding of the American republic, issues of debt and credit were big subjects in local and state politics. The United States had a checkerboard of laws preventing interstate and branch banking. Those laws were designed to keep most banking local, to make sure as much money as possible stayed in the home state and was lent back out to the state's merchants and farmers. In fact, most of the thousands of banks were established by and for those same merchants and farmers.

Many of those banks failed during the Great Depression. So the years between 1930 and 1933 produced a critical redesign in the American financial system. But the old values still guided the new reforms of the 1930s. A key designer of the system was himself a product of that older system, a small-town banker from Utah named Marriner Eccles.

The decentralized structure was preserved, with its thousands of banks. In return, the redesigned system was heavily regulated. The plan was that the banks might be fragile in the particular, not fragile for the whole. Ordinary depositors would be protected if banks failed, which was still expected to happen frequently.[11]

To encourage banks to make home loans, the forms of the home loans were regularized. There were national frameworks to help local banks better assess such loans and manage the risk of holding such notes.[12]

These private-public alliances were centered on local banks to address local needs. As Eccles put it, "I wanted the housing program to be private in character, with all financing done on the grass-roots level by credit institutions of a community for the individuals who lived there."[13]

Though now allied to national standards and federal insurance programs, the credit pools for home loans still came mainly from the local banks. The federal mortgage finance program, Fannie Mae, became a way to shift these pools of money across a more national capital market.

This mix—national regulation and standards along with local, decentralized lenders—worked for decades. By the 1970s nearly two-thirds of Americans were living in their own homes. That level has turned out to be about the highest level that has been sustainable.

Since the 1970s, however, the American banking system became more and more devoted to financing consumer and housing credit. It was a choice framed and incentivized by government policy. A new set of private-public alliances have used financial innovations, like securitization, to make it easier for banks to lend to consumers (especially for houses) than to lend to businesses.

Securitization reduces the risk of investing in housing debt. Fannie Mae, which was a key agent in securitizing housing debt, went private in 1968. Federal laws passed during the 1980s and 1990s deregulated this new sector of credit, opening the way both for MBS and for derivatives based on MBS.

With housing credit now bundled into financial instruments that could be sold to anyone in the world, capital and credit from around America and the world flooded in. Analogous financial moves expanded the flow of credit for student loans and consumer purchases in the form of credit card debt.

The rise of securitization, led by the mortgage-backed securities in the 1970s and 1980s, made investment in household and consumer debt much easier—and with the safety of a bond rating. Treating such debt as a bond made it easier for pension funds, sovereign wealth funds, and other large sources of capital to invest in it. Meanwhile, no comparable widespread financial instrument arose to pool small-business debt.[14]

Laws insulated both mortgage debt and student loan debt from being discharged in bankruptcy. Business debt has no such protection.

Consider the banks' point of view in light of all these incentives. The banks could use their capital either to buy mortgage-backed securities in the markets or to lend to businesses. Making a small-business loan is risky and labor-intensive. The small-business loan may get a good rate of return, but, if one adjusts for the greater risk and greater cost, making that loan may be much harder than reselling mortgage debt.

Recently a team of economists, including Alan Taylor, has shown that across most developed countries, mortgages have gone from about 35 percent of all loans after World War II, to about 40 percent in 1970, to almost 60 percent today. Of all the growth in U.S. bank lending from 1960 to 2010, over half went to U.S. households rather than to businesses.[15] Certain sectors, like construction, real estate development, and finance did well from this, but these sectors do not contribute as lastingly to the core communities of tradable production in the U.S. economy.

Until the Great Recession, these dramatic changes to amp up household and consumer credit were a darling of investors and applauded by politicians in both parties. Helping people take on more debt jacked up aggregate consumer demand. From a macroeconomic perspective—the enshrined perspective of the mass production era—such demand was the key driver of mass economic growth. From a politician's perspective, easier credit to buy a home or to pay for college was a popular cause.

With the inflow of all this money, the proportion of the people living in their own homes did not increase. The scale of their debt *did* increase. It increased a lot. Between 1980 and 2005 the ratio of household debt to net income doubled, from about 60 percent to over 120 percent. This level of debt was unsustainable.[16]

Business Investment: Much More to Do

Since 1945 large businesses have not relied as much on banks for credit. They have more options. They have retained earnings. They can issue bonds. They can sell stock. What large businesses do with their options for raising and investing capital therefore depends on how the owners and managers of these large businesses conceive of their responsibilities as leaders.

In the mid-20th century corporate leaders saw themselves as America's leaders, bearing a major share of responsibility for remaking the country. The American public did not find it too surprising that between 1953 and 1967 Presidents Eisenhower, Kennedy, and Johnson chose businessmen (from GE, Proctor & Gamble, and Ford) to lead the most powerful agency in America—the Department of Defense.

The film writer and director Billy Wilder helped write a scene for his 1954 movie, *Sabrina*, in which one of the lead characters was a corporate titan, played by Humphrey Bogart. The Bogart character asks his younger, playboy brother (played by William Holden) to marry the daughter of a plastics company chief. The marriage is supposed to smooth the way for a merger of the companies. Why should he do this, the Holden character asks. Is it about the money?

> [Bogart character]: If making money were all there is to business, it would hardly be worthwhile going to the office. Money is a by-product.
> [Holden character]: What's the main objective? Power?

[Bogart character]: Ah! That's become a dirty word.

[Holden character]: What's the urge? You're going into plastics. What will that prove?

[Bogart character]: Prove? Nothing much.

A new product has been found, something of use to the world. So a new industry moves into an undeveloped area. Factories go up, machines are brought in, a harbor is dug, and you're in business.

It's purely coincidental of course that people who've never seen a dime before suddenly have a dollar and barefooted kids wear shoes and have their teeth fixed and their faces washed.

What's wrong with a kind of urge that gives people libraries, hospitals, baseball diamonds, and movies on a Saturday night?

[Holden character, giving up]: Now you make me feel like a heel. If I don't marry Elizabeth, some kid's gonna be running around . . . barefoot with cavities in his teeth.[17]

Times and ideals changed. The "shareholder value" revolution, as the sociologists William Lazonick and Mary O'Sullivan have called it, though not required by any change in the law, increased pressure for short-run profits over long-run value creation.[18]

James Michaels, the former editor of the business magazine *Forbes,* wrote the foreword to a book about what happened to the classmates from the Harvard Business School's graduating class of 1949. Some of the graduates had become much-admired CEOs, like Peter McColough at Xerox and Tom Murphy at ABC. Feeling despondent about the current generation of corporate leaders, Michaels decided to hit away.

As I write, it is midsummer 2002. The business and Wall Street people who are in the news today seem a sorry lot compared with most of the [class of 1949]. When I say "sorry lot," I am not just talking about the Ken Lays, the Bernie Ebbers, the Jack Grubmans. I also refer to the dozens of CEOs who destroyed corporate balance sheets during the 1990s and early

2000s. They did so by taking on short-term debt to pay for overpriced acquisitions. They went into debt to buy in their own shares at exalted prices. They showed an utter disregard for probabilities by promising an endless string of 15 percent and more annual earnings gains. And when they couldn't produce earnings, many of them claimed that earnings didn't matter; only EBIDTA [earnings before interest, taxes, depreciation, and amortization] matters. Others made their stock options pay off by gutting their corporate payroll, literally making themselves rich off the misfortunes of their colleagues. All this in the name of "maximizing shareholder values." . . .

I don't know precisely when the term *maximizing shareholder value* came into common usage, but in a way I wish it never had. Too often it means using gimmicks to get your stock up. It is rarely taken to mean building a solid business that adds value for your customers and creates exciting careers for your employees.[19]

In the ten years after Michaels wrote his bitter jeremiad about corporate owner practices, from 2003 to 2012, 54 percent of all corporate earnings among the 449 companies that were publicly listed in the S&P 500—a total of $2.4 trillion—were used by the leaders of those companies to buy back their own stock, almost all through purchases on the open market. Since dividends to shareholders accounted for another 37 percent of the earnings, only 9 percent were left for reinvestment in productive capacities or the employees. The "retain-and-reinvest" approach of major U.S. corporations had been replaced by strategies to "downsize-and-distribute."[20]

Alarmed by the trend, Laurence Fink, the chairman and CEO of BlackRock, the world's largest asset manager, wrote an open letter to corporate leaders in March 2014. In it he publicized his worry that "many companies have shied away from investing in the future growth of their companies."

Instead, too many firms had "cut capital expenditure and even increased debt to boost dividends and increase share buybacks." Fink's argument was that these practices caused him, as an asset manager, to question whether the owners were committed to "sustainable, long-term returns."[21]

Paul Polman, the longtime CEO of Unilever, a global company with more than $60 billion in annual revenue, has observed that "pension funds own 75 percent of the capital on U.S. stock exchanges, representing companies like ours." The funds are supposed to generate long-term returns for eventual retirements. "They firmly believe in that mission," Polman commented, "but many of them have activity systems that do not support it. They might offer quarterly incentives to their fund managers; they might employ short-term hedge funds and others, disturbing the normal economic process. It is increasingly clear now that a lot of this activity actually destroys more value than it builds."[22]

To be fair, however, to the investment community: some of the incentives that push against long-term finance are codified in formal and informal regulations. One example would be asset allocation rules for banks, public pension funds, or insurance companies that require them to hold government bonds or other liquid or short-term instruments. These rules create a tension between efforts to make banks less risky and efforts to encourage banks or other institutional investors to provide long-term credit to businesses.

Also, the present tax system has a relatively high tax rate on corporate income. Dividends and capital gains are taxed at a lower rate.

Private equity owners and active investors often structure the incentives that guide the choices by corporate professional managers. Beyond the world of publicly held companies, the majority of corporate profits now flow through different ownership structures—"master limited partnerships" that must distribute their earnings and are even more oriented to medium-term profits and resale.[23]

From experience, many company board members and C-suite

executives have already come around to the view that longer time horizons improve corporate performance.[24] These decision makers cite better financial returns and increasing innovation as the benefits of a longer-term view.

Yet these boards and executives acknowledge getting acute pressure from investors, including institutional shareholders, to deliver higher earnings in the near term. The institutional investors use short-term investment strategies.

Dominic Barton, the global managing director of McKinsey, and Mark Wiseman, the president and CEO of the Canada Pension Plan Investment Board, have become concerned enough, after surveying top executives, that they recently published, in the *Harvard Business Review*, a joint assault on the "tyranny of short-termism." They bluntly state that these asset managers are "not acting like owners."[25]

Trying to understand declines in the long-term innovative dynamism of the American private sector, both a group at the National Academy of Sciences and then an MIT task force studying the future of American innovation found their investigation leading them away from issues in science or education, and instead to patterns of corporate investment. "[T]he most important factor in trying to understand what happened to American manufacturing," the MIT task force reported, "is the transformation of corporate structures from the 1980s on."[26]

We hope that times and ideals are changing again. If ever there is a time to take a broad view of investment possibilities in America, it is at a time of revolutionary economic change. This is now a time when the leaders of large businesses can and should shoulder significant responsibility for their part in reworking America.

Not every business leader is as outspoken as Unilever's Polman, who at the beginning of 2012 said, "Our version of capitalism has reached its sell-by date." And not every business has, like Unilever, doubled R&D spending at the height of the Great Recession, scrapped quarterly earnings reports, and then doubled its share value.[27] But American business leaders are speaking and acting. Some, like Bill Gates, have used terms like "creative capitalism." Others find their own vocabulary and strategies for linking the future of their business to a longer-term vision of America's future.

One by one, owners and active investors will make critical decisions about their part in reworking America for the 21st century. We can do three things to help them.

We can spotlight their share of responsibility for America's future. We can point out ways to change some of the incentive structures, some of them regulatory, that now discourage long-term finance. Finally, in this and other parts of our book, we can offer strategies for action that may invite visionary investments.

We hope owners and investors will find these ideas inspiring. Or they may be inspired to come up with better ideas of their own for fear that otherwise perhaps "some kid will run around barefoot."

Changing Standards to Encourage Longer-Term Business Investment

The problem of short-termism is not unique to the United States. More-conservative bank lending standards and aging populations with risk-averse investment portfolios tend to encourage investments in government-guaranteed bonds, mortgage-backed securities, or liquid, short-term instruments. Faltering long-term investment has become so serious a problem that the Group of Thirty, organized to discuss financial issues among leading economies, created a working group on long-term finance that issued a recent report suggesting more than a dozen reforms.[37]

Public agencies set investment guidelines for the large sums invested by governments and by public pension funds. Other private bodies set guidelines for industry "best practices." This group of rather sober central bankers urged all of them to set guidelines that would spur longer-term horizons in investment. These would discourage excessive use of benchmarks that reinforce market cycles (like stock indexes). They would strengthen the independence of pension boards to set transparent long-term investment goals. They would change incentive pay to redefine the performance goals for portfolio managers to get away from quarterly or annual metrics, replacing them with time horizons of at least three years, if not longer.

The group also urged both national regulators and international bodies, like the influential Financial Stability Board, to phase in standards in bank and insurance regulation that would not give such preferential treatment to holdings of government bonds. The regulators could instead give more incentives to invest in long-term private corporate bonds and other high-quality private equities. Long-term investments also encounter discrimination in accounting standards, such as the practice of mark-to-market accounting or value calculations with a one-year time horizon.

Another interesting aspect of contemporary accounting standards is that the way they treat investment in a company's equipment differs from the way they treat investment in a company's people. Money spent on capital equipment is accounted as an investment in a depreciating asset. Money spent on improving people is accounted as an immediate cost.

The details are eye watering, but the overall point is clear. Short-termism has been baked into many of the systems that govern the financial management of very large holdings of capital. To put a greater portion of these sums to work at a pivotal period in American economic history entails a lot of detailed work to rewire these structures in a careful and transparent way. Fortunately, some of the groundwork has already been laid to undertake such a project.

In a Land of Plenty (of Capital), Hard Times for Young Firms Seeking It

The Great Recession made an already difficult business finance environment much more forbidding for young firms. These firms are critical for job creation and innovative vigor. The declining rate of new business formation—down 23 percent between 2007 and the beginning of 2011—appears to have prevented the creation of about 1.8 million new jobs.[28]

The U.S. banking industry has consolidated more around the central, "money center" banks. With access to central bank money at nearly zero rates of interest, these banks have many possible investment plays around the world. Their business models to earn large profits do not need to rest so much on lending to all those little businesses. That part of the banking work requires labor-intensive, decentralized, nuanced, and human appraisals of the creditworthiness of young firms around America. The banks are no longer so interested.

The small businesses complain of being credit starved. The banks reply that the businesses are not creditworthy.

A thoughtful appraisal by Karen Mills, a former head of the Small Business Administration, summed up the evidence as "troubling signs that access to bank credit for small businesses was in steady decline prior to the crisis, was hit hard during the crisis, and has continued to decline in the recovery as banks focus on more profitable market segments."

In human terms, these are thousands of disappointed entrepreneurs. Many of them may deserve to be turned away. But the appetite for risk of this kind seems to have gone way down.

Small-business loans are down, a lot. Such loans made up 51 percent of the loan value on bank balance sheets in 1995. The proportion of loan value has now gone from 51 percent down to 29 percent.[29]

Searching for alternatives to bank credit, the smaller firms do not have the same options that large firms do. They can look to the venture capital (VC) sector. That helps some. Yet the VC business is reduced in size from what it was in the 1990s.

There are numerous headlines about VC investments, especially in high-tech companies. And Silicon Valley does indeed do relatively well in attracting VC money.

But even in the high-tech sector, much of the activity has fallen off since the go-go days of the 1990s. Since 2000 there has been "a large decline in startups and fast-growing young firms, reversing an earlier pattern." Initial public offerings have dropped off. It seems that, as a whole, the United States has "experienced a post-2000 shift away from the type of young, entrepreneurial firms that were a major source of innovation and productivity growth for the economy as a whole in the 1980s and 1990s."[30]

VC investors are concentrating more and more on later-stage firms that seem to be safer bets.[31] Moreover, the VC firms tend to concentrate on activities near where those investors live, especially in Silicon Valley of northern California.

Whether it is a local restaurant, a corner coffee shop, or a manufacturer that employs 200 employees, most small businesses are simply not in high-growth industries where an investor could expect a fivefold return on her investment.

These traditional small businesses are experiencing a significant shortage of capital. More than 35 percent of them name access to financing and credit as a major impediment to growth.[32]

VC Funding

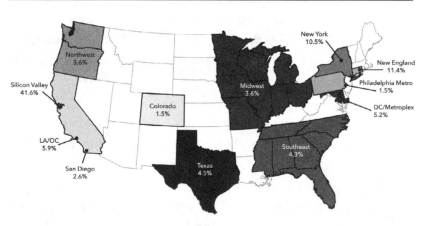

SOURCE: National Venture Capital Association

Small businesses do have a federal agency devoted to their care: the Small Business Administration (SBA). But despite much rhetoric about concern for Main Street businesses, that is not where the money is going.

In 2012 the SBA lent out $15 billion.[33] To get a sense of scale and proportion, the much-diminished annual small and medium-size enterprise (SME) loan market that year in America was still $2 trillion. So the SBA loans accounted for 0.65 percent of that. Incidentally, of the $384 billion allocated by Congress to the Troubled Assets Relief Program (TARP) during the Great Recession, only $334 million ended up going to SMEs, 0.09 percent of TARP funds. The federal government's most important policy intervention for small business does not amount to much more than a rounding error in relation to the size of the small-business portion of the American economy.

Instead, as in the past, a much greater impact can come from encouraging new private initiatives. These may, in turn, need national frameworks or new rules, more than they will need new money. As we have said, America's private sector has money.

In this chapter, beyond our earlier encouragement to owners and investors, we offer two other ideas to get America's money off the sidelines and into play: (1) standards and securitization and (2) new kinds of financial intermediaries.

Standards and Securitization: Allow Businesses to Compete More Fairly for Credit

As we have explained, the long-term tilt of the financial system toward household and consumer credit was the result of deliberate political choices. These began in the New Deal policies that first made it easy to sell mortgages across the country and then, in the Great Society, pushed Wall Street to repackage those mortgages into securities. Further legislation and rules accelerated that securitization process.

That is not all. Following a deep-seated tradition in America, if a business venture fails, the debts can usually be cleared through bankruptcy. The owner can then try something else. That was always part of the American Dream's promise of fresh starts and second chances.

Thanks to federal legislation, as we pointed out earlier, housing and student loan debt usually cannot be cleared through bankruptcy. Tax and loan guarantees further encourage lenders to be aggressive in extending housing and education loans. The federal government thus quite purposefully restructured the market to give banks a powerful incentive to steer credit toward these debtors.

The results over the past ten years have been, and remain, devastating for tens of millions of Americans. The most damaged lives are in the very part of the population that the policies had been meant to help.

Our fundamental recommendation is to address the disparate treatment of loans to business versus loans to consumers. There are two basic ways to do this:

- allow both kinds of debts to be unwound in bankruptcy and curtail tax subsidies and loan guarantees for these credit flows; *and/or*
- encourage innovation in the securitization of business credit.

Well aware of the overextension and abuse of securitization in consumer credit, we do not want to see that repeated. But "plain vanilla" securitization, without the risk distortion caused by blocking off bankruptcy protection or by providing federal loan insurance, did work reasonably well for decades.

The real power of government in freeing up capital for American business investment is in laws and standards. The assumed obstacle in securitizing business credit, allowing many loans to businesses to be packaged and resold in capital markets, is that the businesses are so different. There are actually quite a few differences in the world of consumer credit too. These differences have been overcome by using the development of standards and data analytics that could better assess risk across a great many people and situations.

What made the Federal Housing Administration (FHA) and Fannie Mae possible was not government money, but government standards on houses. Each house is unique, at least in some way. Government standards picked a set of qualities (size, assessed value, street traffic, etc.) that allowed someone in New York to decide whether or not to buy a mortgage on a house in Texas without ever going there. Housing standards allowed mortgages to be treated like interchangeable commodities.

If such a policy could work for houses, perhaps it can work for businesses. Americans already have, in accounting, a common language to describe firms. The secret to making it easier to invest in businesses is not to spend government money, but to make it easier for private capital to be invested.

These loans, initially, could be for firms that had survived a little while, just as the FHA mortgages were designed for middle-income Americans. Start-ups might not be the initial target for such a program. But small and midsize companies with good histories could apply for loans and expand their businesses.

This vision of lending is different from the current SBA rules that require that the applicant be unable to get credit outside of SBA lending.[34] Such rules are the exact opposite of the approach taken in all the successful housing programs. Instead of starting with good businesses, it selects for marginal businesses.

Rather than subsidize marginal firms, Americans can make it easier for good businesses to borrow and have their loans traded. Current SBA rules push money on bad businesses and do little to help actually profitable firms to grow.

Creating channels of business loan securitization, like those for consumer assets, need not increase economic volatility. It could instead reduce it. Easier access to business loans could provide very large productive investments into the American economy, in order to expand real opportunities and give consumers access to better wages—which, in the end, is what they want most.

The idea of doing more to securitize business credit may seem radical to many Americans, but it is already being tried in China and in Great Britain. In China, Alibaba has been involved in financial services for several years. In 2013 the company began to securitize loans it was making to merchants, working with Orient Securities.[35]

In Britain a small financial firm only a few years old—Funding Circle, Ltd.—is currently arranging about $2 million a day worth of loans for small businesses. The three co-founders, 31-year-old friends from Oxford, target enterprises with at least a modest amount of annual sales (more than $80,000) that were having trouble getting credit in Britain's highly centralized banking system (four banks do 80 percent of the lending). Their firm is relatively tiny in relation to the market. It is their approach that singles them out.

Peer-to-peer lending platforms are becoming more common. Most of these have turned to consumer lending. Funding Circle is responding to the crisis in small-business lending, which is as acute in the UK as in the United States. Its strategy, as the co-founder Samir Desai says, is "to create a bond market for small businesses." That means establishing a secondary market where lenders can trade the loans just as bondholders do. Another co-founder, Andrew Mullinger, noted that this was key to getting enough liquidity. "Without that, I wouldn't put any money in it myself."

What that innovation means, concretely, could be seen in visiting a London furniture maker doing customized work, employing a staff of 35. The owner needed a specialized hydraulic press, made in Austria, to apply veneer. He posted a loan request on Funding Circle's site. Investors lent the money at a 9.1 percent rate. The investors could trade the debt on the platform's secondary market, with the debt graded on the basis of data analytics that Funding Circle has designed.

Funding Circle is growing so fast it is having trouble finding office space for its new staff. It is trying to find allies in the banking world, hoping to move to the world of billions of dollars, not millions. Robert Steel, a former vice chairman of Goldman Sachs and a top U.S. Treasury official, has joined Funding Circle's board to help it try.[36]

What inhibits the growth of this idea in the United States? A critical challenge has been to get the legal authority that will allow the creation of these secondary markets. The JOBS (Jumpstart Our Business Startups) Act, passed by Congress and signed into law by President Obama in 2012, was meant to help grow crowdfunding markets in the United States. To date the federal Securities and Exchange Commission has not yet issued the rules to implement this act.

When those rules do come out, they are expected to have the same high hurdles that today keep most businesses from being able to participate in securities markets. The costs to go public with an IPO, once about $10 million, are now more like $140 million. (Easing the pathway to an IPO, making it less expensive, would be another way for businesses to obtain more capital.)

Another way that government standard setting can help is to open the way for securitization markets in long-term debt, other than in housing or real estate. Regulators and international standard setters like the little-known International Organization of Securities Commissions (IOSCO) can set up standardized, relatively simple instruments with disclosure requirements for adequate transparency. Both U.S. and international agencies could create incentives for private institutions to use such instruments, offsetting the usual risk bias against long-term lending.

Our strategy aims at enabling a functioning market—made possible by government standards—to allocate capital more efficiently. Instead of jettisoning securitization, we can use it as a powerful tool to broaden America's advantage.

Beyond Banks? New Kinds of
Intermediaries for Business Finance

Aided by platforms, it should today be easier—and cheaper—to start and grow a business than ever before. In theory this should be a sign of great promise, because Americans have sustained one of the highest rates of entrepreneurship in the developed world. In 2013 an estimated 25 million Americans—nearly 13 percent of the working-age population—were involved in running or starting a new business.[38]

Millennials who came of age around the year 2000 tend to be more interested in creating companies than in working for them. According to 2011 research by the Kauffman Foundation, "fifty-four percent of the nation's millennials either want to start a business or already have started one. They recognize that entrepreneurship is the key to reviving the economy." They described their main obstacles as lack of access to capital and lack of know-how.[39]

Young people want to be entrepreneurs. And entrepreneurs and the companies they start—i.e., new and young firms—are responsible for the largest share of net new jobs.[40]

Yet we see a large mismatch between these potential entrepreneurs and America's current financial system. There are obviously very important issues to be addressed regarding the relationship of large banks and current corporate ownership structures to the level of investment in American business. In addition to that ongoing conversation, we want to inject some new ideas.

A critical issue is whether, in the 21st century, businesses should continue to rely on traditional banks as their principal source of credit and capital. The banks are meant to play the role of an "intermediary," knowing their customer and the local situation. The reality is different.

Banking is becoming more centralized; local banks are playing more the role of data collectors for remote processing. A finance professor at the University of Chicago wrote recently about a bank's computerized refusal to grant a mortgage loan to the former Fed chairman Ben Bernanke. Bernanke had once stated that "the real service performed by the banking system is the differentiation between good and bad borrowers." The professor, Amir Sufi, observed that this episode illustrated a much wider issue, that "banks are bad at the job that is supposedly their main source of value."[41]

But if the banks will not help dynamic young firms, if they are faltering in their older role as intermediaries to businesses, other kinds of institutions may step in. Some of them are big corporations that have become credit mainstays for the firms in their own supply chains and retail networks. Outstanding examples include the reworked subsidiary of GE, GE Capital. GE Capital has been divesting its old business in consumer finance, once so profitable, in order to concentrate on the flow of credit to business, especially the businesses in GE's own network of suppliers and retailers. Another U.S. company that has invested large resources in such business financing is Caterpillar, through its subsidiary, Caterpillar Financial.

These firms can become nonbank intermediaries because they know their customers. Thus they can help manage the risk. GE Capital's Commercial Distribution Finance provided $34 billion in financing for more than 30,000 dealers and more than 3,000 distributors and manufacturers in the United States and Canada in 2013. Most of GE Capital's commercial loans are to midsize companies, spread across multiple industries and geographies and secured by tangible assets to reduce risk. They finance across a range of products, including equipment leasing, franchises, inventory, restructuring, commercial real estate, energy, and health care.

GE Capital has combined its credit program with a new entity created with help from Salesforce, called Access GE. Access GE is a platform that grants GE's business colleagues access to expertise across the company, to help those businesses succeed. This creates a win-win in which the smaller businesses might thrive, while GE strengthens its business base.

Another kind of financial intermediary has also arisen. Like banks, such firms are using data about their customers. But they are doing so in smarter, more nuanced ways. They leverage their data in order to know their customers, mitigate risk, and secure their payment stream. Here are four examples:

• A platform called C2FO, based in Kansas City, Missouri, is a network linking buyers and suppliers to supply working capital. Bridging the gap of the usual months of delays before suppliers are paid, C2FO advances money to the suppliers at lower rates, but involves the buyers in earning the profits from those loans—a rate of return higher than what the buyer would otherwise be getting while the "accounts payable" are being processed. By the end of 2014 the platform was handling more than $1 billion a month of working capital in its marketplace.[42]

• A platform called Kabbage, founded in 2009, is different from conventional lenders in three ways. It operates only from an online platform. It relies not just on a loan application or credit scores; it mines data from the firms, including business checking accounts, accounting software, payment processors, shipping data, and other online tools. Finally, Kabbage uses sophisticated algorithms to assess applicants with automated decision making. A small business can apply for a loan and get a response in just 15 minutes. There is no collateral or interest charge. Kabbage instead takes a percentage of sales for each month the balance is outstanding, perhaps about 2 to 7 percent if merchants repay the amount in a month. Still working at a small scale, but with thousands of merchants, Kabbage has a delinquency rate that is half the industry average.[43]

• CAN Capital is a hybrid between direct lenders and peer lenders. In operation since 1998, it has provided more than $4 billion in loans or merchant cash advances. It does have physical offices but leverages web-based applications and scoring mechanisms. Its core is providing working capital to existing businesses based on cash flow, not credit scores.

• OnDeck has given out more than $1 billion in loans to small businesses. These loans range from $5,000 to $250,000, with an average term of less than one year. The OnDeck model automatically receives payments from the small business on a daily basis. Its terms of service and technology allow the lender anytime access to business banking balances, a radically transparent model. Some businesses like the speed of this model. Debts have a daily pay-down. Knowing that the lender can watch the books on a daily basis also affects the behavior of the borrower.

Right now these alternative institutions can attract some financing from capital markets. They offer the relatively good rate of return that is still available from relatively risky small-business lending. The new institutions, as platforms, can reduce some costs while achieving impressive scale.

At the moment that scale is still small, compared with the traditional banks. The next big step may be the same one that transformed home loans for Americans during the 1930s. As we pointed out earlier in this chapter, that rework of the financial system involved private-public partnerships. Those partnerships standardized lending terms and developed clear underwriting guidelines for a new industry.

Actions Needed

• Business leaders, including members of corporate boards, institutional investors, and corporate managers have a leading role to play in getting capital off the sidelines, more committed to building up American business and creating jobs. With the support from those who study business and finance, these leaders should evaluate the personal goals as well as the formulas and incentive structures that have produced the present long-term trends in net business investment and short-term horizons in assessing the duties of business owners to all their stakeholders.

• In order for American businesses to be competitive in the global economy, they must invest in sustainable future growth for the long haul. That includes workforce development as well as R&D. The expectations of investors as well as policymakers, who set regulatory standards for financial institutions, should be realigned toward such a vision, as critical to the future of the nation.

• National and state governments can address the disparate treatment of household and consumer debt on the one hand and business debt on the other, either with more equal treatment in bankruptcy relief and/or the kind of standard setting that would encourage responsible securitization of business debt.

• Business leaders should also see the profitable opportunities in extending credit to their company's suppliers or retailers, using their understanding of the business, the firms involved, and the data tools becoming available.

• Potential business lenders and policymakers can supplement the role of banks in providing credit for young businesses by encouraging the growth of nonbank financial intermediaries, such as new platforms that both advise and finance firms in their and new financial platforms lending to small firms.

Chapter 5

Share the Knowledge, Innovate the Jobs

In 2013 one of the most powerful weapons that troops from the 10th Mountain and the 101st Airborne Divisions took with them to Afghanistan was network power. Over a thousand soldiers were equipped with a modified smartphone, special software apps, and a secure, easy-to-use radio. The system did not rely on cell towers.

The network pushed powerful information out to the soldiers at the frontline. Soldiers could know where to go. They could see the location of other friendly soldiers as well as that of known enemy combatants. They could see the location of possible roadside bombs. They could draw on real-time intelligence, interpreting data or processing imagery in places thousands of miles away. The goal was to give a 21-year-old platoon sergeant the sort of "situation awareness" that once was the exclusive province of generals—if even the generals had been able to know that much.

Describing this Nett Warrior system, paired with a lightweight "Rifleman" radio, an Army official explained, "What the commercial consumer knows as a smartphone is really a very powerful multi-core mini-computer that is made in high volume at very low cost." The system can be used with a "reticle," a small heads-up display to display information visually, but most soldiers just use the phone, a modified Samsung Galaxy II. America's larger allies have similar systems under development. Such systems have the potential to give soldiers "a revolutionary game-changing capability."[1]

And not just soldiers. Some military veterans, including a former chief engineer from Raytheon, lead a company called DAQRI, a fast-growing business based in Los Angeles. DAQRI has successfully developed and tested several kinds of hardware and software to extend network power and augment reality. One is a "smart helmet." The helmet may at first seem like what any other worker might wear around a worksite—if, that is, the hardhats had been designed by costume designers from the new *Star Wars* movie.

The DAQRI helmet.

Among its many features, this lightweight helmet includes an augmented reality display and an inertial locator system. Integrated, they "augment" the real-life image a worker can see. Suppose a worker is gazing at a tangle of pipes or a complex engine. Using networked data, the worker sees what is in front of him as if it was the object of graphic art, mixed with the real thing. The "augmented reality" can highlight the schematics of the system and add in guidelines of what the worker should do.

Augmented reality user-view from the DAQRI helmet.

In tests the system not only virtually eliminated errors in controlled trials of people performing wing repairs; it also helped others away from the work reevaluate whether their textbook solution to the problem was really best. The company believes that, empowered by technology like this, "the future of work is here."[2]

Our Argument

Take a moment to unpack the story of tools like DAQRI's smart helmet. There are really two stories at work here. American leaders should understand both of them—and how they connect.

First, there is a "sharing" story about all the data and knowledge that a network can pull together and share. If machines as well as humans are contributing data, the network can pool it all, and participants can gain some powerful insights. Part of this story is about how small businesses can also share in such networked knowledge.

Second, there is a parallel "empowerment" story about the way this shared knowledge can be pushed to the outer edge of the network—the edge that is on the frontline, or faces a customer, or is in the field inspecting a pipeline. This is a story about how, thus empowered, a company can reimagine the kind of work those line employees can do.

> • One part of this story is about how important it is for American leaders to think about ways to invest in, improve, and "upskill" the jobs of line employees. We will point out that such a "good jobs strategy" lifts the employees and profitability too. It can very much pay off even in stereotypically low-wage sectors like low-price retail.
> • But our empowerment story is more radical than that. It is about how such empowered employees can allow companies to reinvent what kind of services they provide or tasks they perform. They can redesign their business models to pick up on the revolutionary capabilities that can be pushed outward to the edges of the networks. This kind of "job reinvention" has happened before in American economic history, and, in more imaginative institutions, it is beginning to happen again.

Shared Knowledge and Network Power

Network power can instantly share knowledge in two ways: the accumulated knowledge of the network, including its analysis of available data, moves out to the edge of the network, where it can give small businesses some of the powers of big business and give frontline workers immediate access to insights from the whole organization. Meanwhile, the knowledge of the frontline "sensor" is shared back, reinforcing the understanding of the network.

To understand the opportunity, though, it is helpful to remember how powerful a resource data can be. This was one of the favorable circumstances we discussed in chapter 2.

In this chapter we want to emphasize not just the use of data but the pooling of knowledge that can happen when data resources are coupled to network power.

Imagine Farmer Jane in Iowa. Farmer Jane is thinking about what to plant and how to irrigate. The agricultural equipment supplier John Deere doesn't just handle Farmer Jane's tractor. John Deere connects Farmer Jane to a networked data service. The service processes very large datasets drawn from many sources, such as location-specific weather forecasts and crop-planting histories, combined with information collected from farm equipment sensors, such as data on soil conditions and water levels.[3]

The network can cue the farmer to provide real-time, farm-specific suggestions about planting, harvesting, and plowing—including crop yield projections. Farmer Jane accesses the network through a computer or even a smartphone. Other companies may join in the network, adding their insights—such as Bayer Crop-Science or DuPont or Monsanto. As the farmer operates equipment, the data can constantly be updated and refined. She can then even transmit updated guidance to her planter to get the right seeding or crop treatment.

Preliminary estimates are that Farmer Jane, and all the people involved in her success, make handsome profits from the use of such services. Farmer Jane is also moving to the use of unmanned aerial vehicles as well.

These capabilities enable farmers to cultivate with greater variety and more nuanced choices. The machines are smarter. The farmer is smarter too. Farmer Jane's own knowledge has just been multiplied, minute to minute, by vast, remote resources of data and science.

Depending on the farmer's ecological or growing goals, different kinds of insights can be sought from such a powerful network. The "upskilling" of farmers becomes a cost factor: the cost of training farmworkers to work with and take advantage of all the possibilities. Preliminary evidence suggests the benefits well outweigh the costs.

Cloud services have gone into business, offering network power of many kinds to smaller businesses that cannot afford to amass all these capabilities on their own. But SMEs are still only beginning to grasp the possibilities.[4] A number of companies are trying to push these "cloud" capabilities out to the edge of business networks, as Apple and IBM are now attempting to put artificial intelligence applications, like IBM's Watson, on Apple's mobile devices.

These advances can create more jobs.[5] One way is by being more profitable and competitive, able to grow the business. Or a business can earn money by producing in new ways, and the new ways may require adding new kinds of jobs. Go back to the example of Farmer Jane. Suppose she is empowered to switch from growing just one or two standard crops in a standard way to a more varied menu, tailored to the vagaries of that season's weather or market conditions. She might then need more help to market the variety of products to different customers.

Understandably, big businesses are more alert to these possibilities than smaller ones. Most of them have started investing in data analysis. But these plans are still in their early stages. As of 2014 only 13 percent of even the larger firms surveyed had fully deployed these new plans.[6]

Several major companies, including Salesforce and Apple's partnership with IBM's Watson division, are trying to make data analysis more broadly available. A recent Salesforce product, Wave, is meant to be so user-friendly that a Salesforce official said, "This should feel a lot more like 'Angry Birds' than getting angry at [the] IT [department] because you're not getting the data that you want."[7]

Consider, too, the way such networked information sharing could affect the current model for delivering health care. In an emergency, or far from home, caregivers need the patient's most critical medical information. Most physician offices and hospitals are finally beginning to use electronic medical records.[8]

For a long time many in the health care business or observing it from the outside have been waiting for the day when a "learning health care system" becomes a reality, when an individual's past medical information, past illnesses, medications, allergies, and procedures can be combined with the latest evidence from medical studies and journals to improve medical decision making and reduce errors.

There are some promising examples:

- medication errors may be reduced by 50 percent by giving nurses mobile laptops and barcode scanners to ensure that the drug, dose, and delivery route for a medication are correct and match the barcode on the patient hospital bracelet;[9] and
- mobile devices are allowing doctors and patients alike to access medical records on smartphones and tablets so that an American patient can retrieve her medical records from a hospital in Tokyo, and in turn her doctor can instantly review her materials on an as-needed basis.[10]

But accessing patient information and the best of the existing medical evidence base is just the beginning. It is time to move from our story about the network power of "sharing" to our parallel story about "empowerment" and the reinvention of what businesses can deliver.

"Good Jobs Strategy" Meets the Digital Revolution

We have to start by taking a hard look at the general way in which American firms think about the costs and value of their line employees. We begin this story with what many people might consider the hardest case with the most disposable low-wage employees: low-price retail.

Zeynep Ton is a professor at MIT's business school. She studies low-price retail stores. After years of such study, visiting stores all around America and in Europe, she came to a conclusion that may surprise many Americans. She concluded that retail chains that give their employees good work also, over the long haul, can make much more money. She calls this the "good jobs strategy" in low-price retail.[11]

When such retailers try to solve cost problems by understaffing stores and paying workers less, the results usually go from mediocre to worse. On the other hand, she found that retailers that value their workers, invest in them, and give them valued career paths can do very well indeed.

How does this happen? Methods and processes may be standardized, but workers on the spot feel empowered with discretion about how to help customers. They are cross-trained to handle several kinds of duties and enlarge their sense of responsibility. By keeping staffing levels high, companies have people to afford a "training float." They can give employees predictable hours. They can be ready to provide great customer service when there are surges in business. The employees, knowing the business cares about them, reciprocate in ways that affect bottom lines in a hundred small ways.

Ton knew that her conclusions seemed counterintuitive to conventional wisdom about labor costs in low-price retail. So she recently published her book to detail the strategies and offer the numbers on how and why they were successful.

Good jobs strategies are not easy to carry out. They require disciplined management of operations without adding unnecessary and costly complexity in inventory management and pricing discounts (complexities that usually then have to be juggled by underpaid employees in understaffed stores). Such strategies also require disciplined execution of business plans, so that pressure to cut labor costs does not become the desperate way out of other bad business decisions. But again and again, as she documents, such strategies can work.

A well-known case in the United States is the contrast between two low-price retail chains: Costco and Walmart. Both are public companies. When Costco occasionally announces unexpectedly low earnings, some analysts are quick to pin the blame on the company's generous benefits for employees. In April 2004 a Deutsche Bank analyst told the magazine *Business Week*, "At Costco, it's better to be an employee or a customer than a shareholder." Stock values dropped 19 percent in one day.

The leaders of Costco were undeterred. The stockholders in Costco who stayed the course were well rewarded. Over the ten years from June 2003 to June 2013, Costco's share prices ended up rising by about 220 percent. In the same time period Walmart's share prices went up about 40 percent.[12]

The Starbucks CEO Howard Schultz recalled in an interview that during tough times for his company, shortly after he returned to top management, he got a call from an institutional shareholder. "[The institutional investor] said, 'You've never had more cover to cut health care than you do now. No one will criticize you.' And I just said, 'I could cut $300 million out of a lot of things, but do you want to kill the company, and kill the trust in what this company stands for? There is no way I will do it, and if that is what you want us to do, you should sell your stock.'"[13]

Testing the "good jobs strategy" hypothesis, the Hitachi Foundation has examined whether there really is a business case for investing in frontline workers. Businesses already spend a lot on training (about $170 billion). But this spending, the foundation reported, is "traditionally deployed to the highest educated and highest-paid employees. Training investment is often managed as a benefit for this cohort rather than linking employees to achieving priority business objectives."

The foundation identified nearly a hundred companies in several sectors that appeared to have found win-win solutions. Expanding profits and innovation, they also "extended the ladder of opportunity to their frontline and lower wage workers." What the firms had in common was "a vision and ability to reorganize the firm and engage workers more productively toward key business goals."

To see how this can work, we can visit Baltimore. Marlin Steel Wire Products is a small company in Baltimore that employs 32 people, specializing in custom metal forms like wire and mesh baskets or special sheet metal products for other businesses. Marlin budgets 5 percent of labor costs for training; the average in the precision metal-forming sector is around 1 percent. The cross-trained employees were more valuable, explains Drew Greenblatt, the president, better able to meet client demands, "because employees can move around from machine to machine. It's actually cheaper to run the business this way."

A highly skilled and flexible workforce, able to innovate on the spot, proved its worth, for instance, when Marlin got a panicked call from a major retailer. The retailer had ordered 7,000 wire baskets with particular specs from a Chinese manufacturer, but the supplier could not ship them on time. Marlin "had never made this type of basket," Greenblatt pointed out, "but we can offer speed to our customers because of our engineering skills and cross-training. We produced prints quickly and moved people to cells to produce that work in a hurry." The company's motto is simple: "Quality engineering quick."

Andy Croniser, who started at Marlin in 2007 as a temporary welder, said the approach makes him feel engaged and successful. Marlin has had eight years of consecutive growth, including 47 percent in three years. Despite the Great Recession, "we haven't had to cut an hour from anyone here, that I recall, and wages and benefits at Marlin are top of the line. From top to bottom we have dedicated people and a good atmosphere."

Greenblatt sees the results of his efforts in his bottom line, but he also sees the results when he comes to work every morning. "When I bought the company, everyone was earning minimum wage and I was the only one who owned a home and car. There used to be no cars in the parking lot and I could park wherever I wanted. Now more than half of the employees own a home, 100% own one, even two, cars, and the parking lot has cars double or triple parked."[14]

Our emphasis on the value of a good jobs strategy has become more timely. This era in America's economic history will rely for success on high-value communities of producers and on a lot of specialized production. That means reliance on technical and service skills pushed to the outer, customer-facing edges of the networks. One of the secrets in the success of a "fast casual" restaurant chain like Panera Bread is the good food. But another is the firm's investment in state-of-the-art educational tools, pioneered by companies like Cognotion, to improve the skills of front-line employees.

We find ourselves returning to a recommendation voiced more than twenty years ago, in a book co-authored by a former U.S. secretary of labor, Ray Marshall, with an educational leader, Marc Tucker. They predicted, "The key to both productivity and competitiveness is the skills of our people and our capacity to use highly educated and trained people to maximum advantage in the workplace."[15] That thesis may have been ahead of its time when they wrote those words, in 1992. But its time has surely come now.

Having made our case for a good jobs strategy, we now want to take the next step. We can link that strategy to the new capabilities that go with network power.

Network Power at the Hardware Store

Ace Hardware is in a very old-school line of business. Ace is a neighborhood hardware store. Well, to be more exact, it is really a hardware cooperative with thousands of locally owned and operated hardware stores. The local stores have a lot of independence. What the central organization of Ace Hardware used to do for these stores was to be a centralized purchasing agent, combining buying power. It also became an established brand.

All those local Ace Hardware stores were bound to be worried about the rise of big- box retailers. The little stores had to compete with outfits like Home Depot and Lowe's, as well as with online retailers. It might have seemed to many observers that the day of these little stores was done. Far from it.

Ace Hardware's basic strategy was not to try to compete mainly on price. Hardware stores do not just sell hardware. They sell advice on what to do, and what to do it with. The CEO of Ace Hardware, John Venhuizen, put it another way: "We don't try to say we have the lowest prices, but we will always win when it comes to people-to-people relationships. There's a misconception that retailing is a margin game, but it's not; it's about relationship building."

To empower all the thousands of stores carrying the Ace brand to offer that superior service, Ace Hardware adopted a strategy it called 20/20 Vision. The strategy uses network power to strengthen all those frontline retailers.

For example, one of the initiatives, called Helpful 101, was a training program that blended the best of online and in-person assistance shared across stores throughout America. Stores that completed the program would be certified if the store's customers, also participating in the network, agreed that the store's employees were delivering on the promised service. More than 1,200 retailers have already been certified through the program.

The company's strategy has been successful so far. Ace has held off the big-box and online competition, and most of its retailers reported that 2013 "would be the most profitable year they've ever had." The company is extending the concept to a platform, called The Supply Place, to apply this approach to B2B sales, selling to other businesses in the local community and also integrating the retailers' computer systems to the website.[16]

We are happy the company is succeeding. But that is not the main reason we write about it. The company was testing a strategic philosophy—one that innovated the work at the frontline, upskilling employees operating at the edge of the network, in order to succeed and even thrive.

Instead of "deskilling" employees with technology, this strategy uses network power to enhance employees, make them more valuable and valued. Employees are "upskilled." We believe the possibilities are only beginning to be explored.

Another Case Study for Networked Empowerment: Health Care

Innovators at New York's Paraprofessional Healthcare Institute (PHI) are now testing the proposition that networked technology can extend the insight of a nurse or a physician out to a medical assistant in the field. Although PHI has created elaborate training systems, its leaders have concluded that training the employees to do more is not enough. To innovate the job means, in this case, reworking the health care system that surrounds it.

Typically, frontline workers in health care are marginalized even as they are the eyes and ears on the ground. PHI's training of frontline workers to deliver home and personal care is therefore insufficient. It also has to educate more highly trained professionals, such as doctors and nurses, to listen to all the insights that now can come from these eyes and ears on the ground.

As the next stage of innovation, PHI is equipping home health care aides with tablets. They use the tablets to help assess client health risks and coordinate with the rest of the care team.

Often, in the past, it could take two or three days for home care workers' observations to be processed and acted upon by the nurses or doctors in charge of the case. False alarms and lack of clear and consistent dialogue also led to frequent and often unnecessary trips to the ER or doctor.

In this next stage, armed with their tablets (their link to networked knowledge), home care workers answer 15 screening questions suggested to them on the tablet on a daily basis to monitor for particular health risks. The questions rely on the care workers' trained observations. That information goes directly to the care team. The team can then act according to needs that are being documented in real time.

Thus far, the results of the pilot show that integration of the technology has decreased unnecessary visits to the hospital. It has increased confidence between the client and the aide, as well as between the aide and the care team.[17]

Employees across America are fearful of the way technology can devalue them. With imagination and investment, the networked economy could be a way to *re*value them instead.

Using Empowered Workers to Reimagine
the Business—Innovate American Jobs

Many Americans are understandably worried that technology will displace workers. One widely noted recent study by two Oxford professors observed, after examining the potential for computerization in 702 specific occupations, that about 47 percent of total U.S. employment might be at risk.[18]

The United States has been there before. For example, between 1820 and 1870 the proportion of the U.S. labor force engaged in farming in an industrializing state, Massachusetts, dropped from nearly 60 percent to roughly 13 percent. That was a change, coincidentally, of 47 percentage points.[19]

It was not easy, during the mid-1800s, to envision just what sort of work would take the place of those jobs as hired hands on farms. But by 1870 entire categories of jobs that barely existed in 1820, with titles like "engineers" and "public school teachers," were employing hundreds of thousands of people. Millions of people once employed to work with millions of horses found themselves working with machines instead. Then, as now, there were concerns that the new industries would not be as labor-intensive.

By retelling this history, we do not assume, though, that today's story will have a happy ending. For a great many people the older adjustments were extremely painful. Even where adjustments worked out, not all countries adjusted equally well.

What the past can do, however, is suggest questions. It can prompt ideas about possibilities.

The possibility worth recalling is the potential to reimagine the business and "innovate American jobs."

It goes beyond just imagining how to automate what Americans already do, what they do today. It requires imagining what they could do instead, what kind of service or work might be ideal and might now be possible. Then reimagine the business that delivers it.

America has gone through this sort of change before.

In past eras many American workers had little formal education. Children often went to work. So did the aged. Farms in the 19th century were run by the farmer's family along with hired hands and wanderers doing piecework and, in many cases, with slaves.

The industries of the early 20th century did not rely on slaves, although many had working conditions that sometimes seemed close to enslavement. Bouts of large-scale unemployment were a constant fear and an urban plague.

In 1910, 27 percent of all male workers in manufacturing reported their usual occupation as simply being "laborer." In the transportation sector, 30 percent of the workers described themselves this way.[20]

Americans transformed this labor force. They did it on a gigantic scale. Consider the example of when factories went from using steam engines to electric engines.

In the era of steam power, the typical factory had a single huge engine. The engine got its fuel from coal, so the factory was probably near a railroad siding where the coal cars could conveniently be unloaded. The huge engine spun a vertical drive shaft. All the machines in the facility drew their power from it via a complicated system of belts and smaller shafts arranged horizontally on each floor. Because the power available to machines declined the farther they were from the main drive shaft, factories in the steam era tended to be compact and cluttered. Workers clustered around the big machines to perform their repetitive tasks because, lacking any power supply of their own, they could only do what the big machine let them do.

If you want to picture what such a factory looked like, imagine a four-story-tall brick building with a tall smokestack, set next to a railroad or a river. You have probably seen buildings like this, or the ruins of them.

Electricity could change this whole factory system. Powerful electric motors could be made that were much smaller than their steam equivalents. For one thing, they didn't need to be fed with coal and water.

Eventually, it became feasible to attach a separate electric motor to each machine in the factory. That way, machines could be arranged in whatever ways made sense. Individuals could have their own power—literally their own power supply. So they could have their own workbench. They could do more specialized work with their own power tools.

Businesses were not as tethered to a place where they could get coal deliveries. Businesses started relocating. They began building factories in the long, low buildings we now associate with manufacturing. Tall narrow factories became a thing of the past.

But at the dawn of electrification few businessmen saw any of these possibilities. Few could envision any of these benefits.

The steam way was called "group drive." The electricity option, giving everyone or every machine its own power, was called "unit drive." A historian of this process has observed with amazement that, even after twenty years of debate between the merits of group drive and unit drive, the issue was still up in the air at the end of the 1920s.[21]

The decisive victory of unit drive during the 1930s turned out to be one of the great catalysts of American industrial success in the 20th century. Electrified factories were a key reason why American productivity per worker soared even during the Depression years. These redesigned factories formed the foundation for the production miracles during World War II and the postwar American prosperity that came later.

As electrified factories proliferated, their owners and managers realized that when they innovated the jobs and the whole way they imagined their business, they also needed to invest more in their workers. To make best use of the new facilities, machine operators needed to work more in interdependent teams. The workers had to be left more on their own, to be given more autonomy than was the norm in the old factories. Frontline workers had to be able to read, write, reason, and communicate. In short, they needed to be much more educated.

Despite this demand, and even though such industries hired heavily and paid well by the standards of the time,[22] in the early decades of the 20th century there was still much resistance to the idea of having universal education continue through high school. Some said that high schools were elitist. Others objected to their expense. Still others argued that the schools paid insufficient attention to moral education. Some questioned whether all children were intelligent enough to benefit from additional years of school.

Yet, on this issue of universal high school, businesses and community leaders joined forces. They won the fight. The result was that by the mid-20th century America had the most skilled, literate, and well-paid industrial workforce in the world. This, then, was the workforce capable of operating more modern machinery, capable of building new automobiles and fixing the old ones.

When businesses made the leap, it was a win-win. The businesses did better. The employees became more capable and were paid more.

Creating more valued career pathways is not an equation with just one factor in it. The electrification story shows that a strategy to innovate the jobs also was a strategy to reimagine the business. The workers had to step up, getting the training they needed both from the firm and from public education. And the education system had to step up too.

This history is a reminder of possibility. Americans have proven that they can summon the imagination to conceive of a different workplace. The easy, initial route is to stay with the established model. Automate what people do now. Deskill workers. A company has a worker now doing a low-skill task. Replace the worker with a robot.

What if, instead of reimagining the worker (person to robot), the employer reimagined the task? Instead of doing the same thing with a machine, why not combine the person with the machine and do a different, better thing—a more rewarding and profitable task?

It has happened before. But it took imagination and investment to see those ways to redesign businesses, to see how much more fruitful that could be.

Why should Americans think this is an idea that can work only once?

The "New Artisans"

GE has been giving an example of how to reimagine a business. In its case GE is putting particular reliance on smarter machines. The old model was that GE would sell a business a machine that it needed. Pretty straightforward.

The new model is that GE instead analyzes what task the business is trying to do with the technology, and the assumed cost to do that. Then GE offers a deal: it will provide a mix of machines and services to perform that end task.

The machines are "smart," with thousands of sensors reporting back to GE how well they are working. So the deal is not just a transaction to buy a piece of equipment. It is a deal about the whole performance of the business task. GE had to "abandon its traditional 'box seller' mentality [sell you the gadget in the box] in favor of solution-based sales that focused not only on pain points but also on exactly how to enhance the customer's operating performance."[23]

If the business gets better performance for less money, the deal is that the business gets more profit and GE gets more revenue. GE then monitors its machines' performance continually through new networked software. It stays with the whole task, servicing the machines or adjusting the technological solution, to achieve the customer's end goal at lower cost.

Profiting from these win-win solutions, GE has been making hundreds of millions of dollars in added revenue from the success of this transformed business vision. It relies on smarter machines, "digital ubiquity," and also on a different kind of workforce—a networked mix of hardware and software people, of builders and servicers. It is not the old paradigm of technology displacement and replacement, but a new paradigm of "connectivity and recombination."[24]

Many Americans know that "the quality of the service improves when the worker combines technical expertise and human flexibility." The greater power of machines does not need to be a story of replacement. It can be about complementarity of humans *and* machines, including highly capable robots. That includes the mass movement toward more and more customized products and services, provided by what Lawrence Katz has called "the new artisans."[25]

Thinking about the workforce in this way would be a big shift in mindset for many American executives and managers. Underestimation of their workforce (which can be a self-fulfilling prophecy) and disappointments with the skills of their workers have led managers into the habit of deskilling frontline workers, taking away their judgment and flexibility. What could then be more natural than to replace them with robots.

To consider a different pathway, we have some suggestions for business and for government.

More Data Sharing among Businesses

Business must take the lead in using networked data analytics and applying those possibilities to the workforce. Many businesses will have difficulty doing these tasks on their own. Some firms wonder, with some cause, whether "big data" is overhyped.

New businesses are emerging that can help businesses collect data and show them how to use it. The firm Salesforce is already a major force in this realm. Companies like Salesforce and new kinds of business organizations may be able to join forces to pool data that can collectively benefit all, but are impossible or too costly for any one firm to undertake.

The health care sector provides an example of this. Physicians, hospitals, and insurance companies—some of them rivals—all have access to complementary data that could be of use to all, if they can find ways to help them share. There may be a role for governments or nonprofits to help create clearinghouses where sharing can be done with appropriate protections, solving some of the difficult technical problems in combining seemingly incompatible databases.

The NIH has set a promising precedent in its BD2K initiative (Big Data to Knowledge), pooling data for the collective benefit of biomedical science. Another approach uses a distributed architecture to link and analyze data from many kinds of sources. The U.S. government's Food and Drug Administration has the Sentinel project to identify adverse reactions to drugs. The participants keep control of their data, but they make it available for this ongoing safety and public health analysis.

The private sector is also short on sufficient talent in data analytics and statistics. But the deeper problem is in the way companies organize their work on data. As a McKinsey study pointed out, firms may have "to redraw organizational charts so that analytics are not simply slotted into the IT department but are part of cross-functional execution teams." The instinct to guard data, not share it, runs deep.[26]

Upskill the Workforce and Reimagine What Workers Can Do

When information technology first began making very large impacts on companies, in the 1990s, a team of economists including Erik Brynjolfsson noticed that the biggest returns to IT innovation came when organizations innovated the work processes that used the new technology. Enterprises gained the most when they changed the organization, not just the machine.[27]

The health care sector again provides a large example of what can be done. This sector has a lot of polarization between high-wage and low-wage workers. The trend is accelerating. Growing health care needs combined with resource constraints mean more paraprofessionals, largely in low-wage positions.

For instance, there are more than 570,000 medical assistants working today, with median earnings of about $29,000 per year, and medical assisting as a profession is projected to grow at a rapid pace. Training and preparation for this position is uneven—often inadequate. Many medical assistants carry training-related debt.

An even lower-skilled, lower-paid job category is that of the home health aide. It may seem jarring to imagine home health care aides as "new artisans." We are used to seeing them more as laborers, doing hard, stressful work helping an elderly patient eat or changing the bed linens.

Our argument challenges leaders to imagine what such jobs could be, should be—for the benefit of everyone involved—and then to think about how to get there.

To take the case of the medical assistant or home health aide, imagine that

- the aide is also enabled, at the edge of a health care network, to observe the patient through wearable or handheld networked sensing abilities, like the products now being developed by DAQRI or like Microsoft's HoloLens, and is thus virtually joined by a nurse or a physician in gathering information about the patient's condition;
- the aide is part of a network in which the information about the patient appears on a "dashboard" that can access all the relevant, up-to-date information about that patient, programmed to warn anyone involved about the need for extra attention to certain medical indicators or possible drug interactions;
- the aide is placed in a career pathway, developed by both management and labor, that identifies gaps in

education, offers flexible options to address them, and shows ways that the aide can gain more skills and play more valued roles with experience; while

• the work itself can be integrated into the training, using the practical experience and sharing ideas among peers, linked in a network.

Play this out a bit, and it is not hard to see how the humble medical assistant or home health care aide can become much more. Already, many nonclinical tasks often do not require the physician's or, in some cases, the nurse's advanced training, and therefore can represent a misuse of high-level skills. Advanced practice providers, such as physician assistants or nurse practitioners, can complete tasks that do not require physician-specific skills. Wider use of technology, such as electronic health records or apps, could allow some physicians to help many patients at home, according to a study examining the medical workforce.[28]

Imagine a new way of organizing health professionals to optimize their roles in precisely the right way. Sensors, wearable devices, and remote monitoring may make having a strep test or monitoring anyone's vital signs possible wherever the person is. Networks and smartphones have made all of that data easily transmittable. Big data, open data, and high-powered analytics can enable the patient and the professional to have just the right information at their fingertips wherever they are and streamline critical communications with the rest of the caring team.

Health care is being pushed to the frontlines, whether we are ready or not. The frontlines are no longer defined as the doctor's office or the emergency room. The frontlines are wherever the patient is, when the patient needs care. We can even conceive of a return to house calls.

Trained frontline workers can transform the way care is delivered and optimize the use of nurses and doctors who are already stretched. As the level of patient complexity is understood, complicated individual cases are routed to the highly trained physicians, and less complicated routine care can be delegated to paraprofessionals armed with technology and decision support tools.

Appropriately trained, paraprofessionals can take on greater responsibility for administrative duties and for basic preventive and chronic care. They can serve as health coaches and support patient self-management. By taking on routine tasks, these staff further free up skilled doctors and nurses to attend to the more complex aspects of the health care.[29]

The biggest obstacles to changing the system are not technological. They are institutional and cultural and social. Today's America regards frontline health care workers the way industrial America regarded its frontline workers a hundred years ago—as unskilled laborers. There is no generally accepted standard for frontline care.

This fastest-growing employment group in the country is also among the lowest paid. Therefore retention is a very significant problem. Treated and trained as day laborers, people have less incentive to stay in a given role. On average, managed care entities hiring home health aides see upwards of a 40 percent attrition rate on an annual basis—which may come as little surprise, given the long hours, frequent periods of isolated work, and pay rates consistently below $10 per hour.

Creative Joint Investments in Workforce Training

No single organization usually wants to shoulder the responsibility for innovating the jobs and the associated task of upskilling the lower-wage part of the workforce. One creative model for a training program that shared the costs was developed in Philadelphia. The National Union of Hospital and Healthcare Employees, part of the AFSCME, which is part of the AFL-CIO, cut a creative collective bargaining deal in 1974. All the employers had to pitch in 1.5 percent of gross payroll to a training fund. At first there were only nine employers. Now there are more than fifty, from hospitals to community clinics.[30]

The pooled funds are administered jointly by employer and union representatives, each side filling half of the seats on the board. The fund itself is a nonprofit reporting to this joint board. It has a rather anodyne title: the District 1199C Training and Upgrading Fund.

This little-known fund changed the world of a woman in her 50s named Debra Burton. When she was 18, Debra was on her way to becoming an all too common American statistic. She dropped out of high school. She was a single mother.

Debra had gotten off the usual highway of advancement. For an African American single mother in North Philadelphia, there were not too many on-ramps for getting back on that highway. She could hear and see the traffic going by; she was now one of the millions left behind, with few options.

Debra's education had been a mess, and, even as she got her life together, full of determination, there was no easy way to repair the damage. Eventually, she obtained her GED, but this credential has little meaning or evident value to many employers.[31]

Debra found work at the bottom of the health care system in what can be a dead-end job, as an entry-level health or nursing aide. She spent many years in that work, staying in her community, looking for ways to improve herself. Over the years she thought she had picked up what she called the "head knowledge" about how to do more, but that was not the same as "book knowledge." Debra had none of the usual formal credentials. Her pay and opportunities remained low.

Already into her 40s, Debra thought it was not too late to turn her head knowledge into the credentials she would need to advance. She quickly encountered all the old gaps in her education. The nonprofit fund provided teachers who worked with her part-time in completing preparatory and technical training for two years to get her up to the level at which she could do college-level work.

First, Debra enrolled in a behavioral health technician program at the Training Fund, which led into an associate's degree in health and human services offered through a partnership of the Training Fund and Philadelphia University. The joint labor management program reimbursed her tuition expenses, helped with the supplemental education she needed, and arranged some more tutoring.

As in many traditional college structures, the pace for a part-time student is slow. Think about the challenge from Debra's point of view. Working hard to make ends meet and play her role in her family, it was hard for Debra to carve out time to do the commutes for classes. Juggling her commitments, she could manage to complete one course at a time. "The work was hard and took long hours," she remembered.

Debra had to complete, as is standard, 20 such courses to earn an associate's degree at her college. But the program was innovatively designed to help her get through what otherwise would have seemed an impossibly long journey.

The equivalent of 7 of the 20 courses could be attained through the Training Fund's own elaborate vocational education program. The remaining 13 courses were taught in eight-week increments, not the usual semester length, and were also offered on-site at the Training Fund. Nevertheless, this curriculum combined with Debra's time constraints required her to stick with the program, year after year after year.

Lives are often too complicated to be able to manage such long journeys. Most students in community colleges do not complete them and earn the associate's degree. Debra did.

The Training Fund stayed with her, helping with tutoring, with tuition, and with encouragement. Finally, at age 51, Debra earned her associate's degree. Armed with that credential, she could also get a much better-paid job in the North Philadelphia Health System.

Debra was understandably proud. She has now started part-time study to earn a bachelor's degree. "Never in my wildest dream did I think I would have a college degree. I'm excited."

Debra Burton in her home in Philadelphia.

Although we are staggered by the effort our existing structures require—in the early 21st century—in order for women like Debra to get the education and the credentials they need, the strategic vision of the union and the employers paid off for her, as it has for many others over the years. The organizations realize how much they can gain if they design valued career paths, linked to innovative training, to keep entry-level jobs from being dead ends.

Unfortunately, creative shared solutions like the Philadelphia fund are still unusual. Extensive research by the Robert Wood Johnson Foundation found that "[m]any health and health care organizations devote considerable resources toward developing clinical and professional staff, but they rarely make more than a minimal investment in a sizeable segment of their workforce: front-line employees."[32]

From 2005 to 2012 that foundation managed a major seven-year experiment to learn whether well-designed training programs could transform such common, vicious cycles into virtuous ones.

It required an effort: hospitals had to think about career paths and change their usual routines. An outside team evaluated 17 such programs. One of them was the Philadelphia program that Debra Burton had used.

The researchers found that such good jobs strategies in health care worked. Employment stabilized. In one setting, turnover rates went from 90 percent down to 25 percent or lower. Employees gained more credentials; they usually improved their wages. The quality of frontline patient care also improved. Given the way the U.S. health care system is organized, better patient care may not add much to a hospital's bottom line. Some institutions consoled themselves at least with the report that they could bill at a higher rate for the more credentialed workers! The institutions were glad they had participated, glad they had taken the trouble to develop ways to upskill their employees. More confident and engaged employees had strengthened the institutions.[33]

All this remains within the existing conventional model. This is training the people, not innovating the job. Our suggestion is that many jobs in health care, and millions across America, might also be innovated in ways that reimagine the business too.

Legal Frameworks for Networked Sharing

In order for networked data to be used, the data must be open or shared. Opening data to the public is also likely to have significant social value. Individuals can make better-informed decisions. So can governments. And so can the watchdog agencies that want to make governments more transparent and accountable. We detailed the significance of open and shared data in chapter 2, as one of the tools Americans can wield in the new economy.

The engineered production of data resources also carries with it great issues of its own, notably privacy. Addressing these data governance issues holds the key to unlocking the full positive potential of the digital revolution.

The networked world has many kinds of information sharing.

And most people value privacy, but tend to judge what privacy they consider appropriate on the basis of the context. For example, by paying with a credit card, you let the credit card company know where you are located, but few Americans regard this as a violation of a right to privacy, in the context of processing their transactions and providing them with a verifiable billing statement. On the other hand, they would be quite upset if their location data were compiled into profiles sold to third parties or disclosed to the government. One of the best articulations of this principle of "contextual integrity," by Helen Nissenbaum, stresses that the "right to privacy is neither a right to secrecy nor a right to control." It is a "right to *appropriate* flow of personal information."[34]

In the absence of comprehensive privacy protections, Americans are uneasy. In 2010 the Federal Trade Commission recommended a "do not track" registry to provide privacy protections online. In 2012 the White House proposed a "Consumer Privacy Bill of Rights." Neither idea has advanced much.

As we mentioned in chapter 3, the sharing of more data will be impeded if users believe the networks are insecure or if they believe their data is not stored safely. Shared data is good. But as governments and other entities release more information, they have the task of protecting citizens and consumers. The current rules do not do enough to keep people from being "reidentified" by linking one source of data with another.[35]

As governments experiment with legal, policy, and technical solutions, a useful foundation does already exist. Though originally developed in the United States in the 1970s, to deal with another era's privacy concerns, there is wide international support for the Fair Information Practice Principles: individual control; transparency; respect for context; security; access and accuracy; focused collection; and accountability.[36] The challenge is to apply these principles in practice and find the balance to do it in a mix of industry self-regulation—codes of conduct that illustrate alternative ways to implement principles like these and build trust—

and government regulation, consumer awareness, and technical standards.

The privacy challenge must be addressed head-on. But even as data governance issues are being explored, there is ample room to rework American businesses and workplaces. Some of the most valuable data needed to support innovation does not even relate to individuals. Much that does relate to people can yield its value in formats that remove markers of personal identity. New tools are already available. Companies can already put their own information and information about their own customers to work. Network power holds great promise to empower thousands of small firms and millions of frontline employees, for the benefit of both.

Actions Needed

- All business leaders should follow the example of those who have already learned that a good jobs strategy for line employees is a best practice, especially as the economy becomes more advanced and the level of production and service delivery goes up.
- Firms should look hard at whether pushing out networked knowledge could raise the capabilities and value of their frontline employees. Innovating these jobs can mean reimagining what the whole business produces and delivers.
- Small businesses should examine new ways they can get stronger by sharing data, working with partners and third-party platforms.
- Health care institutions and health care platforms, in particular, should invest in line employees and reimagine what services they can provide.
- Business and labor can turn to proven examples of how, working with nonprofits and local public institutions, they may be able to share the costs of upskilling the workforce.

• For policymakers, more data sharing requires that they work through governance and privacy issues. The best approaches are not rigid. They look to the context of how the data is being used and balance a guiding set of principles in ways that build public trust.

Chapter 6

———

Better Made, in America

In the last chapter we discussed ways to rework the character of work itself, in a networked economy. In this chapter we widen our focus to reworking whole communities of producers. We start, though, with the story of an unusual small business.

Local Motors

The alarm goes off early in the morning for Jay Rogers at his home in Phoenix, Arizona. It is 5:30. About to be another hot day in the valley of the sun. Shake off the cobwebs. Limber up. Brew the coffee. It is time to believe again.

Jay is a true believer. Every day he goes to work he steps out the door knowing that he will have to believe that a small, inventive company can still succeed, believe that there is a market for their products, believe in the American Dream. And every day he will have to inspire others to believe right along there with him.

John "Jay" Rogers is the co-founder and CEO of a small business called Local Motors. He is wiry, fit, looks like a veteran—which he is. A firm, convincing speaker, he exudes confidence, like the guy who can see the road ahead. The road ahead though, for Jay, was not always so clear.

Jay was a child of privilege. His father was a real estate magnate in Houston, and circumstances were comfortable. But then his father was ruined by the savings and loan crisis of the late 1980s, and circumstances changed.

Jay had gone to Princeton. Like so many of his classmates, he went to work for an investment bank. Then Jay took a different kind of road. He joined the Marines. He became an infantry captain. He was deployed in Iraq and other garden spots.

After seven years of service, Jay left the Marines. He returned to the world of business, but not back to finance. Instead, after earning an MBA at Harvard, he pursued his fascination with design, engineering, cars, and motorcycles. He joined with others to build a business as a boutique manufacturer of unusual vehicles.

Interesting. More interesting is that Jay and his colleagues who have joined him in this young firm, Local Motors, are not just building unusual cars and cycles. They are prototyping a different *way* to build them, a different approach to how things can be made in America.

Jay Rogers, in front of the Local Motors "microfactory" in Phoenix, Arizona.

Technology is enabling a level of personalization by the consumer, of local production. "The point is that the individual is really the one who could have the power." This could bring back the excitement and creativity of craft in what he also calls a "third industrial revolution."

To design his cars, motorcycles, and powered bicycles, Jay looks to something he and others call co-creation. That means there are thousands of people joining in an Internet-organized community of designers. Enabled by new computer-assisted design software, the community of co-creators exchanges and votes on open-sourced ideas for each key component. They debate about the best overall look, the best chassis, the best side panel, or the best engine. Open-sourced means open designs. The innovations can spread, open to constant tailoring by more craftsmen and makers.

To software developers in America, these practices may seem familiar. In the world of hardware, they are newer.

Local Motors awards prize money and credit for winning ideas. Many components are ready-to-use items from other companies, like the vinyl wrap produced in partnership with 3M that takes the place of paint on some vehicles. Some designs really are meant to be "local," designed to suit a local environment, like a Boston winter, and produced locally.

To produce its vehicles, Local Motors relies on "microfactories." Ford's Dearborn plant covers 600 acres. The Local Motors microfactory in Phoenix is the size of a high school gym—an immaculate gym with flower plantings, soft music, and a relaxed team of professionals at work.

Local Motors even has a "mobifactory," built to fit into a shipping container. It can be hauled around by a truck and is being adapted for use by the U.S. Army to fix and fabricate needed parts in the field.

The larger vision, as Jay puts it, is to illustrate that "{w]e can develop a hardware system—that's commonly known as a vehicle—five times faster and with a hundred times less capital put into it."

Rogers and his colleagues imagine a hundred such microfactories, quickly rolling ideas out on the road.

These microfactories could customize vehicles for their communities—a Boston car, a Los Angeles car, a Beijing car—involving local consumers in the creative or even the building process. Jay thinks the third industrial revolution may be about happiness, not money. It is the satisfaction of participating in creation.

Local Motors is still just a small business. Its future is not assured. But part of its experiment is about the future of small business itself.

Traditional industrial auto companies rely on scale. They look to sales of hundreds of thousands of units to offset their capital and labor costs—setting up a big factory with heavyweight machine tools, elaborate supply chains, centralized distribution, and a large labor force—and still be able to make a profit.

Jay is investigating whether smaller, nimbler production, enabled by technology, can offer another approach. He wants to find out whether producers using different ways of making things can instead think of healthy profits on small, custom production runs. Maybe a lot of these runs, a lot of tailored vehicles, can add up to a big profit. But that is a very different idea; it is a 21st-century version of an older artisanal, craft mode of production for hard goods.

Last year Local Motors organized a competition to design an attractive and functional car that can be produced with 3-D printers. These are machines that "print" the components in layers in a small facility, not stamping out steel frames in giant presses. The winning car design, using relatively few parts, was built in public and driven around at a manufacturing conference in Chicago, or, to be more precise, the car was "printed + subtracted + formed and placed."

Getting the financing for new ideas like these has been a high hurdle for Local Motors. Jay discovered the hard way that today's financial system is actually not very interested in serving innovative small businesses. In his experience, venture capital may be eager to push money into "another corporate Twitter messaging service." For ideas like his, he had to scramble among friends or other enthusiasts to find investors in a different model for American makers.[1] As we discussed in chapter 4, Jay's experience with the way the American financial system now serves smaller businesses is not unusual.

Fortunately, after years of effort, Jay has found some private backers. He also has co-workers who share his vision and are excited by it.

In Jay's case, his idea is getting more notice. In 2014 one of the world's largest hard goods companies—GE—partnered with Local Motors to try out this new approach in a new way.

GE does not want to make cars. It is interested in the Local Motors approach to innovation and production. The large firm wanted to see whether approaches like this might be extended to more of the economy, in this case as a way to design other cutting-edge products and bring them more quickly to market. And if small companies end up building hundreds or even thousands of microfactories, they may look to companies like GE to supply the means.

Bridge the Misleading Divide between "Manufacturing" and "Services"

Read a little about the American economy, and you soon encounter what seem to be rival agendas. The spectators crowd close to the brightly lit boxing ring. The announcer pulls down the microphone:

> • In this corner, he shouts, is Dave Detroit! The onetime world champion, the battler for American manufacturing. He fights for people who make stuff! Who create new technology! He represents the spirit of America! Half the crowd cheers. There are a few jeers: "Aaah get outta here, you're in natural decline!"

• Beckoning to the other corner, the announcer calls out the bespectacled current champion of the world, Steve Cupertino! Steve stands up for the knowledge economy! He wields the power of software! He represents the new spirit of America! The other half of the crowd cheers. There are a few more catcalls: "No jobs!"

A battle like this is going on, at least in print. To pick a couple of examples: Suzanne Berger and her colleagues on the MIT Task Force on Production in the Innovation Economy published an outstanding book in 2013 called *Making in America*. There they vehemently refute an apparent "claim that a nation can thrive if its economy is based on services alone."

Another excellent book, by Enrico Moretti, titled *The New Geography of Jobs* and published a year earlier, discusses the "pale ghosts" of America's manufacturing centers. It explains that manufacturing is dying for deep structural reasons, and that the future lies with "the creation of knowledge, ideas, and innovation."[2]

Call off the fight. Raise the arms of both fighters. They can both be right. In fact, they should be allies. They are really on the same side.

Both sides want good producers. Both want plenty of innovation. Jay Rogers and Local Motors are excellent examples: they are "manufacturers"; they are also "knowledge workers" par excellence.

The arguments among the experts have been distorted by the way the statistics have been compiled over many years. Areas of the economy are put into various categories in order to measure the activity. Some categories that seem to cover physical objects ("if you drop it on your foot, it hurts") are labeled as "manufacturing" or "goods." Other categories are labeled as "services" or, even more confusingly, "information"—e.g., knowledge.

Over decades of economic work, these habitual divides have become culturally ingrained. They get locked in. Economists have to rely on these categories because that is the way the data is organized. It is hard to organize the data any other way, because then it would be hard to do comparisons with the older data.

These divides become ways of seeing the world. The popular image of manufacturing seems manual and outmoded to some. That then provokes an ardent defense by others.

All the sides concede that the landscape of American producers has changed. Because of the changes these old classifications no longer make as much sense. On the inside within today's businesses, many of these divides fall away. What takes their place is a complicated world of increasingly networked producers.

Think about the iPhone (or any smartphone). Is it a good, or is it a service? It is actually both. Take out the service portion, and it is a polished metal brick.

The smartphone is a bundle of goods and services. So is a restaurant. The smartphone maker has produced durables (buyers hope). The restaurant produces consumables (buyers hope).

Producers are software developers. They are engineers. They are cooks. They may be producing the software for a video game, a turbine blade for a jet engine, or a slow-cooked barbeque brisket. And, by the way, all of them use physical objects—often quite specialized objects—to produce these things.[3]

Most innovation comes from *producers*. On the frontlines every day, they are the ones confronted with problems to solve, the ones who see opportunities to grasp.

There are more and more producers. In energy, production of solar or wind energy is advancing in ways that could turn millions of homeowners or local businesses into producers, each contributing energy to a grid. Each may be employing both hardware and software to do it, linked to a network.

More and more of the objects are encoded with software. Software producers are not classified as manufacturers. But cars are software vehicles. There are tens of millions of lines of code, for instance, in the Chevrolet Volt.[4]

As a digital layer begins to coat most everyday objects and experiences, the role of programmers grows. Millions of new combinations come into focus. New kinds of entrepreneurs are needed to explore the possibilities. A giant firm like GE finds itself tapping the ingenuity of such tinkerers by forming a partnership with a self-described crowdsourced invention platform like Local Motors or the firm Quirky, which we described in chapter 2.

When they looked more closely at what went on in the "manufacturing sector," a team of McKinsey analysts noticed that a large proportion of what happened there actually consisted of services. From 30 to 55 percent of manufacturing employment consisted of service activities.[5]

The same was true in the supposed "services sector." For instance, even classic service businesses like Walmart and Amazon have spent enormous sums to develop complex technological and communication systems as part of their service delivery operations. These are not turnkey products that they just bought off the shelf. They involve satellite communications and other special hardware.

A group of experts led by John Zysman calls this transformation of services "dramatic, pervasive, and far-reaching." They observe, "[T]he distinction between products and services blurs, as manufactured products are increasingly embedded within and recast as services offerings. Clearly, traditional sectoral boundaries break down. . . ."[6]

Struggling with the statistical categories, the McKinsey researchers tallied nearly a trillion dollars of service inputs into manufacturing, then counted $1.4 trillion of goods going into services, and finally shrugged. "[T]he traditional manufacturing/ services perspective does not account for the synergies between the two economic realms. . . . The old manufacturing/services divide obscures a complete and accurate view of the role of manufacturing in the economy."[7]

Companies as diverse as Google, Apple, GE, Caterpillar, John Deere, Ford, and Microsoft all understand such integration. Companies that do not understand it pay a price.

For example, some service entities, like government agencies or banks or stores, have had notorious difficulties with technology acquisitions. Some of the latest fiascos have occurred in the recent rush among large retail stores or large government agencies to address cybersecurity dangers. As service agencies, they do not consider technology strategies part of their core operations. One reason for their difficulties is that such businesses have lost the capacity to master and integrate deeper technology innovation into their service delivery. They thought of technology as living in a different sector.

Berger and her MIT colleagues summed up their findings this way: "[I]n most of the firms in which we carried out our research the traditional line between 'manufacturing' and 'services' has become so blurred that it no longer serves to distinguish separable and distinct activities or end products. . . . [T]he activities that create most value—the ones that are most difficult for others to replicate—are bundles consisting of services and objects. . . ."[8]

The Taylorist Paradigm and America's Knowledge Workers

Peter Drucker called the ideas of the famed efficiency expert Frederick Winslow Taylor (1856–1915) "perhaps the most powerful as well as the most lasting contribution America has made to Western thought since the Federalist Papers." International organizations referred to Taylor's system as "a characteristic feature of American civilization."[9] Taylor's "principles of scientific management" laid out, in excruciating detail, how to break down every workman's task and organize it more efficiently.

One of Taylor's early followers was the industrialist Henry Ford, a pioneer of assembly-line methods for mass production. In his dystopian fantasy of the future, the English satirist Aldous Huxley—writing in 1931—set his *Brave New World* in the year 2540. The inhabitants of this brave new world regard Henry Ford as their messiah. Their calendars mark the year as 632 A.F. (After Ford). They pray to "Our Ford." They worship the assembly line for liberating the world from want.

But Huxley was writing a satire, not a celebration. In his brave new world, humans are hatched, bred for specialized roles. In the command economy of the world state, all citizens are taught from birth to consume as many standardized products as possible, because constant consumption is what keeps the economy and society stable.

It is hard to overstate the cultural influence of "Taylorism." The image it stamped on ways to viewing the economy did not just leave an impression on an English writer in 1931. Most Americans also equated much of American industry with routinized large-scale production.

In this view, manufacturing had a few distinct, defining features: cavernous factories and smokestacks on the outskirts of cities; masses of relatively low-skilled workers—nearly all of them men—in dark blue or gray overalls and caps; two or three shifts a day when men would clock in and clock out, with the occasional wail of a siren marking the end of one shift and the start of another. The economy seemed to be dominated by a small number of giant, highly integrated corporations in which professional management was separated from ownership, the professionals—the knowledge class—separated from the working class.

In the era of large-scale production, Americans remade many of their country's institutions in this image, this stylized view of the core of their economy. It is not a cultural image that was very flattering to the workers, at least not very flattering to their skills. "It is," Mike Rose explains, "as though in our cultural iconography we are given the muscled arm, sleeve rolled tight against biceps, but no thought bright behind the eye, no image that links hand and brain."[10]

The stylized view, overstating just the manual part of this labor, can obscure the skills many Americans gained in this era. As we pointed out in chapter 5, the new production technologies actually required more skilled kinds of jobs than had been needed in the past. Mass production allowed millions of low-skilled laborers to find productive jobs where they could acquire new skills and build careers. Workers in these industrial centers had (and still have) the opportunity to work in teams, solve problems on the assembly line, and get on-the-job training from more experienced colleagues. Even assembly-line work combines skill, creativity, and precision.

Despite these nuances, in the eyes of many the Taylorist paradigm equates American production with mass output. It propagates an image of mindless assembly lines organized by mindful efficiency experts.

That image is a triumph of historical myth over historical fact. There was a reality underneath it. But there was much more as well.

The reigning image of the mass production era was exaggerated by the enormous attention given to Taylorism (and to Ford). Significant parts of U.S. manufacturing during the second economic revolution looked nothing like these large centers of production with their layers of professional managers.

There were many companies, large and small, doing specialty production at that time. Some of these firms were large integrated anchor firms like GE and DuPont, inhabiting a world of extremely specialized work (atomic bomb components) as well as a world of mass production (light bulbs). Other firms also did big but specialized work, like making small numbers of ships or locomotives. Networks specialists made batch sets or very particular machine tools, furniture groups, jewelry, and many other products.

While the large mass production firms were centers of national attention, a good part of the production was actually being done by skilled workers using flexible working methods and machines that could adjust to constant change, organized by resourceful executives, and often in firms that remained family owned. They did not compete primarily on price. They competed on quality, style, and innovative novelty—"endless novelty," in the words of their best chronicler, Phil Scranton.[11]

Today even the physical work throughout the economy remains

quite demanding in cognitive skills. It requires plenty of brain-power to be a skilled waitress in a busy restaurant. Yet the "tendency to denigrate entire categories of work and workers is amped up in our high-tech era."[12]

In the conventional stereotype, the future "knowledge workers" complete college; they get their liberal arts rounding. As for the majority of Americans who do not have a college degree, well . . . leaders publicly wish that somehow all of them did, and subsidize banks to extend more debt so they can try.

The Alcoa Foundation discovered the cultural power of the Taylorist paradigm when it asked an outside group, Why is it so hard to get young Americans to pursue careers in skilled production work? The questioners were puzzled because these are now jobs such as programming for computerized numerically controlled machines, jobs that may pay *on average* more than $52,000 a year.[13]

There is a striking contrast between the United States and Germany. There manufacturing enjoys good social status and employs 22 percent of the workforce (the U.S. figure is 11 percent).

Several factors contribute to the German manufacturing miracle. But behind all of these factors lie a single idea: a belief among all the stakeholders in government, industry, and labor that processes of production truly matter. They matter not just for productivity but also as a way to develop human capital. "Germany innovates in order to empower workers and improve their productivity," but in the United States, with its Taylorist mindset, there is instead a cultural habit that invites attention to how to "reduce or eliminate the need to hire those pesky wage-seeking human beings."[14]

The Alcoa Foundation investigators reported back, "Young people [in America] tend to think of manufacturing in terms of routine, manual labor, involving assembly lines and 'dirty' work." "One community college student said, 'If [manufacturing] was a last resort I'd probably have to go in, but that's definitely not what I want to be doing.' Another student told us: 'My parents don't really want me to be working in those kinds of jobs. This is why I'm going to college.

I really respect all those people because it's really hard work, but minimum wage doesn't satisfy what you need to live."[15] The young people also had little idea what these jobs really paid.

Another unfortunate cultural hangover is from the more recent past. It is an image of high labor costs for American workers and the belief that American workers are much more costly than highly skilled foreign workers. This image is less true today than it was at any time in the prior half a century.

Labor costs include both wages and benefits. In a high-profile and relatively comparable industry like automobiles, American labor costs are about on a par with workers in Japan. American workers classified as being in manufacturing are the most productive in the world, adding over 50 percent more value a year per worker than their counterparts in Japan. And this is according to an analysis done in Japan.[16]

The American automobile industry and its labor force did go through a terrible reckoning. During the Great Recession the Big Three restructured deeply, including their labor relationships and costs, in painful negotiations involving their unions and the U.S. government. By 2012 GM directly employed only 49,000 hourly workers in the United States, down from 78,000 in 2007. But there the decline stopped.

In 2011 all of the Big Three had labor costs that were competitive with any other auto producer in the United States ($56 per hour in total compensation for GM; $55 per hour for Toyota). All of the Big Three now make a good profit on every car they sell, and they are selling plenty of them.

The BMW decision to center global production of its SUV line in South Carolina was an important signal. This is not just a regional production center. It is the lead factory for global production of this line. In 2012 BMW declared its intent to invest another billion dollars in the facility, which built more than 300,000 vehicles that year, 70 percent of them to be sold outside of the United States.

Since 2012 American auto plants have been running at nearly full capacity, and expansion is underway. Tens of thousands of new workers are now being added. A "hiring spree," one observer called it, "as car makers and parts suppliers race to find engineers, technicians and factory workers to build the next generation of vehicles."[17]

The issue is not whether America can travel through a time machine and return to its past. The issue now is whether, having already gone through the wrenching shakeout, Americans are well positioned to change the trend lines, to move them upward again.

Producer Communities as Ecosystems

A pair of experts, Gary Pisano and Willy Shih, have written eloquently on the "rise and decline of the American industrial commons."[18] We share their concern. We only think the term "industrial" may be too narrow. We see these communities as networks of producers of many kinds. We see them as ecosystems.

One of the best-known examples today of a producer ecosystem is the one in Silicon Valley. Another is the historical heart of the machine tool industry, in the Ohio Valley.

A specialty steel manufacturer moved to North Canton, Ohio, in 1901. It was then a family-owned company called Timken. Timken soon acquired a steelmaker, so that it could make the particular kinds of steel needed for the specialized bearings and other products it sold.

Over the years Timken became a center for innovative and increasingly advanced manufacturing. As many other American factories were shutting their doors between 1980 and 2010, Timken's sales were quintupling. New plants opened and expanded in South Carolina and in Europe. Rising to Fortune 500 status, Timken became a key sponsor of research consortia, working with colleges and their students in North Canton and in Akron, letting students in on tests to build ultra-large bearings for wind turbines and other new designs.

Networks of specialty producers like this, with highly skilled workforces and connections to related institutions for research and training, are familiar to observers of Germany's famed *Mittelstand* of thousands of manufacturers. They are becoming defining features of China's production economy today. America used to have more than its share.

Timken serves as a reminder that, though the image of American manufacturing was one of mind-numbing work by semiskilled workers, the reality has often been different. Searching for "endless novelty," these companies frequently relied on retained earnings, investing for the long haul, investing in the skills of their employees. DuPont invested patiently for ten years during the 1930s in the work that finally produced nylon. The results were the kind of spectacular innovations that led to America's golden age.

Yet the half-hidden world of these American problem solvers is endangered. Funds for government-sponsored R&D are dropping. And the networks of makers are often viewed by the financialized part of the economy through their version of the Taylorist paradigm, as more interchangeable cogs.

In 2013 Timken was still flourishing. But the principal shareholders broke up the company. The shareholder move was led by the asset managers for the pension fund of the California State Teachers Retirement System. The shareholders wanted to spin off the steelmaking.

Timken's chairman, Tim Timken, and its CEO, James Griffith, opposed the move. They protested that the integration of the production with the steelmaking had been essential over the long haul to the company's ability to solve problems. It was part of their marketing strategy to be sure of getting the particular steel they needed for new and unusual innovations.

Management was overruled. Stock prices were predicted to be higher in the short run from the spin-off; it was deemed the best value choice for the pension fund.[19]

The asset manager's analysis was, in effect, a version of the old paradigm. From that point of view: I see these units. Here is one unit to do materials, like steel. Here is another unit to do industrial components. In the short run, if the materials unit is not doing so well, it should be sloughed off. The units should be rearranged for short-term profit and shareholder value.

The value of a specialized innovative network that had thrived for a hundred years with a skilled workforce did not fit easily into short-term calculations of yield for an institutional investor. During the past thirty years, as a significantly higher proportion of the American economy has passed into the effective control of financiers and institutional investors, such calculations have had enormous cumulative effects.[20]

The Timken example is not unusual. In chapter 2 we mentioned how close Dow Chemical came to being broken up by a private equity play during 2006. Amid a September 2014 effort to break up DuPont (a company that is also flourishing), one analyst explained, "[T]here's a lot of investor skepticism about the value of those R&D links. Most investors prefer simpler, more-focused portfolios."[21]

Such results do not help the odds for America to rebuild and strengthen its own *Mittelstande*. "[H]ow likely is it," an MIT professor who studied the process asked, "that either [the new companies emerging from the breakup of Timken] will be so active in strengthening the Ohio industrial ecosystem? Judging by the records of other companies that have gone through similar restructuring, I am not optimistic."[22]

We tell the Timken story not because we are against all corporate restructuring. Sometimes such restructuring can be very constructive.

We tell the story as a caution against the possibility that many Americans, including canny portfolio investors, may not yet adequately understand producer communities as ecosystems. They may not know how to attach an appropriate value to the role that companies and other institutions play in a dynamic community of producers.

Another activist investor group went after the still-flourishing

DuPont again, this time with a larger war chest and assisted by the California State Teachers Retirement System, in January 2015. Watching this, a Yale professor named Jeffrey Sonnenfeld observed that the activists were going after "the good guys." "This can't be good for long-term investors," he added, "or for the industrial base and economic health of this nation."[23]

Most Americans are taught about ecosystems in school. They learn about interdependence, for instance, the way trees can prevent soil erosion or absorb carbon from the atmosphere.

If investors think an ecosystem is doomed, that a company like Timken is part of a dying line of business, then of course they will act. If the ecosystem is healthy and growing, however, as it was in this case, then it is important for all the stakeholders to enlarge their concepts of value, to understand the way these communities are taking form.

The investors are often key stakeholders in a community that offers strong longer-term prospects. So, as farmers used to say, they would have to be pretty desperate for short-end money if they start selling their seed corn.

Some of the most interesting studies of these producer communities have been done by a group of scholars associated with the Harvard professor Michael Porter. Porter and his colleagues have done much to popularize thinking about what they call clusters.

These clusters, they stress, are not single industries. They are clusters of complementary activities that can embrace multiple, connected industries. For instance, the motor vehicle and car bodies industry is only one among the fifteen industries in what Porter calls an "automotive" cluster.[24] These complementary specialized activities range from research to design to fabrication to marketing to lawyering.

The Job Multipliers from Healthy Producer Ecosystems

Over the last five years, Houston, Texas, has had the best job growth of any major metropolitan area in America. Since the beginning of

2010 the Houston area has added 420,000 new jobs to its employ-ment base, an increase of 17 percent.[25]

A simple explanation could just exclaim, "Energy!" That is indeed a big part of the story. Yet hardly any oil or natural gas is actually taken from the ground in the Houston area. Houston is an export hub, but very little of the job growth is in the direct employment of people loading ships, trucks, or pipelines.

Clearly, as everyone living in Houston knows, the story has a lot to do with the production of energy. Drill down, and—technically speaking—the energy sector seems to account for only one in ten jobs in the region. And the Texan statisticians, like most others, feel obliged to categorize employment into the separated catego-ries of "goods producing" and "service providing." In Houston the second category seems about four times larger than the first.[26]

Drill down some more. During 2013 in Houston, the sector creating the most new jobs was the one labeled "professional, sci-entific, and technical services."

This is a category that includes employment in law offices, accounting and bookkeeping, architectural and engineering firms, geophysical surveying (a big part of exploration for energy sources), testing labs, computer systems design, management consulting, advertising, and more. Statistically, jobs like these are separated from counts of employment in "goods producing" work.

That separation disappears in the life of the energy production community. Consider where innovation and dynamism happen in energy production. Exploration innovations, new drilling tech-niques, different ways of refining products, financing petrochemi-cal R&D: the answers can touch most of these "service" categories as well as the more obvious ones that statisticians conventionally associate with goods.

Drill deeper still: the Houston employment growth relies on tens of thousands of people flowing in every year. Most recently these have come mainly from elsewhere in Texas and the rest of the United States. But they also come from neighboring coun-tries, like Mexico. To enable and draw this inflow, more jobs are needed in food, health, education, and construction. In fact, the Houston construction boom has been held back by a shortage of skilled construction workers. As one business organization put it, trying to explain why thousands of skilled jobs remain unfilled, "High schools eliminated shop classes, the construction associations focused on concerns other than training, and builders relied too heavily on the undocumented workforce to pour concrete and frame homes."[27]

Houston is a booming production ecosystem. It is hard to separate out which part of that community provides the innovative dynamism that drives the others.

It is clear that, at least in the last year, for every new "goods producing" job added to the base, more than three "service providing" jobs were added. There appears to be some sort of multiplier relationship. In Houston it appears to be about threefold, or a total of four jobs with every goods-producing one created.

The multiplier runs both ways: it is a synergistic relationship. As the figure below shows, these trend lines in Houston seem to have run side by side in this way for at least the last ten years.[28]

Goods-Producing and Service-Providing Employment

Houston Metropolitan Statistical Area

■ Goods-Producing Jobs

■ Service-Providing Jobs

SOURCE: Texas Workforce Commission

It is also worth noting that Houston's energy production community is a high-technology sector. It is about as capital-intensive as any production activity can be. Health care, the second-largest production community in Houston, is also quite capital-intensive.

Yet whatever technology does, however it affects the statistics around "productivity," high-tech advanced production in Houston is clearly not a job killer. Far from it.

The Houston experience is not at all unusual. Studying what he calls the "innovation" sector, Moretti looked at companies that were hubs of Internet-related innovation, as in northern California. They may not look as if they directly employ so many people. But "for each new high-tech job in a metropolitan area," he found, "five additional local jobs are created outside of hightech in the long run."[29]

The Houston example can inform the way we think about the potential of a future American economy. It is a case of advanced, specialized production that is, simultaneously, both close to American markets yet also able to add value to networked products being composed globally and shopped across the world.

The United States has nearly 250 industry-specific clusters—some based on old anchors like medical devices in Minnesota and proximity to the Mayo Clinic, and some new, like the automotive cluster that has arisen in South Carolina or the aerospace clusters in seemingly improbable places like Wichita, Kansas, and Duluth, Minnesota.

Strategies to Grow Ecosystems and Create Jobs

In the case of the iPhone, much of its high-end component value is now provided by suppliers based in countries like Japan, South Korea, and Germany. These countries are not low-cost producers. They, like American suppliers, also subcontract certain tasks to lower-cost labor. The suppliers are based in these other countries, like Japan, because they have built up, over time, their own hubs, highly skilled and well-paid networks that can bundle the innovative production and services Apple needs for its iPhone.

In designing its production network, Apple has been responding to its surrounding circumstances. It is adapting to the fact that "[a]cross the entire industrial landscape [of America] there are now gaping holes and missing pieces . . . [where] critical strengths and capabilities that once served to bring new enterprises to life have disappeared."[30] Because of choices made decades ago, a core part of the high-value constantly innovating production ecosystem for information technology is centered in Taiwan, not in Silicon Valley.[31]

But to see how success can work, consider too the example of Gorilla Glass, the material on the front of the iPhone. The American supplier is a firm, Corning, that has been around for over 160 years and is based in, well, the small town of Corning, which is in south-central New York. Once best known for its cookware, Corning is at the cutting edge of work in advanced materials, especially glass and ceramics.

Corning uses fabrication facilities in the United States and foreign locales (including Taiwan). But the *hub* of its production community is in the United States. Because the research and design involve materials, it needs at least some significant fabrication capability close to its headquarters, in order to test processes and try out new designs. This is sometimes called a "lead factory" model.[32] That variety of activities creates an ecosystem of researchers, trainees, network production managers, and others.

What are the ingredients to help good hubs grow? Some of the growth can be pure serendipity. The main reason Microsoft is in Seattle, and not in Albuquerque, is that two young men, Bill Gates and Paul Allen, had grown up in the Seattle area and wanted to relocate their business to their hometown. In 1978 the business of programming computer operating systems happened to be an embryonic and unusually portable ecosystem.

More deliberate strategies can concentrate on four kinds of ingredients: *leadership in private-public alliances; people; innovation; and the networks—the infrastructure—that connects the community to others.* In Wichita, Kansas, for example, the aerospace cluster has become a strong exporter, thanks to a carefully wrought alliance organized by a National Institute for Aviation Research and including Wichita State University, NASA, the FAA, and private firms like Lockheed Martin.[33]

Successful implementation of an economic growth strategy requires developing a pipeline of high-skilled workers, entrepreneurs, researchers, and visionaries. They need a base of effective anchor institutions and infrastructure. Patience helps, a lot. Short-term, visible successes may get headlines, but effective strategies have to be sustained.

In a McKinsey study of possible "gamechangers" that could kick-start American economic prospects, one of the top five was to increase America's "competitiveness in knowledge-intensive industries." If you imagined that by "knowledge-intensive industries" the authors meant the products of Silicon Valley, you would be wrong.

In the authors' view, knowledge-intensive industries are makers of innovative goods that involve a lot of R&D and advanced production, such as aerospace, automobiles, and medical equipment. If these ecosystems could again become as healthy in relation to the American economy by 2020 as they were in 2000, they estimated the result would be 600,000 net new jobs. If America could get back to the position in industries like these that the country had in 1990, the result would be 1.8 million net new jobs.[34]

It is doable. As the McKinsey report pointed out, the problem is not with labor costs; the challenges are to restore the other ingredients of healthy producer ecosystems, the ones at the heart of the four recommendations that follow.

Leadership in Private-Public Alliances

Mississippi's Golden Triangle is in the eastern part of the state; the three points of the triangle are the small cities of Columbus, Starkville, and West Point. The three-county area has a metropolitan area of about 130,000 people. For more than a century, it has been a part of America that people often felt they had to flee if they had any hope of a better or different life.

Agriculture was the area's first industry, based on plantations in the era of slavery. Through the 20th century most of the industrial base consisted of factory jobs. These industries had come down from the unionized northern states starting in the early 20th century. By the end of the 20th century many of these operations had disappeared, some moving on to ever-cheaper labor in Latin America and Asia. The median household income in the three counties that make up this region has been only about 60 percent of the national level. The population is about 50–50 black and white.

In the early 2000s an unusual group of local leaders came together to try to change the future of their communities. The partnership was led not by city or state government, but by a nongovernmental economic development coalition, a merger of a city chamber of commerce and a county economic development organization, which eventually was called Golden Triangle Link or just plain "the Link."

Joe Max Higgins Jr., an Arkansas economic developer, was hired to lead the Link. He promoted a black woman from local Lowndes County, Brenda Lathan, from the reception desk to be his director for business research and development. Now the Link's senior vice president, Lathan became Mississippi's first black female certified economic developer. Twelve years later Higgins and Lathan still work in tandem, Lathan offering a softer side to the high-energy Higgins, each able to finish the other's sentences.

The Link helped connect all the other participants. These included the state, county, and local governments; utilities; engineering companies; and especially educational institutions like the local research university, Mississippi State, and, crucially, East Mississippi Community College (EMCC).[35]

Joe Max Higgins Jr. and Brenda Lathan.

These Americans in Mississippi were figuring out how to use the emerging economic revolution to create hope in a region where, for a long time, hope had been in short supply.

They looked at the global economy and thought of how people in northeast Mississippi might contribute. They analyzed ways to mobilize available investment, both private and public. They worked hard to improve and reinvent their local education system. They believed in the abilities of their people, so they insisted on strategies that would produce good jobs to lift people up, not just any jobs.

Because the starting point was so challenging, the initial strategy was to attract big, outside manufacturers to the area. This has succeeded. Beginning in 2003 American Eurocopter (Airbus) located a helicopter facility in the Golden Triangle Industrial Park. The Link team, working with the Tennessee Valley Authority, also developed a certified automotive megasite, a piece of land jointly developed in a private-public partnership to promote clusters of aligned businesses. That was snatched up by the Severstal Columbus (Steel Dynamics, Inc.) mini–steel mill. The team developed another megasite. And that one was selected by the Paccar company, a world leader in producing trucks for long-haul commerce, to set up one of North America's most advanced factories for truck engines. A huge new Yokohama Tire facility is also now being built. Yet another industrial park is being developed.

The first companies to arrive feared that in such a destitute, deindustrialized area they would not be able to find skilled workers to manage their computerized, robot-heavy modern factories. EMCC's Golden Triangle campus went all out to train local people for these roles. Its Center for Manufacturing Technology Excellence is led by Raj Shaunak. Shaunak's family is Indian; he was born in Kenya, educated in England, and immigrated to Mississippi. Now, as a retired businessman, he brings plenty of passion to the center's work training young people in the skills and disciplines of cutting-edge 21st-century production work.

The success of the first companies made it easier to attract additional ones. The pool of skilled workers grew. The expanding presence of internationally trained managers for these factories, plus researchers at Mississippi State, has begun to lead to small spin-off start-up firms. The publicly funded Mississippi School of Math and Science, an outstanding mixed-race school that blends advanced technical education with a rich humanities curriculum, fits easily into this region and sends its graduates to the nation's finest universities.

The Golden Triangle remains a part of the country with above-average challenges. But the Link has brought investments of over $4.6 billion to northeast Mississippi, creating 5,600 jobs. It is a place where Americans believe they are moving forward and creating opportunities for the entire range of its population in ways that few would have thought possible a decade ago. Higgins drives around with a license plate he has personalized to read "2EqLast." Second equals last.

A few years ago the Federal Reserve Bank of Boston set about figuring out why some communities turned themselves around when their old industries faded and why some did not. Singling out ten such success stories in their report *Lessons from Resurgent Cities*, the researchers isolated the factors they had in common. Number one was leadership jointly from the private and public sector. As in the Golden Triangle in eastern Mississippi or in the cities highlighted in the Boston Fed's report—cities like Fort Wayne, Indiana, or Grand Rapids, Michigan, or Greensboro, North Carolina—the common theme was that business and public leaders joined to offer this sort of leadership.[36]

Sometimes the business leaders took the initiative. Sometimes it was a civic leader, like a mayor. But in every case these communities analyzed their assets, looked at the kinds of producers they could attract, and developed purposeful strategies pulling together. They do not view their fellow citizens in the way predators view prey.

They may not use fancy words like "ecosystem." Whatever words they use, these people who care about their community see the connections among the many factors we call attention to in this book.

Those responsible for core businesses in a community have to make business decisions. We understand that "creative destruction," brutal a term as that is, is vital to a dynamic American economy that is creating more opportunities for good work. In Grand Rapids the once-proud furniture businesses were dying. The city saw opportunities to diversify their producers, including a "Medical Mile" joining in strong producer communities surrounding health care.

In Mississippi one of the civic leaders, Joe Max Higgins, knew that some of the old low-wage businesses, including a plant owned by Sara Lee, were going away. Regarding his search for new producers, he said, "I'm not even interested in factories that aren't going to pay a lot more than people are already making here. Why would I be? If you are going to create jobs at that level, you are forever dooming your area."[37] His part of Mississippi had been through two hundred years of that sort of history.

Note our wording: "private-public," not the usual "public-private." It does not mean the public sector is not vital. We offer many examples where it was, and is. But business development is a path to more good work. We use "private-public" as a way of signaling that, at least in America, private actors must be willing to take the initiative, accept major responsibility, and bear a large share of the costs.

These alliances are beginning to win bipartisan political support. President Obama awarded a couple of initial grants to support "hubs" of production. The concepts have demonstrated enough promise that, at the end of 2014, a bill co-sponsored by Senator Sherrod Brown (D-Ohio) and Senator Roy Blunt (R-Missouri) was passed with wide support. It set aside funds to support fifteen more such "hubs" to nurture advanced manufacturing capabilities over the next ten years.

Why are these alliances so important? They are there to solve what social scientists might call a "collective action" problem. Suppose that a number of players might benefit from a solution but, on their own, none of them individually have the authority or resources to handle it for themselves and the others. In a productive ecosystem the three most common kinds of "collective action" problems for companies are: (1) attracting and training people; (2) supporting enough R&D; and (3) building out the networks the businesses need—from roads to broadband.

People and Training

Communities may do many things to attract and hold talented people. A common issue is training in needed skills.

A journalist touring the training facilities of leading German companies like Daimler, Siemens, and Bosch kept noting the puzzlement of the Americans, shaking their heads at how much money the companies were spending on training and on apprenticeships with local schools. The issue of who paid for the facilities "came up at nearly every stop on the tour, we Americans asking about what costs mean for ROI [return on investment] and the

Germans telling us to look beyond ROI to the longer-term benefits, for the company and society."

The journalist was sympathetic. But she admitted, "[I]t's hard
to imagine many American firms, generally focused on short-term
financial gain, building the kind of in-house training centers we
saw at every German plant: immaculate, state-of-the-art facilities,
complete with robots, the latest computerized machining tools,
and a raft of uniformed instructors overseeing busy trainees."[38]

The German model is not replicable in America, and it has
disadvantages all its own. But plenty of Americans do care, just
as much as Germans do, about "the longer-term benefits, for the
company and society." Americans can fashion their own incentives
and private-public partnerships. If employers are committed to providing good work and rewarding skill, both the employer and the
surrounding community should work together, each doing what it
does best, to design flexible training programs. Some of these may
be formal apprenticeships; some may be programs in local colleges
that make use of experts and equipment offered by the employers.

A workable solution is for companies, with this common interest, to put in a share of the needed funds along with their input on
the kinds of skills that they need. A local government might then
also pitch in some money. This creates a community resource:
more work-ready individuals for all.

As an example of what we mean, consider the Edison Welding
Institute (EWI). Headquartered in Columbus, Ohio, the institute
was set up to pool expertise and provide training in arc welding or
soldering, of course, but now offers much more than that. Additive
manufacturing (3-D printing), laser processes, ultrasonic technologies, computer modeling: these are all part of EWI's menu for
trainees and research in advanced production work in many sectors. Many of the companies doing this work are relatively small.

EWI gets its money from its members and customers: more
than 220 companies along with state, local, and federal agencies. It
received one of the initial federal "hub" grants in 2012, as part of a

consortium with Ohio State University and the University of Michigan. Base funding comes from member companies; much of the revenue comes from projects for clients in industry and government.

The private-sector members of EWI may be competitive rivals. But they all invest in EWI for the common good of their communities of producers. With outposts in Ohio and near Detroit, Washington, DC, and Buffalo, EWI offers regular training courses taught by its staff of more than 130. It has full-size test labs and $20 million worth of its own capital equipment. Working with students at Ohio State University, EWI helped build the Buckeye Bullet 2, the world's fastest car powered by a hydrogen fuel cell (303 mph).

Unlike such organizations in Germany, called Fraunhofer Institutes, EWI relies primarily on private-sector support and private initiative. It therefore has good reason to be highly responsive to its members.

In the Golden Triangle of Mississippi, there were public partners in the form of vital early federal recognition from the Tennessee Valley Authority that this three-county area was doing the work to attract good business. Local authorities organized training support, working with the employers and their state-of-the-art equipment, through a local community college and a university.

Another kind of interesting formula is the one we recounted in chapter 5, where a local union partnered with local employers to pool a percentage of gross local payroll that will be used for common training. The fund is administered by a nonprofit, supervised by a board appointed by employers and the union, half and half. The fund is a long-term project, working with students over periods of years. Some employers are fully interested and committed; some not so much.

Innovation and R&D Investment: Recommendations for Government

Most economic growth comes from new technology.[39] An economy can add people. It can add machines. But without technological progress, the economy will not grow as much.

Government investment has played a vital role in American research and development (R&D), especially in sponsoring basic research. Government policies sustained productivity growth during the 1930s, not least by the public investments in transportation infrastructure such as roads and highways.[40] The government's role in fostering technological innovation was vital as well. The initial markets for transistors and microprocessors were for government procurements.

When considering the challenge of increasing U.S. investment in R&D, it is crucial to understand that the two parts are very different. R&D is a continuum.

At the *R* end is *basic research*, which focuses on achieving greater insight into or discovery of particular phenomena. It is undertaken without much consideration of practical end goals, applications, or products, and is the stuff of scientific breakthroughs.

Applied research, by contrast, is focused on a known opportunity or challenge, with the goal of achieving feasible solutions. This segues into what is often referred to as *advanced development*, which takes the output from applied research and figures out either (a) how to incorporate it into existing products or solutions, or (b) uses it to create new products or solutions.

Finally, *D* is for the most part what companies do: *product development*, the creation of products (or services) that they will bring to market. The diagram below illustrates this R&D continuum.[41]

On its good days, capitalism can do a fine job at continuously increasing investment in *D* with little help from the government except for the usual corporate tax breaks. Even in the public sector, investment in development has remained relatively robust. But *R* has fared less well for a number of reasons, foremost of which is the failure of various "peace dividends" over the years to redirect public funding from the U.S. defense-industrial establishment (and also from the moon shot–era NASA) toward scientific research. The steadily diminishing percentage of federal funding that has

Research and Development

R Rd RD rD D

| Basic Research | Applied Research | Advanced Development | Product Development |

SOURCE: Machine Design

gone into basic research, at universities and elsewhere, has also disproportionately favored the life sciences.

The private sector did fill in some of the gap, but not as anticipated. Increasingly lacking the spun-off benefits of government-funded research, and for the most part also lacking their own research facilities, more and more companies are sponsoring university research—research that is usually more applied than the basic, long-term projects that research universities were able to carry out when government funding was plentiful. The tide of research that therefore used to flow from the government to the corporate sector has thus been reversed. It is now flowing in the other direction.

This reallocation of roles in supporting scientific research is dangerous to America's long-term technological competitiveness.

- First, it means that companies are for the most part no longer developing their own basic research facilities. This reinforces the relatively lackluster private sector investment in corporate R&D more generally.

• Second, companies that do invest in research are more interested in funding applied (or "directed") research rather than the basic research that drives scientific and technological breakthroughs.

• Third, *all* sources of grant funding for university research—public and private alike—now tend to be shorter term, fragmented, harder to secure, and smaller in dollar terms—a result of shrinking budgets and also the increasing number of universities, many of which believe they must perform "research" to attract faculty.

A look at one prominent grant-making institution, the National Institutes of Health (NIH), is instructive. Securing an NIH grant is so competitive that the average age at which researchers obtain their first grant from the institution is 42, while the median age of all NIH grantees is 10 years older.[42] Grant fragmentation is also taking a toll. Many researchers complain that both companies and grant-making bodies will now fund research only in stages. By the time any subsequent round of funding is secured, students and researchers working on a particular project have often moved on. And all this assumes that a grant is made at all. At the NIH the overall percentage of successful research-grant applications fell from more than 32 percent in the late 1990s to about 17 percent in 2013[43]—and the NIH's success rates are higher than those of many grant-making institutions.

The United States is still the world leader in basic research at universities. But its hegemony is under threat, for all the reasons cited above. We cannot prove from official macro data that R is faring much worse than D, because perplexingly everyone from government statisticians to corporate accountants persist in lumping together these two very different activities. But we do know that between 1996 and 2011, the most recent period for which we have comparative data, U.S. spending on R&D has been between 2.5 percent and 2.8 percent of GDP. In South Korea, by contrast,

R&D Expenditure as a Share of Economic Output

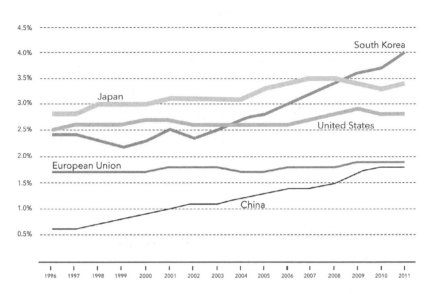

SOURCE: National Science Board Science and Engineering Indicators 2014

R&D spending rose from 2.4 percent of GDP to 4 percent over the same period, while in China the increase was from 0.6 percent to 1.8 percent. The chart above illustrates these trends for selected countries.[44]

We know what is causing this relative U.S. stagnation in funding levels. Fixing it will require a longer-term approach by both government funding institutions and corporate sponsors. It will also require a rethinking of the entire peer-reviewed grant-making process, which tends to favor the known over the adventurous, and lacks consistency both across disciplines and over time. To be more specific:

- Every federal grant-making institution should have a strategic plan that explicitly addresses the different kinds of research activities that can contribute to its missions, specifically addressing the balances between evolutionary versus revolutionary research, disciplinary versus interdisciplinary work, and project-based versus people-based awards.[45]

• Instead of focusing resources almost exclusively on individual research grants, the National Science Foundation (NSF) and especially the NIH could support the creation of high-quality national laboratory facilities for remote biological research, using robotics. Early advantages in bioengineering, such as genomic sequencing, could lead to the development of personalized medicines and other breakthrough applications.

• Networked technology is enabling the conduct of remote biological experiments at high-quality laboratory facilities, since such experiments are usually already carried out by robotic instruments. For example, the Emerald Cloud Laboratory, which is launching now, is meant to unleash biological research by allowing anyone to conduct high-end experiments, using the Internet, and without having to spend the millions of dollars on his own lab.[46]

• Congress and the executive branch should commit to raising R&D expenditures to 3 percent of GDP (preferably more), and sustaining them at that level, linked to mechanisms that will increase the stability and predictability of federal research funding. The NSF was originally intended to provide such insularity from short-termism in basic research.

• Congress should also make the Research and Experimentation Tax Credit (usually called the R&D tax credit) both permanent and higher. It is worth taking a moment to understand how these are set up now. In an effort to avoid giving tax credit for money the company would spend if there was no credit, these credits— federal and state—usually use a "baseline" approach.

Companies have to calculate a historical baseline R&D spending rate, and show they are going above it to get the credit (on up to 20 percent of the qualifying spending). This is called an "incremental" credit. In other words, the current R&D tax credit system is fundamentally complex and incremental. Many other tax credits and deductions, including for business costs like advertising, are not set up this way. Moreover, young firms, or firms that have not yet earned large profits, do not get much from the system as it is currently structured.

• This aspect of the tax system seems ripe for overhaul and reevaluation.[47] Most claims for this credit are already being audited, and most of the audits sustain the current claims.[48] An increase in the rate of the alternative simplified credit from 14 percent to 20 percent would not be unreasonable. Such an increase, according to one study cited by the President's Council of Advisors on Science and Technology, could create 162,000 jobs.[49]

Innovation and R&D Investment: Recommendations for the Private Sector

Although we believe the government role in financing R&D is vital, we do not believe the government has a dominant role to play in fostering American innovation. "Technology," the Columbia University economist Richard Nelson has explained, "is partly in books and mind, partly in the fingers and organization." The books can be a public good, but the applications come mainly from specific investment and learning by companies and people deeply involved in the work.[50]

The various technology companies that have emerged in the past decade alone have transformed almost every aspect of our lives. But innovation in large and longer-lived companies is less healthy, and many have been scaling back significantly on their research activities. There are at least two reasons why this is happening.

One is financial. Corporate America today is profitable, yet reinvestment in R&D has been flat. Corporate labs have flourished when firms have some freedom to focus on the long term. Some of the relatively new companies, like Google, are making significant commitments to R&D. But they know they are bucking contemporary fashion.

The other reason is organizational. As Clayton Christensen famously wrote back in 1997, in big companies good managers tend to direct resources toward protecting established lines of business, usually by investing in incremental improvements that help profit margins. He cited Microsoft as an example, noting that while the company has an abundance of creative talent and ideas, it then seemed to devote the majority of its vast resources to defending its existing franchises.[51]

Most large companies find it hard to apply "creative destruction" to their existing businesses. Their research labs—if they have one—continue to create technological and scientific breakthroughs. They partner with U.S. research universities, which are still among the best in the world. But they struggle to bring innovation to market.

This is primarily a structural problem. Big companies are structurally evolved to be adept at things other than the transfer of innovation, even from their own labs. They service huge markets with gradually evolving products, homing in on those that bring the highest short-term profits and rewards to shareholders. This means focusing their resources on production, distribution, sales and service channels, and being skilled at developing and marketing incremental improvements in their products.

The often process-ridden and bureaucratic structure that makes them so good in that domain renders them immensely inefficient in addressing small markets and in handling substantial innovations. And even when a substantive innovation crosses the divide to become part of an existing product group, its incubation is taken over by that group's product development team. Many such innovations—especially if they are transferred too early in their development—thus fail to gain traction. They wither on the vine, only to be "rediscovered" by more-agile start-ups—sometimes founded by ex-employees who quit rather than see their ideas stifled.

The late Peter Drucker's classic solution to this problem of status quo smothering of internal re-creation was to recommend that "The search for innovation needs to be organizationally separate and outside of the ongoing managerial business. Innovative organizations realize that one cannot simultaneously create the new and take care of what one already has."[52]

When large companies try to do this in parallel with their legacy businesses, they can succeed. Microsoft, for example, scored a major hit when it fenced off its innovative Xbox gaming platform and hardware from the beginning. That division now accounts for $1.7 billion in annual revenues. But failures far outnumber successes.

Another model may be that of Teknekron, one of the most innovative companies that almost no one has ever heard of. In its heyday this firm showed that it was possible to deliver innovations to the marketplace with startling consistency (its core team is long retired). Founded in 1968 by a group of academics from the University of California at Berkeley along with a handful of entrepreneurs, Teknekron was from the outset intended to be a new kind of company—one that would focus solely on incubating cutting-edge information-technology research and innovation into a constant stream of profitable, sustainable businesses.

During the next 30 years Teknekron spun off businesses with a cumulative initial market value of almost $5 billion in today's dollars. In that period Teknekron produced a compounded *average* return on investment of more than 50 percent a year. Its success rate in forming viable companies from the start-up phase was also about 50 percent—some four to five times the usual rate for high-technology start-ups (with or without venture capital support).

Teknekron called its approach the "open corporation." This provided a platform on which the three key elements of tech transfer—(1) sources of innovation, (2) what Teknekron called "catalytic" entrepreneurs, and (3) innovation users (i.e., customers)—were combined to accomplish the incubation process. The platform was sustained within an existing corporate structure, kept small enough to prevent the encroachment of bureaucracy, but large enough to give the entrepreneurs immediate corporate substance, credibility, and stability.

Teknekron was a large-scale innovation incubator providing broad support to "catalytic" entrepreneurs. "In contrast to the more traditional company," Teknekron's co-founder and CEO, Harvey Wagner, explained in 1991, "identifying and nurturing entrepreneurs and connecting them to sources and users of innovation are the open corporation's raisons d'être and the main driving force of corporate growth."

Specifically, Teknekron's main functions were to "seek entrepreneurs; help connect them to sources and users of innovation; teach them the elements of business that they might not know; nurture them during their learning period until their efforts stabilized; launch their units as affiliated companies so that they could achieve further growth independently; and finally spin the affiliates out by public or private sale when they were fully matured and too big for continued affiliation with the parent." Nor was that all. The company also performed "corporate services best accomplished as a group (such as employee benefits, insurance, and legal matters)."[53]

Teknekron's enviable model has drawn attention from management gurus (Tom Peters is a fan) and from federal research labs and economic-development agencies. But no major corporation has single-mindedly attempted to reproduce Teknekron's model, unwilling to commit the steady focus, patience, and financial long-termism that would be needed. But if the United States is to maintain its lead in global innovation, perhaps the time has come to become more single-minded.

Americans have succeeded before when they invested in their ingenuity. As the economic historian Michael Bernstein has shown, the new industries of the 1930s like electronics and aerospace recovered almost immediately from the downturn in 1932.[54] A lack of investment in those new industries contributed to the continuing Depression. Many investors and banks sat on capital, unwilling to invest. The innovations were there; the productivity gains were there. But the engines that can bring economic opportunity to millions of Americans need the fuel of private investment, without waiting for a world war to bring giant government subsidies and loan guarantees into the mix.[55]

Networks: Public Co-investment in Transportation Infrastructure

The United States has for decades underinvested in its infrastructure; its roads, ports, electricity transmission, and waterways have been especially neglected in comparison with those of other advanced economies. High-quality physical and electronic networks are essential to almost all communities of producers.

Major investments are needed, but they would be rewarded with multiplier effects in job creation and economic growth. One major estimate assesses the job-creating impact of a nationwide infrastructure investment program at between 1.5 million and 1.8 million jobs.[56] The broader indirect benefits over decades are harder to estimate, but the mid-20th-century investments yielded benefits so large that they are incalculable. A further benefit of infrastructure investment is that it is one of the few government spending measures almost guaranteed to draw significant private capital into the mix.

One of the political challenges faced by proposals for huge

infrastructure investments is that they are sometimes presented as instruments of macroeconomic stimulus, with proponents appearing to be relatively indifferent as to how or where the money is spent. Thus we again emphasize the significance of private-public alliances in which infrastructure investments find private co-investors willing to place their own bets on the value and management plans of the proposal. There are various ways to construct such alliances. Infrastructure banks are another approach, used in Europe and being tried on a small scale in states like Florida, Pennsylvania, and Texas.[57]

Governments are already spending large sums to attract producers. One investigation tallied up $80 billion every year that state, county, and city governments are giving to companies, mainly in tax benefits, and this estimate is probably very low. It can be beneficial to win the auction. But the winners, desperate to get the plant, frequently overbid. "A portrait arises of mayors and governors who are desperate to create jobs, outmatched by multinational corporations and short on tools to fact-check what companies tell them."[58]

One recent study sponsored by the Kauffman Foundation has examined firms that received relocation incentives and compared them with firms that did not receive such inducements, using the example of the program in Kansas. The conclusion was that "there is no concrete evidence that [such programs] are effective in generating jobs in Kansas."[59]

Communities can seek a better balance, offering investments that will benefit the whole community, making it more attractive to more than one company. Assistance to a single firm is just that. To form needed alliances, more of the burden then falls on a single firm. Few such firms may be willing to shoulder it by themselves.

Also, privileging one company too much may create a competitive advantage for that firm that discourages others. Thus reliance on one company can discourage or weaken the broader alliances that might build up more resources for the community as a whole. In today's economy, more than ever, productive communities can rarely rest securely on one company. The healthier ecosystems usually involve a network of firms, some of which may be competing with each other.

Communities extend across political boundaries; governments and the private sector alike should collaborate with that in mind. In the successful cases it is common to see groups that cover multiple jurisdictions, cities and counties. The growth of economic clusters is not bounded by where a city or a county may happen to have its borders. Regional cooperation is essential.

A stark example of what happens when a region does not collaborate is the Detroit metropolitan area, which includes six counties. While there are many reasons for Detroit's decline as a city over the past half century, one aggravating factor has been not only the lack of a regional outlook but even the outright competition among the city and the counties.[60] As opportunities return to the area, this competition makes it harder for the city—and the region— to rebound because it creates an endless loop of luring companies away from the core, moves jobs outside of the city and increases the number of unemployed, and further tears at the social fabric of Detroit while draining away its tax base. An enlightened approach to regional cooperation is no panacea, but success for all is more likely when Americans recognize that they are all in this together.

Greer is a small town in South Carolina of about 20,000 people, situated halfway between two larger cities. To the west is Greenville, which has already been successfully shifting from a textile-based economy to a new diversified, advanced-tech economy mentioned earlier. Spartanburg, to the east, was richer during its textile heyday but—having had one dominant company (Milliken) rather than several competing companies—was slower to make the adjustment. It has now become a center for advanced automotive manufacturing, with the BMW facilities at its core.

In between them lies Greer, which has based its prospects on an innovative plan for an *inland port*. Greer is 212 miles from an actual ocean port, in Charleston. But it has set up an "inland port" that has all the attributes of a normal port, except the water.

The idea is that exporters located in Tennessee, Kentucky, Ohio, or Arkansas can suddenly be closer to world markets by *trucking* their goods to Greer, and then having them loaded into containers and put onto railcars for quick shipment to the coast. The inland port opened in October 2013, with the full cooperation of the port in Charleston. It has cut the shipment time for inland exporters very significantly (and there are energy savings from not having to send trucks on crowded Interstate highways to the coast).

Greer could see the communities of producers growing up around it. Its business leaders, including the Norfolk Southern Railway and Greer's mayor, Rick Danner, saw ways they could work together. The result is a shrewd private-public alliance, adding infrastructure and creating jobs.[61]

Today's Networks: Widen and Share the Data Highways

America has risen along with the networks that linked it together— its waterways, its railways, its highways, and its airways. Building and sustaining these networks has been a primal duty of American government. The Constitution expressly empowered Congress to establish "Post Offices and post Roads."

In less than thirty years the Internet has become the most powerful global platform offering access to information. Broadband access runs hand in hand with per capita economic output.[62]

Americans may assume that, having originated the Internet, their networks are the world's best. They are not. Their networks are pretty good. Overall, they are about on a level with those in most developed countries, if not quite as good as those in Japan or the Netherlands, and certainly well behind those in world-beating South Korea. And quality varies considerably from state to state and city to city.[63]

Since, far more than any other nationality, Americans helped originate most of these network systems, what explains the not-so-awesome development of high-quality networks in the United States? One hypothesis: lack of competition. In the city-state of Singapore, with a population of about 5.4 million, three competing companies have launched a price war on gigabit fiber home Internet access. Citizens there can enjoy gigabit broadband speeds for just $40 a month.[64]

Another hypothesis: lack of public investment. South Korea has made lowering the cost of Internet access a national priority. China announced in 2013 that it would invest $323 billion to improve its broadband infrastructure.[65] It is a stunning investment. In contrast, when the Obama administration rolled out a broadband investment plan in 2011, it called for only $15 billion in spending and aimed to expand broadband wireless by fewer than 10 million citizens.[66]

Not waiting for the national government, several of America's local governments are stepping up. Currently there are nearly 400 local governments in the United States offering some kind of municipal broadband Internet. This number includes 89 communities with a publicly owned fiber-to-the-home network reaching most or all of the community, 74 communities with a publicly owned cable network reaching most or all of the community, and over 180 with some publicly owned fiber service available to parts of the community.[67]

Although it is too early to extrapolate too much from these early experiments, one survey concluded that, so far, such local investments produced "far-reaching, positive economic impacts" that offset the cost.[68] The finding is hotly contested by incumbent cable companies. They argue that the municipal services are often subpar, providing inferior but taxpayer-supported competition, which is unfair and bad for the consumer.[69] The chairman of the FCC, Tom Wheeler, has come down strongly in favor of municipal broadband. He cites the benefits of facilities-based competition.

Unmoved, the incumbent Internet service providers (ISPs), the cable and telephone companies, have urged state legislatures to block municipal broadband networks, and 21 states, to protect incumbent providers from facing government-funded competition, have adopted laws banning or restricting municipal broadband. In response, Wheeler has indicated that he may invoke national authority to open up this commerce. He believes that the FCC has the legal power to "preempt state laws that ban competition from community broadband."[70]

Meanwhile, from the private sector, Google has tried to take matters into its own hands. It has financed Internet networks up to 100 times faster than basic broadband in three cities (Kansas City, Austin, and Provo). It has started talking about expanding this initiative to nine more metro areas around the United States.[71]

This debate, like the current debate over net neutrality, is framed by a sense of scarce spectrum and a limited amount of network bandwidth. Most Americans think of 4G (fourth-generation wireless technology) as the state of the art. It is not. The fifth-generation wireless race has already begun. South Korea, Japan, China, and Europe are busy planning for 5G service this decade, with speeds ranging from 1 to 10 gigabits per second.

In our recommendations that imagine widespread telepresence for global digital delivery of American services (chapter 3), our observations about the data insights that can come from huge streams of data in the Internet of Things (chapters 2 and 4), the networks that could empower frontline employees (chapter 5), our interest in this chapter in opening up scientific work with more Internet-based laboratory research, or in our recommendations that imagine much richer networks for mentoring and teaching (chapter 8), we are counting on very powerful networks indeed.

An agenda to rework America should therefore include an aggressive effort to explore better ways to utilize spectrum, with more efficient use of spectrum available today, more use of unlicensed spectrum that powers Wi-Fi, exploring possibilities in underutilized low bands, like the 225–400 MHz range currently reserved for the military, and very high bands.

Until recently the model of allocating spectrum in dedicated, exclusive slices seemed to have served America well for the last century. But technological improvements now open the way to move, over time, to a completely different model.

The new model is a concept of shared spectrum, just as cars can share a highway without anyone's having to build walls between the lanes. Bluetooth, Wi-Fi, and garage door openers already live in exactly the same band. A dynamic, real-time system can manage access for various users with various priorities. In 2012 a presidential panel recommended the first steps, now being implemented, which put marine radar bands at 3.5 GHz (gigahertz) into such a shared management regime.[72]

This sort of sharing is possible because the means of discriminating one signal from the next can now be done on more than one frequency. A variety of applications and radio systems can coexist in the same regions of spectrum. Coupled with the low cost of much more sophisticated receivers and even new antenna technologies, these developments permit the use of small cell sizes that create more use of exactly the same channels, as if more spectrum had been added. Over time the current view of spectrum as a scarce resource can evolve into one of a new abundance. These invisible but essential resources can support an economy that will increasingly depend on wireless communication.

In addition to better use of the usual spectrum, an FCC commissioner, Jessica Rosenworcel, argues that, in thinking about the use of the electromagnetic spectrum, it would be possible to go beyond—way beyond—the usual 3 GHz ceiling and look at spectrum up to 60 GHz or more. Because this part of the spectrum has a shorter transmission radius, solutions may involve many more small-sized antennas packed close together. The FCC has begun looking into these possibilities too.[73]

One of the transforming initiatives in modern American economic history was the creation of a highway system that could link a giant country, beyond the railroads. The build-out of the U.S. "route" system in the 1920s and 1930s was an extraordinary achievement, complemented by the Interstate Highway System program launched during the 1950s.

The build-out of America's telecommunications networks could eventually have a comparable impact—and with less need for dynamited roadcuts. It is another example of how private-public partnerships can remake America once more.

Actions Needed

- Getting past some of the misleading and divisive labels, the American economy will thrive if American leaders in all sectors recognize and nurture ecosystems of networked communities of producers that usually go beyond any single company.
- To do this business leaders should offer leadership in developing private-public alliances to solve problems no firm can solve alone. Sometimes a public official like a mayor may take a lead, sometimes it will be in the private sector, but the strongest alliances are private-public partnerships in which local businesses assume much of the core responsibility for making it work.
- Leaders in these alliances should especially look to talent development—attracting people and sometimes setting up new entities that provide needed training; sponsoring needed facilities for research and product innovation; and building up needed networks that connect companies and communities.
- In supporting R&D, government leaders should focus especially on the R part, and especially on basic research, balanced to support less established lines of work and building up national research facilities that—

using network technology and information sharing—can empower many scientists.

• Business leaders not only need stronger R&D efforts of their own; they must also address the challenge of how to support truly disruptive innovation—either through more long-term commitments or through incubators that combine investment with practical assessment and advice.

• Policymakers should prioritize innovative efforts to expand the speed and quality of the telecommunications networks that are becoming the railroads and highways of the digital economy.

Chapter 7

Match Americans to Opportunities

If it was functioning well, the American labor market would do a reasonably good job of matching Americans to opportunities. Employers would be able to signal what skills they need. Job applicants would be able to signal clearly what they can do. Educators and trainers would respond quickly to gaps.

But the American labor market does not work nearly as well as it should. Credentials are out of date and often not very meaningful to employers. Job applicants have trouble knowing what skills are desired and finding flexible ways to learn them. Educators and trainers are out of sync with a fast-changing economy.

As an illustration, consider a common and important middle-skill career path: work in information technology. These IT middle-skill jobs are in firms all over the economy.

A typical entry-level job in this field, the one with the most openings, is at a help desk (in New York City, which has higher than average salaries, the average advertised annual salary for such a job was about $66,000). Studies of the career paths of IT professionals make it clear that the entry-level job does not necessarily require a college degree. The help desk entry-level needs certain basic skills, none of which are necessarily correlated to a BA degree program.

That help desk job could then lead to roles in advanced computer or network support (average NYC salary of about $80,000 and higher) and on up to network and database administrators—with even higher salaries. Different skills are needed to advance along the career path. For instance, a help desk worker who wanted to be a network support specialist might learn to master software tools like Solaris and Apache web server.[1]

This is not an unusual example. Another key entry-level point in the business world is in sales work, such as retail sales. Again, few of the formal skills for this job are necessarily correlated to a BA degree program.

Yet, more and more often, employers looking for an IT entry-level employee, like a help desk worker, require applicants to have a bachelor's degree. Why?

From the employer's perspective, the existing educational system usually does not train people with the specific skills the employer needs. The menu of credentials to choose from is pretty limited—a high school diploma, an associate's degree, or a bachelor's degree. Not knowing what this signifies for their needs, a usual default approach for the employers is to just require the bachelor's degree as a recruiting filter. This gets coded into the human resources (HR) department software. It becomes a routine.

This practice is called up-credentialing. For now, employers can often get away with up-credentialing a job and still acquire someone because, at this moment in history, labor supply is relatively abundant, including the supply of college graduates looking for work.

The old labor market system, with its credentials, was designed in its basic elements more than a hundred years ago. It worked reasonably well in serving the older world of training "blue-collar" factory workers and "white-collar" office workers. But that world has been changing rapidly. It is becoming a "no-collar" world with fast-changing skills and job categories.

Now the employers have trouble signaling what they really need. The available credentials do not signal well what people actually know or can do. The applicants do not know how much education they really need to buy. All overcompensate. Or they *try* to overcompensate, since most Americans do not complete college. The majority who try fail to earn a degree. They are often left with only large intractable debts to show for the effort.

It is worth breaking down some of the ways the now out-of-date labor market system sets up failure:

- Employers are often unhappy that they are not getting someone with the right "hard" skills (technical training) that are needed. It is not easy to identify those skills and attach them to established academic credentials.
- Employers are also often unhappy that they are not getting someone with the right "soft" skills, in speaking or writing. They find it is hit or miss as to whether the usual academic credentials will mean the person has such skills.
- The job applicant has trouble figuring out just what the employer needs, how to get those skills, and how to demonstrate credibly that she or he has what it takes.
- Most Americans (about three-quarters between the ages of 25 and 64) do not have a bachelor's degree.[2] So up-credentialing redoubles their sense of failure, of being shut out.
- For the Americans who do have a bachelor's degree, returns are good in many cases. But a large fraction now find themselves underemployed, doing work that does not require such a degree, or just unemployed.[3] Their degrees are often in subjects that do not line up well with the labor market, so they merely join the pool of good people with no particular skills.

An unusual combination of researchers and scholars recently studied the problem of "middle skills" in America. They were consultants from Accenture, analysts of labor market data from a firm called Burning Glass, and scholars from the Harvard Business School. Their conclusion is ominous.

> Underemployment is rampant for both middle-skills workers and recent college graduates. Too few have highly marketable skills; too many have pursued courses of study for which there is little demand. Ballooning student debt threatens the future of graduates and looms over the federal budget. Employers find it hard to fill occupations ranging from healthcare technicians to technical sales and service. Companies cite fears about the availability of skilled labor as a major deterrent to their growth plans.[4]

Demographic Trends Tightening the American Labor Market

For a generation Americans have gotten used to a labor market in which the wage rates for most Americans have remained flat. But the American labor market is beginning a historic transition.

The most obvious question about a market is the relation of supply and demand. The supply of labor in America is a fundamental factor.

For more than thirty years the labor force grew at a rate much faster than that of the population, contributing to the abundant supply of workers still in the economy today. The large-scale entry of women into the labor force was a huge onetime event that took off during the 1970s. Another key variable was the return of mass immigration during the 1970s, for the first time since the 1910s.[5]

The impact on the labor market of these two demographic factors has leveled off. The disproportionate labor force growth tapered off during the 2000s and the early part of this decade, as shown in the chart below.[6]

The trend is now going sharply the other way, for the first time in generations. The population growth rate is expected to remain close to the 1 precent annual rate of growth shown in the chart.

Population and Labor Force Growth Rates

Civilian Noninstitutional Population and Civilian Labor Force.

CATEGORY	1950–60	1960–70	1970–80	1980–90	1990–2000	2000–10	2010–13
Population Growth	1.1	1.6	2.0	1.2	1.0	1.1	1.0
Labor Force Growth	1.1	1.7	2.6	1.6	1.1	1.1	1.0

But the Bureau of Labor Statistics has predicted that the rate of labor force growth will drop. It was projected to drop over the course of the 2010s by about 30 percent.[7]

Basic issues of supply and demand then again come into play. The demand for labor and the supply of workers were very tightly balanced from the time the Great Depression ended, in about 1940, until the late 1960s and 1970s. Union power was therefore also at its height. More than thirty years of disproportionate growth in the workforce then affected the general supply of labor, which, absent an equally disproportionate elevation of economic demand, has long affected general wage levels.[8]

But as we show, this pattern is changing again. So the agenda for America's economic future should envision a different kind of labor market, one that may have better prospects for good wages if the right workers with the right skills can be matched well with the right job opportunities.

Why has the pattern of labor force growth changed? Part of the labor force shrinkage was caused by the Great Recession, as people gave up looking for work. But quite a lot of it, at least half, is the result of deeper demographic trends.[9] The workforce is aging; baby boomers are retiring.

In addition, young people are not entering the workforce as much as they once did. This decline started in the 1990s and has continued steadily. It is evident even in summer work. About 77 percent of young people between the ages of 16 and 24 were working in the summers of the late 1980s. By the 2010s that proportion had fallen to about 60 percent, remaining there through July 2014.[10]

If these demographic trends persist (as expected), the American labor market will tighten. As more baby boomers retire, more and more businesses will be looking for skilled workers from a stable or shrinking pool. If the labor market problem is *not* solved, the future of American business—and job creation—becomes *really* cloudy.

Yet there is a brighter side. If the problems can be solved, good matches of people with opportunities could be rewarded with much better wages in a tighter and responsive labor market. These trends can provide a historic opportunity to reverse decades of skill mismatches and sluggish wage growth. If Americans can utilize some of the ideas and tools we describe, there could be a large opening to distribute the rewards from a well-matched, high-functioning labor market, one where it is much easier to identify needed skills and get the education or training to line up with them. More young people may be tempted to join the workforce, balanced with their education. More Americans at any age may find it easier to retrain and take advantage of new opportunities.

Understanding Skills Gaps. Jobs Requiring Few Formal Skills

Across many industries and occupations, there are widespread mismatches between the skills that are needed in today's workforce and the skills job seekers possess. That situation affects millions of Americans.[11]

This surface data only hints at the deeper mismatches. For the last four years, blue-ribbon panels of leading scientists have been working hard to understand the fit between American talents and the emerging opportunities of a networked world economy. They have done this work as part of the nonpartisan President's Council of Advisors on Science and Technology, or PCAST.[12] The PCAST broke the problem down into three broad parts of the workforce.

At one end was the segment with the *highest formal skills*, with advanced degrees for professional and scientific work. There are oversupplies in some subjects and undersupplies in others, with broad concerns about the breadth of training in the so-called STEM disciplines—science, technology, engineering, and mathematics.

The public assumes that this STEM training requires college or graduate degrees. In fact, quite a lot of this sort of work does not necessarily require those kinds of formal academic credentials.[13]

At the other end of the workforce, the PCAST found jobs requiring *few formal skills*. There the labor supply for those jobs was relatively ample. But, responding to a McKinsey survey, 45 percent of American employers said a lack of skills is a leading reason for entry-level vacancies.[14] Employers and job applicants alike are concerned that the opportunities for career development are limited because too many applicants and jobholders have weak foundational skills.

In 2012 GE reinvested massively in its Appliance Park, near Louisville, Kentucky. It had the goal of hiring 2,500 new workers. Of the 730 hired in the first phase (out of 10,000 applicants), 23 percent had to be terminated in the first year. This level of turnover is unacceptable in a quality production operation.

Google partnered with Flextronics International to assemble the MotoX smartphone in Fort Worth, Texas. Over the course of ten weeks, the company had to hire 6,500 workers to yield the 2,500 employees needed to begin volume production. Workers were surprised at and unready to handle the sophistication of the skills required in these modern facilities. "We hired people off the couch," one plant manager remarked.[15]

The need was not so much for formal academic skills as for basic competencies. The workers were held back by the weak American skill base—compared with that of other developed countries—in literacy, numeracy, or ability to do basic problem solving in a technical environment.

The Paris-based Organization for Economic Cooperation and Development (OECD) is well known for its survey of student achievement. It has now added an ambitious effort to identify the kinds of skills adults need in 21st-century work. It has measured levels of attainment of those "adult competencies" in 24 countries. Their assessments of literacy, numeracy, and "problem-solving in technology-rich environments" may sound similar to some academic categories, but the measures are not really the same.

In 2013, the first time these job skills were measured, Americans were assessed as significantly below the average in *all* of these categories, compared with their counterparts in the other 23 developed countries. While the U.S. literacy score was competitive with that of Germany and other major global economies, the numeracy and problem-solving skills of American adults ranked well below those found in most OECD countries. [16]

The President's Council of Advisors on Science and Technology, for its part, observes, "[E]mployers in the private sector, government, and military frequently cite that they cannot find enough employees with needed levels of mathematics skills. This lack of preparation imposes a large burden on higher education and employers. . . . Reducing or eliminating the mathematics-preparation gap is one of the most urgent challenges—and promising opportunities—in preparing the workforce of the 21st century."[17]

Employers, especially smaller ones, find it difficult to step in and provide this kind of training, which they believe job applicants should have received in school. So companies tend to address this problem in other ways.

- They can "deskill" the job, making the tasks easier for anyone to learn and perform. Not expecting employees to have the ability to advance, the employer may treat them as short term. The employees respond accordingly.

Also, not seeing much room for the employees themselves to add value, employers choose to compete even
more just on cost, a path encouraging outsourcing and
more reliance on part-time and temporary workers.[18]
This is the trend we pushed back against in chapter 5.

• Or, if the job cannot be deskilled, the employer may
up-credential it, as we discussed earlier. The company
will post a job announcement requiring a college degree
for a job that does not really need one.

Office jobs for executive assistants or insurance claims clerks
do not require a BA degree level of training. Only about 20 percent of the people holding these jobs have a BA degree (and many
of the 20 percent did not have the degree when they were first
hired). Yet employers required a bachelor's degree in nearly half of
the almost 900,000 postings for such office jobs in 2013. That is
up-credentialing.

Similarly, many entry-level IT positions—like help desk
positions—do not require skills that go with a college degree. Yet
postings increasingly ask for one. Still more up-credentialing.

The examples we have given above are extreme, but the trend
is visible across many job categories, as the figure below shows.[19]

The BA is being used as a recruitment filter. And why not,
employers might ask themselves, if the labor supply is there?[20]
Because of the demographic trends we discussed at the beginning
of this chapter, the labor supply *is* often there.

We want to emphasize that, for millions, college can be invalu-
able in preparing for life and career success. Yet because many college graduates are actually underprepared and ill matched for the
job market, and because many of the up-credentialed jobs do not
actually require college-level skills, results for the graduates are
often disappointing. Despite what most parents have heard, the
college degree alone is no golden ticket.

A recent study of how students fared after graduating from

BA Degree Requirements

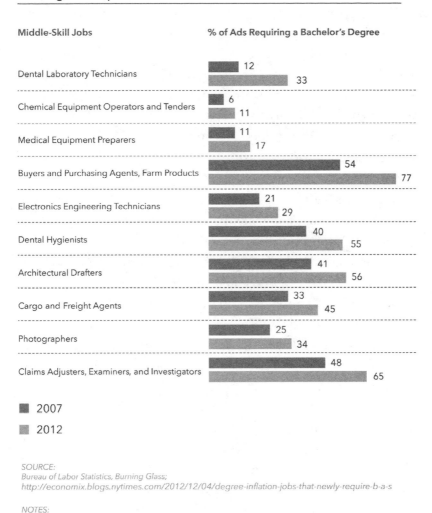

Middle-Skill Jobs	% of Ads Requiring a Bachelor's Degree
Dental Laboratory Technicians	12 / 33
Chemical Equipment Operators and Tenders	6 / 11
Medical Equipment Preparers	11 / 17
Buyers and Purchasing Agents, Farm Products	54 / 77
Electronics Engineering Technicians	21 / 29
Dental Hygienists	40 / 55
Architectural Drafters	41 / 56
Cargo and Freight Agents	33 / 45
Photographers	25 / 34
Claims Adjusters, Examiners, and Investigators	48 / 65

■ 2007
▨ 2012

SOURCE:
Bureau of Labor Statistics, Burning Glass;
http://economix.blogs.nytimes.com/2012/12/04/degree-inflation-jobs-that-newly-require-b-a-s

NOTES:
2012 data is from Nov. 1, 2011 to October 31, 2012

college leads with the example of Nathan, who graduated with a degree in business administration and good grades. Nathan now drives a delivery truck. Though a bit philosophical about his situation, he acknowledged, "I feel like I'm not using my degree at all."

Nathan's situation was not unusual. Two years after graduation, this study by Richard Arum and Josipa Roksa found that half of the thousand college graduates in this survey were unemployed, employed part-time, or employed full-time, making less than $30,000 a year.[21]

The Arum and Roksa findings line up with the conclusions from a McKinsey survey of recent graduates. There is no need to read the executive summary of their report; just read the chapter titles: "Overqualified," "Underprepared," "Regrets," "Haven't done the homework," "Disappointed," "Can I help you?," "Liberal arts?," and, the last chapter, "Do it yourself."[22]

The situation is often even more desperate for the millions of Americans who, after being told they must, tried hard to go to college and could not complete. Perhaps it was the array of course requirements, the time required away from work or family, the commuting commitments, or the costs that simply were not sustainable, year after year, in complicated lives.

These college "dropouts" get little or no credit for the college work they have done. They have years lost from their lives. They may be saddled with large student loan debts that cannot be cleared in bankruptcy. By 2009, the last year with good data, student loan burdens were drawing off 35 percent of the annual income of college dropouts. Yet such college dropouts have virtually no advantage in wages over those who did not go to college at all; in 2011 their wages were even lower.[23]

The crude statistics commonly used to show correlations between educational levels and wages miss a lot of what is really going on. The skewed imbalance in salaries, in which a minority of people get the high-paying jobs and the rest do not, is a function not so much of education as of skill-to-job matching. One-fourth of bachelor's or advanced-degree holders will one day earn a lower median wage than holders of associate's degrees. About one-fourth of the college graduates are making less money than almost half of those who have only a high school diploma. One-third of the associate's degree holders will earn less than high school graduates do.[24]

More education does not necessarily mean better pay. One senior executive in the personnel business, Mara Swan, said, "There's always been a gap between what colleges produce and what employers want. . . . But now it's widening."[25]

Understanding Skills Gaps: Middle-Skill Jobs

The *middle-skill* segment of the workforce category identified in the PCAST study makes up the largest proportion of the workforce. Middle-skill jobs have usually required some postsecondary education, though not necessarily a college degree, and typically pay wages in the range of $40,000 and up. As we mentioned earlier, many IT jobs are middle skill. Such job needs are expected to rise as fast as high-skill employment and to be the largest single part of all job growth.[26]

Jobs in skilled production work include those of an electronics engineering technician or an operator/programmer of computer numerical control machinery. They usually require some specific postsecondary education. They pay well, in the $50,000 range and up. But employers find a much smaller labor pool to recruit from and have difficulty finding qualified workers.[27]

Employers systematically indicate that they are struggling to fill jobs across skill levels with qualified candidates. One survey of 2,000 U.S. companies in 2011, when the U.S. unemployment rate was almost 9 percent, found that 30 percent of all companies and 43 percent of those in manufacturing had positions open for more than six months that they could not fill. Another survey found that "a lack of adequate middle-skills talent directly or significantly affected the productivity of 47% of manufacturing companies, 35% of health care and social assistance companies, and 21% of retail companies." A more recent survey looked not only at how long positions were open but also at needs for duplicate postings and resources devoted to recruitment. This study confirmed large gaps, especially in areas of economic importance such as health care, computer and mathematical positions, and technical sales and sales management.[28]

Moreover, unfilled vacancies are a weak metric for measuring how companies address the middle-skills shortage.

• Where specific skills are needed, the larger firms may offer their own training programs and higher wages. More of this spending is devoted to managerial level workers, in the belief that they can add more quickly to the company bottom line. In recent decades large company investments in training are often constrained by investor-owners who have difficulty valuing any training that does not produce a market value payoff within the time horizon of the owners' or investment managers' exit strategy, which may be no more than about three to five years.

• Where specific skills are needed, the smaller, younger firms cannot afford to do the training. Most firms cannot sponsor apprenticeships with local high schools, even if the schools welcomed them. Or, if the small firm has the money, it might fear it would lose the person it had invested in training. So even though the business community as a whole may need the welders or computer programmers, no one firm will step up on its own to pay to train the welders or programmers. Theorists call this a "collective action" problem. We offered ideas to help address such problems in chapters 5 and 6.

• Another scarcity problem for the younger, smaller firms is that, where there is scarcity, the little guys will be outbid for the available talent by the big guys. In Silicon Valley, supposedly crawling with IT talent, it is easy to find owners of smaller businesses complaining that Google is vacuuming up most of the good people. The high bidders for scarce talent tend to be larger, older firms (which Google is now). Over time, if the scarcity continues, this trend will produce a less dynamic economy, one more dominated by the entrenched older firms.[29]

Perhaps the gravest symptom of all is this: perceiving that they cannot readily solve a shortage of workers with relevant skills, companies will form plans that require fewer such workers.

Companies do not like to embark on ambitious plans and then watch aghast as job notices go unfilled for three months. Instead, if they perceive that suitably skilled people will not be available but still want that value added, then the firm will slot that part of the networked production process to a foreign supplier, such as high-cost but available and suitably flexible clusters of producers in places like Taiwan, Germany, Japan, and Singapore.

A dispassionate survey of available evidence about skills short-ages, supplemented by fresh employer surveys, was recently carried out by the MIT Task Force on Production in the Innovation Economy. Those experts concluded that the problem was indeed very real for a significant fraction of jobs. The task force also warned of the "huge problem in years to come when the aging of the current workforce leads to a massive wave of retirements."

Yet the most important observation of the MIT group was about the need to look ahead. In addition to the filling of present gaps and the replacement of retirees, it emphasized new kinds of training needs. The new economy requires "training for jobs that demand new combinations of book learning, hands-on experience, proficiency with digital technology, and ability to manage relationships face to face and with distant collaborators—these are the labor market challenges we face today in the United States." We agree with that observation.

We also agree with that task force's follow-on conclusion. Given the disincentives in current corporate structures and the weaknesses of the existing public structures, it stressed that "[m]eeting these challenges will require very different institutions than those that trained the workforce even in the recent past. . . ."[30]

The Labor Market as an Ecosystem:
The Worker–Trainer–Employer Triangle

Working with a group from the Markle Foundation, the PCAST study of workforce training offered a useful way of visualizing a whole system of interactions that should occur in America's labor market. In the figure below we show a triangle in which each corner is trying to signal the other about needs and capabilities.[31]

Right now this interaction does not work well. There are several matching services, but few integrate all three angles. They do not have a common vocabulary or common platforms. The platforms are sometimes proprietary and closed off to the general public. The platforms do not "learn" from what happens in the interactions.

One of the more innovative developers, Felix Ortiz, founder of

Employment Triangle

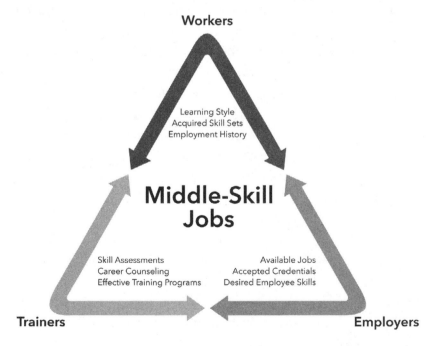

Workers

Learning Style
Acquired Skill Sets
Employment History

Middle-Skill Jobs

Skill Assessments
Career Counseling
Effective Training Programs

Available Jobs
Accepted Credentials
Desired Employee Skills

Trainers

Employers

Viridis Learning, suggests that few evidence-based employment decision-making tools currently exist on the market. It seems to him that employers might have no better than an estimated 50 percent success rate at hiring qualified middle-skill workers.[32]

One cause of this skills disconnect appears to be that the three major players—employers, job seekers, and training and education providers—are not adequately engaged with each other.

> • The system fails most employers. In a substantial McKinsey study of education to employment, less than a third of employers felt they were successful in getting the talent they needed. Those were the employers who connected with education providers and with youth. Others were not so engaged or tried to connect but found the existing structures did not work for them.
> • The system also fails most young job seekers. Although their perspectives were of course very different from those of the employers, the majority of them—regardless of whether they went to college—felt that the education system had not prepared them for an entry-level position in their chosen field.
> • The only contented group was the educators. They thought they were doing a fine job and producing graduates ready to learn. The McKinsey researchers found that the educators seemed to be living in a "parallel universe."[33]

To be fair, as Dennis Yang, president and chief operating officer of Udemy, points out, "Universities weren't designed to change curricula and introduce new classes at the pace required by changing industry requirements." After all, he notes, "we now live in a world in which half of today's jobs didn't exist 25 years ago."[34]

We believe that Americans should consider deep innovation and redesign in the way we have approached problems of personal development for the last hundred years and more. Those approaches, like the spread and standardization of today's high schools and colleges, were radical changes that transformed America. Those approaches worked well in their time. The times really are changing. It is our turn to do what Americans did when they coped with the second economic revolution: rethink the system.

Much of the current debate about education reform occurs in the framework of the existing system. In that system a critical variable is the classroom teacher. So Americans have been locked in heated debates about how to improve teacher quality and teacher accountability.

We respect those arguments. Many of us have participated in them. Teachers matter. But our aim in this book is to look beyond the teacher as miracle worker and more to the system in which teachers and many others try to help people live the life they want.

In the next chapter we will spend more time on education itself, on ways to help people juggle life and learning and new ways to learn.

In the remainder of this chapter we call for five kinds of actions:

1. companies should better define the skills they need and join in private-public alliances to develop the human talent they will need;
2. develop a broader, more flexible, and useful system of credentials to show what Americans know and can do;
3. reverse the modern trend toward disconnection of "academic" from "career and technical" secondary and post-secondary education;
4. build a much more interactive and functional digitized labor market to improve the functioning of the worker-trainer-employer triangle; and
5. help Americans move more easily to where they can find opportunities.

Invest in Talent Supply Chains[35]

In a better-functioning labor market, credentials are more clearly connected to job and learning requirements. These are usually practical skills, many of them involving creativity and problem-solving skills in real-life situations, skills not easily replicable by machines.

The private sector should take the lead in defining its needs and structuring career paths. None but the largest companies can do this on their own. So the best solutions would require much closer alliances between educators and leaders in the producer communities. Academic credentials at all levels can better blend theory with practice, priming students with broadly applicable credentials that employers understand and validate. Better academic credentials can lead to more flexible and abbreviated follow-up to attain more specialized credentials, constantly kept up to date in a changing market.

In other words, employers can devote the same energy to sourcing their human talent as they devote to their other supply chains. Earlier we mentioned the troubles GE had in Kentucky and Flextronics had in Texas in recruiting thousands of new workers. As one of the GE Appliance Park leaders recalled, "We didn't even have a pipeline of emerging manufacturing talent, because it had become all about sourcing goods."[36]

If businesses and unions step up, educators and trainers should meet them at least halfway. One of the Flextronics managers in Fort Worth, where the equipment was state of the art, commented, "Nobody coming out of college these days is knowledgeable or excited about doing this kind of work. We can't afford to only hire people who are over 40 or bring people in from abroad."

One of the solutions both firms developed, out of desperation, was to design relatively short and flexible education and training programs that would build up to the work, ultimately leading to an industry-recognized certification. Employees who made the commitment were usually rewarded. Turnover dropped. Also valuable was a vision of how skills could progress. This built a culture of achievement, which can be very important. This is a point we made in chapter 5 as well, when we used an illustration drawn from the health care workplace.

In this vision, we are seeing new kinds of educators and trainers, with or alongside traditional schools or community colleges, all changing, all offering several kinds of credentials, validated and taught in new ways. Some of the building trades, like that of electricians, have well-established certification and training setups.

For example, more than 70 years ago the International Brotherhood of Electrical Workers (IBEW) and the National Electrical Contractors Association (NECA) created an electrical-training alliance. It works through local affiliates that use apprenticeships and also deploys a blended learning program, combining remote online education with personal coaching. This training alliance—privately funded—has enabled hundreds of thousands of workers to earn recognized credentials to be wiremen or installers.[37]

Credentials better linked to job requirements are a cure for up-credentialing. Yet it is exactly the absence of certified skill standards and well-developed, flexible training programs that characterizes much of the middle-skill workforce.

The Burning Glass researchers noticed this gap. "Jobs resist credential inflation when there are good alternatives for identifying skill proficiency. [Examples include] many health care and engineering technician jobs . . . because those positions are governed by strict licensing or certification standards, well-developed training programs, or by measurable skill standards such that employers do not need to look at a college degree as a proxy for capability."[38]

American employers may be willing to pay more for appropriately skilled workers. A McKinsey study found that 86 percent of U.S. employers surveyed would pay more for a job candidate with the right training and hands-on experience—a higher proportion than in any of the other eight countries surveyed.[39]

We understand that employers (and some unions) already have respected credentials in particular jobs, as we have mentioned in discussing some of the building trades. As in the case of the IBEW-NECA alliance, we have seen impressive illustrations of what is possible when all the relevant parties work together.

In Kentucky, facing a shortage of people with the skills to work in an automotive plant, Toyota started working with a local community college on the Automotive Technical Education Collaborative (AMTEC). This has grown into a network of 30 community colleges and 34 auto-related plants in twelve states. Joe Welgan, a maintenance manager at Nissan's plant in Smyrna, Tennessee, says he and his colleagues know what to expect if someone has that credential—"It's a validation."[40]

In the electrical-training example, the credentials have relatively specific applicability—to help a person get a job as an electrician or telecommunications worker. A missing and potentially vital credential would be one that could signal solid ability in skills of broad applicability.

More Flexible and Useful Credentials

Employers often want to find someone who can take "book" skills and apply them constructively in some practical setting. These skills might not be calculus, for example, but they might just involve "numeracy," the ability to understand and work with materials that are presented in numbers or some abstract forms, like shapes and graphs. Such a credential might reveal the kind of adult job skills that the OECD surveyed, but might not necessarily line up with all the skills, including those for college prep, that are meant to be represented by a high school diploma.

The existing certificates tend to be too rigid or narrowly oriented. They may point to the quality of college prep (e.g., grades or AP test scores in particular subject disciplines like calculus). Or, less often, some have vocational courses or tests for a specific kind of job. But graduation from a multiyear secondary school in vocational education in some particular field may also be too rigid. Most students may need or want to shift their career pathway in these early years, often more than once.[41]

We would welcome a more open-ended system in which individuals who took the equivalent of a year or two of postsecondary education, perhaps not enough to earn a degree, could actually get value for their investment by showing what they had learned, at least up to that point, in some widely valued skills. The process therefore does not have to require the completion of college or the expenditure of excessive time or money. Already able to get recognition for some of their skills, learners could tackle the next stage when ready and able.

The building up of such alternatives poses some big challenges, of course. We can call them the three Cs—content, credentials, and a compact.

Content. Working with the private sector, developers of new credentials must base them on well-understood definitions about what skills most importantly make up something like "numeracy." The work should be open and evidence based, inviting evolutionary revision. We want to repeat that opening clause: "working with the private sector." That will be key to the "compact" part, described below.

Credentials. Any credential should be digitally portable, at least as secure and movable as a person's money. It should be backed by credible assessments that could involve simulations and other state-of-the-art techniques, not necessarily the traditional paper tests.

Compact. The only concrete proof that employers buy into the system is for a number of firms to join a compact promising to respect the credential in their HR policies in a way that job seekers will hear about, notice, and understand. That is why the employers have to be brought into the conversation, the process of developing the credential. It is why the content must continually evolve, just as employers' needs evolve.

The most-needed credentials are those that would show that the person has good, practical skills to embark on a career pathway, offering maximum flexibility to show value to more than one kind of employer. Since the credentials should signal significant value to many employers, it is reasonable to ask companies to back up that judgment, concretely, in their hiring processes. Not all employers would need to join in. A critical mass would be enough. Indeed, a healthy competition may develop among rival credentials, each arguing that it is better judged, of broader use, of greater credibility.

Such new credentials could work outside or inside of the traditional context of college degree programs. Many colleges might eventually regard credentials like these as useful or revealing milestones within their more elaborate degree programs. All of these attainments should be a "ladder" for each person's goals and career pathways.

Reverse the Modern Trend toward Segregation of "Academic" from "Career and Technical" in Secondary and Postsecondary Education

The emphasis on college prep has pushed out most of the old "voc-tech" classes in many of America's secondary schools. But our argument is not a plea to restore lots of dedicated vocational schools for students who cannot or should not join the highway to college.

Instead, we believe practical skills should be in the mainstream of American education. We should not concentrate on more ways to push 14- or 15-year-olds (or their parents) to decide to segregate themselves from "the rest of us," in social status and our culture.

As long as career and technical education is a defined separate track of secondary or postsecondary education, a second tier, we expect it may be seen as socially inferior. As long as it is seen as an inferior choice, both these skills and these jobs will be misperceived in popular culture. The Taylorist cultural image we discussed in chapter 6 will be reinforced. And these careers will not attract as many Americans as they should.

Such an informal but very real segregation of educational pathways will remain a marker of "two Americas." As the emerging employment picture is already showing, there is no compelling reason to regard one particular path as necessarily superior to another, either in earnings or in brainwork.

In arguing for a system that connects education more tightly to the world of work, we do not belittle the value many Americans can find in a liberal arts education. For those who can afford it, at the time in their life when it makes the most sense for them, such programs can offer a long menu of educational possibilities, along with opportunities for self-discovery and social development. We are not against any particular course of study. We believe everyone who can or wishes to do so should be able to study what he or she wishes. We want parents and students alike to have more choices and more information.

America has had these debates before about the "academic" versus the "practical." In the 19th century, absorbing the industrial revolutions, Americans argued heatedly about whether mainstream academic institutions should include the contemporary vocational subjects. A separate "Bachelor of Science" degree was introduced by Harvard in 1851. But even then, Harvard's professors stoutly resisted any intrusion of practical subjects like "engineering" into their newly added study of natural sciences.

Schools that taught applied, practical skills were regarded as trade schools. Hence MIT was founded as an "institute," not as a "college." In that day the only "professions" were those that required formal study—divinity, law, medicine, and perhaps the military. All others "were of a lesser nature, of the sort that could be learned 'on the job.' Farmers, merchants, and manufacturers pursued vocations." And work like law enforcement did not rank even as high as that.

In 1847 Yale created the separate Sheffield Scientific School. It had different terms of study, and at Yale, as at Harvard, "the scientific students were considered second-class citizens, too benighted to aspire to the only worthy degree and therefore to be treated with condescension. At Yale, for instance, Sheffield students were not permitted to sit with academic students in chapel."[42]

By 1900 those older segregations had fallen away, and the basic credentials and patterns we know today had been set. Yet America's leading philosophers thought the system was not going far enough. William James argued for reducing the length of Harvard's baccalaureate program down to three years.

Most eloquently and persistently, John Dewey advocated the unity of theory and practice as the best way to learn both. It was a tenet of pragmatic philosophy. "Culture," he wrote, had to operate "in the conditions of modern life, of daily life, of political and industrial life." Education, he believed, should "frankly adapt itself to the central role of vocation in human life."[43] His ideal progressive schools always tried to integrate academic subjects with craft work and practical skills. One latter-day descendant of Dewey is the director of MIT's Media Lab, Joichi Ito. Raised in Japan and America, Ito attended college but earned no degrees. A renowned innovator, he emphasizes practical skills as the tools that liberate problem solvers, creators, and explorers.[44]

Today many Americans may regard those old arguments as quaint relics. They are not. In the study of many of today's practical skills, from advanced production to software development to networked service delivery, new gaps, new segregations, and new hierarchies of social status have opened up in the structure of our educational systems and curricula. Future generations, looking back on today's system, may wonder at today's classifications and hierarchies that do not seem to be justified by any objective appraisal of the cognitive skill, rigor, or creativity involved in the varying fields.[45]

On the southernmost coast of Georgia, right above the border with Florida, sits Camden County. It is close to the Cumberland Island National Seashore and the large Kings Bay naval base. The county has one high school, Camden County High (CCHS). CCHS is a big school, graduating about 600 students a year. Its ethnic makeup mirrors the county, about 25 percent black, and about 40 percent of the students qualify (by low family income level) for reduced-price lunches.[46]

CCHS made the decision to mainstream practical education into its high school curriculum. The ninth graders go to a "freshman academy." After that, all students select one of five other academies for the rest of their high school work (transfers are possible). The academies are in health and environmental sciences; engineering, architecture, and industry; business; fine arts; and government and public service. All have career/technical curricula. In the government and public service academy, a student in the "law and justice" curriculum might conduct a mock crime scene investigation, write reports, and prepare a case, taught by a former Navy-Kings Bay NCIS professional named Rich Gamble. "We emphasize a lot of writing," he explains. "I give them issues where they have to defend themselves, in very few words, because courts don't like you to waste words."

Most schools with career and technical education have a "pull-out" model, where students leave school for courses at a technical center. CCHS is different. It is "wall-to-wall," with everything in the school built around its component academies.

Rachel Baldwin, a career instruction professional at CCHS, explains,

> In the past, we've encouraged all kids to go to college, because of the idea that it made the big difference in income levels. . . . The recent evidence suggests [it] really goes back to something like "grit." I think you are more likely to learn grit in one of these technical classes. The plumber who has grit may turn out to be more entrepreneurial and successful than someone with an advanced degree. Our goal has been getting students

a skill and a credential that puts them above just the entry-level job, including if they're using that to pay for college.

The results have been interesting. In 2001 CCHS had a graduation rate of 50.5 percent. The graduation has since risen to 85 percent. The school also has the best AP scores of any school in southern Georgia. Baldwin borrows a naval expression, that "a rising tide raises all ships." She clarifies that their AP students "thrive in Career Technical options (we have more than 20 AP course offerings), along with students who would be considered traditionally 'vocational' in the past. Our administration and faculty, believing in 'all ships rise,' recognize and provide strong support for both achievement at higher academic levels and meeting the new technical demands of the workplace."

After a report on CCHS was published in the *Atlantic* by Jim Fallows, one reader wrote in to note how, as an educator himself who had grown up in that part of the state, he agreed with the approach. He concluded, "The era of the 'collars' is over. I wish I didn't go to school where vocational and 'college prep' were segregated."

Such "edutraining" approaches offer students a richer menu of options and life sequences. These alternatives also affirm the pride in and social status of many kinds of skills. For those parents who might be aghast at their children's being locked into taking "shop," our ideas are all about no one's being "locked in." As we will detail in the next chapter, different kinds of educational designs could offer students many different ways to connect theory to practice.

An exciting initiative, Pathways to Prosperity, was launched in 2011 by a group of scholars at the Harvard Graduate School of Education to explore just such possibilities and share concrete ideas. The movement now already includes officials from ten states, several foreign countries, and the help of a nonprofit foundation, Jobs for the Future.[47]

The existing routines and credentials, including the standard four-year BA model degree program to be followed directly after high school, were standardized a long time ago, mainly in the 1890s. Those older routines and structures are now unnecessarily rigid. They are not working well for most students or most employers.

We also challenge the rigid social and cultural expectation that has evolved alongside these structures. It is the expectation that good students, with good social status, will do college prep, followed promptly by four years of college and a degree. That is an expectation that most Americans have not attained and are not likely to attain. Most Americans should not believe that they are on the low way, having failed somehow to get on the highway.[48]

The historical pattern in America has been job innovation and upskilling for the vast majority of Americans. From farmers and hired hands with no formal education to laborers with primary education, to employees with universal secondary education, with constant changes in the nature and value of the associated work: that has been the American way.

A Truly Digitized, Networked Labor Market

All through this chapter, we have emphasized our impression that today's labor market is full of mismatches. People do not know just what skills they need. Employers do not know just how an applicant relates to their needs. Educators and trainers are not sufficiently plugged into the labor market at all.

In a better-networked labor market, each part of the employment triangle would interact with the others in multisided platforms. For that to work best, a job applicant would need to be able to represent, digitally, what she or he has done and can do. Some of the new credentials we are advocating would facilitate that. An employer would have to digitally represent its needs too. And we emphasize the ingredient missing now from the standard two-way matching platforms: the educators and trainers.

Building on the hundreds of millions of member profiles

already in its databases, LinkedIn has begun working on ways to digitize all the inputs to the labor market, to create what the company calls an "economic graph." Over time the platforms can then become much more sophisticated in identifying and suggesting possible ways to match Americans to opportunities.

Our vision is that, aided by such platforms and perhaps by capabilities sponsored in the nonprofit or public sector, Americans can look at the condition of the labor market as well as a farmer can look at a daily weather report, and find it just as up to the minute. (We have no view on the forecasting.)

On the basis of an early analysis of how a more connected labor market might improve employment, one analyst recently estimated that the positive impact could be very large—boosting employment by 700,000 to as many as 1.8 million workers. "This would involve both better matching of workers to existing jobs as well as creation of new jobs through better exploitation of business opportunities."[49] Creating such digital platforms is a challenging task. But we believe it is doable.

Many such platforms are possible, not just one. As with weather reports, there are local ones and national ones. Like farmers looking for rain, Americans looking for work will be most attentive to their local conditions, even as they study what is going on elsewhere. Here again there is a potential role for local or regional private-public partnerships to make sure everyone has as much information as possible to plan for the future.

Make It Easier to Move to Opportunity

The traditional way for Americans to advance themselves is to move. They move to find something better. With geographic mobility came the creation of new communities.

Between 1930 and 1970, and especially from the 1940s on, two regions of the United States fundamentally changed their relationship with the rest of the country. One was the American South. The other was the American West. Both regions became far more productive parts of the United States.[50] Tens of millions of Americans moved, including millions of black Americans who left the South for new destinations in the North and West.

All this movement created hundreds of new communities. "Aerial views of Los Angeles County as of 1960 reveal cluster after cluster of housing tracts geometric in regularity."[51] The term "suburbia" passed into common use and meaning.

This kind of mobility is packed with economic energy. American schoolchildren had learned that the frontier had closed in about 1890. That closing of the "frontier" was bemoaned as a sort of metaphor for the end of national possibility. But in the 1940s, 1950s, and 1960s frontiers seemed to be reopening for relocation, with new chances all around. A young new president in 1961 even made "New Frontier" the reigning metaphor of his administration.

Contrary to what many people believe, the United States is a less mobile society than it was in the 1970s, both in terms of geography and in terms of employment. Americans move less frequently and they change jobs less frequently than they did in the past.

The scale of American mobility is now greatly diminished. In every single year from 1945 to 1965, about 21 percent of Americans changed their residence. Between 2010 and 2013 that percentage dropped by about half. In every single year from 1947 to the mid-1970s, about 3 to 3.5 percent of Americans made even longer-range moves, from one state to another. Then that mobility also tapered off. Now it is also about half the former rate.[52] A lot of Americans feel stuck.

The least mobile workers tend to be those with the least education. They are stuck most of all. This is another reason they are most likely to be unemployed; they do not—or cannot—move to opportunity.

Obviously this has not always been so. What is happening now? Perhaps information about new opportunities is not being passed through family networks as efficiently. Perhaps people are stuck in houses they cannot afford to leave.

A big factor, though, is one of the simplest. It takes cash to move, and cash is in short supply. The unemployment insurance program in the United States has the same structure now that it had when it was first created during the 1930s. The system does not provide any incentive for unemployed workers to move. It even discourages mobility, because the checks are adjusted to costs of living. If an unemployed worker wanted to move from a low-cost city like Lynchburg, Virginia, to a higher-cost city like Houston, the unemployment check would still be based on the salary the worker had earned in Lynchburg.

There are other disincentives to moving. If someone is on a waiting list for a rental housing voucher (and the waiting lists are usually long), she might be reluctant to move and lose her spot in the queue. If someone is eligible for Medicaid or food stamps in one state, he might fear becoming ineligible by moving to another state with different standards.

Some experts have suggested supplementing unemployment compensation with relocation vouchers. Vouchers could be offered to people who lived in areas where unemployment was regarded as too high, above average. This could address a longstanding aspect of poverty that experts call a "spatial mismatch" of poor people or underprivileged minorities concentrated in the wrong part of a city—or just the wrong city. Such vouchers could cover some of the costs of moving somewhere new. Such a policy would help not only those who want to move but also those who want to stay, since there would then be fewer people competing for the scarce remaining jobs.

This is not a new idea. An early version of it was tried out during the 1970s and worked. One version of such assistance, the Moving to Opportunity program sponsored by the former Housing and Urban Development secretary Jack Kemp, worked reasonably well.

Relocation aid could be combined with migration aid too. Dayton, Ohio, has launched a "Welcome Dayton" initiative, a private-public partnership to attract immigrants. It is meant to draw them not just from foreign lands but also from other cities. Other cities in the Midwest are doing the same.[53]

One solution to the problem of "place-based" welfare assistance, like Medicaid or food stamps, could rely more on a networked approach. The United States is increasingly moving to "portable" forms of federal assistance, for instance, in health care. The problem of conflicting state standards is difficult, but one of the advantages of federal poverty programs like the Earned Income Tax Credit is that they are geared to the individual, not to the place.

Another issue related to skills and affecting labor mobility is the role of legally mandated credentials—or licensing. Licensing has a long history in the United States, starting with jobs that involved obvious issues of public safety such as piloting ships. Formal licensing structures expanded greatly at the beginning of the industrial age as professions such as law, medicine, engineering, and accountancy sought to define themselves in ways that their customers and the broader public could have confidence in.

Some have argued that these efforts were in part designed to define professions in a manner that excluded competent but disfavored workers, such as midwives, from professionalized markets. The argument is that licensure laws create legally enforced monopolies that pull up the ladder, restrict entry, and hinder mobility. Ultimately, arguments about licensing are really arguments about enabling innovation and new entrants in the provision of services balanced against appropriate concerns about public safety.

With the rise of the knowledge-based service economy and the decline of traditional industrial jobs, licensing now plays a much larger role in the U.S. labor market. Securities brokers, nurses, and teachers have become more typical of the workforce than assembly-line workers. But in some states licensing extends well beyond those professions, applying even to hair braiders or florists.

In a recent important study of these trends, Morris Kleiner and Alan Krueger found that during the early 1950s less than 5 percent of the U.S. workforce was in occupations with entry restricted by state licensing laws.[54] By 2013, they discovered, 29 percent of U.S. workers were required to have a government-issued license to do their jobs. Another 6 percent were employed in jobs where there was a program for voluntary government skill certification. A further 3 percent expected their jobs to involve licensing or certification in the future. Kleiner and Krueger's research did not determine whether this growth is primarily a result of expanding the coverage of licenses, or of shifts in employment patterns toward licensed jobs.

Kleiner and Krueger found that licenses are more common at the higher end of the wage spectrum than at the lower end. Common professions employing affluent Americans—medicine, law, securities dealing, accounting, and engineering—all require licenses. So do important middle-income professions such as nursing, teaching, and the mechanical construction trades. While some lower-income occupations such as taxi driving and working at a barbershop do often require licenses, licensing is less typical of lower-income workers. According to Kleiner and Krueger, occupational licensing is also correlated to an 18 percent wage premium. As a form of labor market regulation, licensure now covers substantially more employees than collective bargaining through unions.

Licensure requirements should not become an arbitrary barrier to new entrants to skilled jobs. As new types of skilled work come into being with technological change, those who are first to acquire those skills should not be allowed to prevent others from following in their path. There should be clear, transparent paths, open to all, to skilled work.

The U.S. Supreme Court recently upheld a broad challenge

to the "public safety" rationale used in keeping people out of certain trades. The Federal Trade Commission had challenged North Carolina's dental assistant licensure rules.[55]

We think states and localities should look for ways to manage their licensing systems to encourage labor mobility and to give workers incentives to develop their skills. For example, in many professions licensing is either national in scope, as it is in securities brokerage, or have national examination systems and national credentials databases, as is now the case in medicine.[56]

In any agenda to match Americans to opportunity, government policies should consciously prioritize approaches that empower Americans to seek out fresh chances—the original American Dream—while at the same time encouraging the widespread development of a more skilled workforce. We believe these two goals can, and must, be pursued together.

Actions Needed

> • Companies should better define the skills they need, giving as much attention to developing and assuring the supply of human talent as they do to the rest of their supplier network. They should help foster private-public alliances to develop the human talent they will need.
>
> • Alliances that include leading employers should develop more flexible, low-cost, and useful systems of credentials to show what Americans know and can do. Employers, or groups combining them, should update and maintain sets of credentials that they respect.
>
> • Educational leaders, public and private, should reverse the modern trend toward segregation of "academic" from "career and technical" secondary and postsecondary education. Instead, they should evaluate ways to mainstream combinations of theory with practice.
>
> • Alliances with employer participation should build

platforms to create a much more interactive and functional digitized labor market that represents constantly updated data from all parts of the worker-trainer-employer triangle.

• Policymakers should make benefit systems and occupational licenses more portable in order to help Americans move more easily to wherever they can find their best opportunities.

Chapter 8

Prepare for the Life You Want

The 20th century has rightly been hailed as America's human capital century.[1] The 21st century could be another . . . but in a totally different, individualized way.

When a McKinsey group sized up several game changers that could supercharge the American economy, "talent" was at the top of their list. They estimated that improving skills development from kindergarten to postsecondary education could add $1.7 trillion in added annual GDP by 2030. This was a larger impact than any other set of changes the group considered.[2]

The group did not analyze the possible impact of pre-K—better early childhood education. This could also be very significant.

Education is at the top of practically all agendas for America's economic future. In this book we look beyond the current debates about teachers or testing.

Those debates are very important, but we want to enlarge the conversation—to reconsider the deep structures of American education that were designed to succeed in the 20th century. Fortunately, Americans have entered an era when it has never been easier for anyone to tap high-quality educational resources—anywhere, anytime. The challenge is to design new structures to empower all these possible learners.

We began the last chapter with the example of middle-skill training for IT jobs. We explained the mismatches in that labor market and the way these well-paying jobs were being up-credentialed. Suppose those problems were solved: the employer stated the need, and applicants understood what they needed to learn and earn.

How, then, might someone get this training in a high-quality but more flexible fashion? We begin this chapter by illustrating an answer to that question.

As one test of how to train IT professionals at the entry-level or above, the Defense Advanced Research Projects Agency (DARPA) ran a pilot study in which the Navy placed a group of novice IT pupils in a rigorous 16-week Digital Tutor program. This program was carefully developed, at significant cost, by observing and employing expert techniques being used by teachers of these skills.

The sailors who completed this program were then put in a competition that tested their knowledge and skills both against other students who had completed much longer conventional programs and against veteran IT professionals (with seven to nine years of experience). In all the assessments the Digital Tutored sailors outperformed their competition by "wide margins." The program is scalable.[3]

The point of this story is not that such alternatives are cheap. If they are to be done well, they often are not.

Nor is the point of the story to emphasize how human beings can be replaced by computer teachers. The real lesson is much more interesting.

Excellent human teaching is being embedded in software that distills and extends it. That new teaching tool requires plenty of human professionals, but they may be playing different roles in a redesigned process. The systems could be designed to serve many, many more learners—at all ages—than our education system is currently serving today. The educational system and the credentials it awards can be enriched by supplementing it with fresh blends of many kinds of educators and trainers cooperating and competing—businesses, unions, libraries, museums, science centers, and more.

For an America of potential learners to tap all this available knowledge requires providers to make significant investments in human "navigators," counselors to help learners find what they need, since the world of training and credentials should become much larger and varied. These navigators should be able to blend professional insight with customer service. And they, too, should be working in structures organized to operate at scale.

The point of the story about the Navy's Digital Tutor experiment to train IT professionals is, above all, about designing new ways to empower individual learners. Each of them can get keys to unlock vast, hitherto inaccessible storehouses of knowledge.

We Did It Before, Up to a Point

What made the 20th century so remarkable for America's human capital was a movement that gathered steam toward the end of the 19th century. Most state and local governments in the United States joined the movement to build up public education. The resulting achievements were stunning. Just between 1892 and 1940, high school enrollment rose from about 5 percent of 14- to 17-year-olds to about 75 percent.[4] Already by the 1920s more Americans had finished the equivalent of high school than was the case in any other country in the world, distinctly ahead even of western European countries.

School structures in that era were more accessible and forgiving than they are now. They were better able to handle students dropping in and dropping out. There was more practical education, with more scope for influence by local companies (which had often been part of the private-public alliance that had built the school system in the first place).

In the years immediately after 1945, while federal spending declined sharply, state and local spending doubled. Most of this state and local money went to schools and to roads.

Not only did high school completion rates climb; college attendance took off as well. The federal government sponsored college education for returning veterans with the GI Bill, and many colleges entered periods of rapid growth to accommodate them. Entry to top universities, especially public ones, was easy and inexpensive for anyone who could do college-level work. At the University of California at Berkeley in 1960, anyone could be admitted who met the university's stated requirements, and most qualified applicants did attend. And tuition was free.[5]

Until 1970 high school and college completion rates steadily rose.[6] Then the rise slowed. High school and college completion rates have remained fairly flat since the 1970s. Women have made further gains, offset by declines in the rates for young men.[7] Over the past decade high school graduation rates began inching up again. High school graduation rate gaps remain large in many districts and states, however, for students from low-income families, students with disabilities, and African American, Hispanic, and Native American students in comparison with their more advantaged peers.[8]

The impacts of school failure and individual choices are dramatic. In fact, there are 6.7 million 16- to 24-year-olds in the United States—17 percent of this age group—who are disconnected from school or employment. About half of them never attended school, went to college, or worked after the age of 16.[9] The rest are "under-attached"; they have some education and some work experience, but it is very limited.[10]

That data raises serious moral issues about whether America is living up to its creed of being an opportunity society, but it also has dramatic implications for taxpayers and our economy and society. In 2011 alone, these 6.7 million disconnected youth cost the taxpayer $93 billion in lost revenues from a lack of productive workers and increased social services and $252 billion to society, tallying earnings lost and losses to victims of crime.[11] In total, the lifetime economic burden of these youth in 2011 was put at $1.6

trillion to the taxpayer and $4.7 trillion to society. But millions of these "opportunity youth" accept responsibility for their futures. New pathways for personal development should give them more on-ramps to get back onto a constructive road.

For the United States to turn the 21st century into another human capital century, we are looking hard at the new tools for *learners* and their need for *navigators* for help in how best to use these tools.

Learner Power

In 2001 the Massachusetts Institute of Technology decided to make its course materials available to the whole world, free of charge. The initiative is called OpenCourseWare (OCW). The program, "a permanent MIT activity," provides open access to lecture notes, exams, problem sets, and virtually any and all other content from MIT courses. The completely open, completely free initiative offers material from 2,150 courses. It has apparently reached at least 125 million people. MIT is quite happy to see teachers everywhere "remix" its material.[12]

As more and more content becomes available online through platforms like Khan Academy, Coursera, edX, Udacity, and others, millions of people around the world are teaching themselves on hundreds of different subjects. The most interesting frontier of experimentation is how teachers can use this enormous support to remix—or rework—the way they educate.

A radical experiment is occurring at Clintondale High School in Michigan. Clintondale is on the north side of Detroit. The school was ranked among the worst 5 percent in the whole state. Its principal figured that the school had "nothing to lose" by trying something new.

In 2010 he "flipped" every class in the ninth grade, a grade where more than half of the students had failed science and almost half had failed math. To "flip" a class meant posting videos of the instructional content, available on YouTube, allowing the students to watch them again and again, practicing at home to get the idea. As one student put it, "Whenever I had a problem on the homework, I couldn't do anything about it at home. Now if I have a problem with a video, I can just rewind and watch it over and over again."

Then the time in class would be devoted to hands-on practice of the material, with the teacher coaching and intervening as needed, instead of giving a lecture. Thus much of the traditional classwork became homework; the homework practice was done in class with the "coach" standing by. That's the flip.

Failure rates in the ninth grade dropped: in English from 52 percent down to 19 percent; in math from 44 percent to 13 percent; in science from 41 percent to 19 percent; in social studies from 28 percent to 9 percent.

The next year Clintondale flipped all of its classes. Failure rates dropped from an average of 30 percent down to 10 percent; graduation rates rose to over 90 percent; college attendance went from 63 percent to 80 percent. Meanwhile, Clintondale's students went from 64 percent low income to 81 percent low income. Tina Rosenberg, who wrote about Clintondale, concluded that "the biggest effect of flipping classrooms is on the students at the bottom."

Some of the videos are "homemade" by the teachers, aided by a local firm. Some use Khan Academy or other sources from the growing pool of quality online material.

The experiment is still just that. There is some improvement, but there is still a long way to go. Every aspect—the videos, the teacher roles—needs more work. But the educators at Clintondale are charged up. A ninth-grade science teacher said he now feels like an "educational artist." He felt liberated. "There's so much more time to educate!"[13]

Some universities are developing programs taking an entire degree program online—a spectrum from "full [residential] immersion" to "digital immersion," all of it enhanced by technology to help students find personal academic pathways and tailor course work as much as possible to their individual needs and learning styles. At Arizona State University its president, Michael Crow, is creating a model for the "New American University."

Crow is a passionate defender of America's research universities as marvelous knowledge enterprises. What Crow attacks is the evolving assumption that research excellence goes hand-in-hand with a culture of exclusivity.[14]

Instead, Crow believes that the New American University can thrive in research while also being far more inclusive. His own university, ASU, offers powerful empirical evidence that his proposition is true. While excelling in metrics of research productivity, the university is opening its doors as widely as it can. It is innovating the design of courses so that students from every kind of background can succeed. It is pioneering ways of reaching students that imply a "scalability [in higher education] previously considered improbable if not undesirable."[15] He is adapting the original vision of the American public university, with its relatively low costs and more open admissions, for the 21st century.

Other university presidents are joining in this movement. In 2014 the heads of eleven public universities in the United States (including Crow) created the University Innovation Alliance. The alliance represents schools enrolling more than half a million students. They have pledged to share best practices with the common goal of making "high-quality college degrees accessible to a diverse body of students" and "increase economic opportunity and mobility." They will work together to combine strengths for maximum impact.[16]

Using a different approach, concentrating above all on the teaching mission and less on research, Western Governors University (WGU) is a private nonprofit online school. It was established in 1997 by the governors of nineteen states and supported by over twenty major corporations. By 2003 it was the first institution of higher education to receive accreditation from multiple regions (four of them).

WGU provides wide access by setting tuition at a fraction of the cost of most institutions. It is the only online, accredited university in the United States that offers, at scale, bachelor's and master's degrees solely on the basis of demonstrated "competency"—the knowledge the student can demonstrate, regardless of the amount of time the student has spent in "class."

According to a recent White House report, "Because competency-based learning allows students to advance as soon as they demonstrate mastery of course materials, the average time to complete a bachelor's degree at WGU is 34 months."[17] The WGU programs combine a variety of learning materials with a "mentor" to help, and a series of assessments to gauge competence in the subject.

Program quality can be high. In 2014 WGU's teacher education program was ranked as the best preparation program of any kind in the country for future high school teachers by the National Council on Teacher Quality and *U.S. News & World Report.*

Another goal for WGU is to retrain adults who may be changing jobs and need fresh training. The average age of its over 48,000 students is 36. In 2013 most students paid about $2,890 per a six-month period, during which time they could take as many courses as they could handle. The tuition rate had not changed in five years.[18]

Education reform today is a nationwide political battlefield. Most of the arguments center on how to improve the system within the existing model.

Our strategy starts from the premise that the current economic and technological revolution is the right moment to consider different models. We believe these will require a willingness to rethink basic structures, innovation as deep as that involved in the shift from steam engines to electricity.

If just as a mental exercise, we should ask ourselves, How would we design the best possible way of teaching very large numbers of young people, from many different backgrounds, if we could design the system today, from scratch? Then, if some good ideas emerged, we would work on how to get from here to there.

Start with the wider availability of high-quality educational content. Some of the best courses, the best teachers, and the best materials are available to everyone in America, often at modest or no cost. By itself, that is not the solution. But it can be part of a solution.

The first-wave innovations in online learning, though vastly democratizing the availability of quality education, seem mainly to be serving individuals who already have the know-how to take best advantage of them. That is a typical pattern for early adopters of revolutionary technologies. But that is just the first wave.

Meanwhile, a predictable but unfortunate debate has already emerged between the evangelists of "digital" education and the fierce defenders of "immersive" education. The argument is unfortunate because practically all educators know and accept the following:

> • Subjects are not all alike. Some are clearly more sus-
> ceptible to remote education and programmed skills
> practice than are others. This has long been true, even
> when self-education came just from books and copy-
> books.
> • Students are not all alike. Some need more personal
> time and attention. Some may whiz through the math
> course and stumble over English literature; some just
> the opposite. *All* students benefit from individualized or
> personalized learning.

The debate about "personal" versus "online" is a first-generation debate. The next-generation systems, already beginning to emerge, will combine the best of both. The most effective and flexible approaches for the future will be blended.[19]

Caring teachers and educational designers and specialists will always be at the core. But they can be coupled to and supported by online content and shared knowledge available with networked technology. These methods can apply to immersive residential experiences as well as to immersive digital ones.

One simple benefit of technology is to make potentially superior course materials widely available. For example, a lecturer at San Jose State University taught a relatively standard electrical engineering course, "Introduction to Circuit Analysis." Some sections of the class were taught using lectures with the San Jose State way of teaching the course. The experimental section used content material from an MIT intro course, viewed online videos and the MIT course's problem sets. In the experimental section the San Jose State lecturer still met the students in person and handled questions. He used class time for peer-to-peer instruction and problem solving. The conventional class had pass rates of 55 percent; the blended experimental class had pass rates of 91 percent.[20]

Americans have arrived at a turning point in the history of education. Imagine we are in the kind of phase that American education was in 150 years ago, before all the current institutional models were set firmly in place. We need to ask ourselves, How might we design anew? What models make sense for a networked society? And, most important, what models make the most sense for Americans who want the opportunity to benefit from lifelong learning?

As we recall the past of America's educational designs and contemplate the future, we stress three points:

1. Put the learners and their individual ways of learning at the center—anytime, always—in more flexible educational approaches that blend a world of available content with personal help.
2. Use new tools for learning and networked support to empower individualized learning.
3. Consider fundamentally different designs that help stu-

dents juggle life and education. Constant lifelong learning must be taught as a life habit.

The Educational Design Toolkit: No. 1—Gamification and Simulation

In addition to the availability of knowledge by way of online resources, the basic design of educational materials is evolving rapidly. The textbook becomes an e-book, which can become a video presentation. The next stage is to explore what the entertainment world already knows about the learning that occurs in games and simulations, in "edutainment."

Dimension U is an online gaming platform geared toward young people, but with a difference. It is focused on general math and language principles. The platform awards prizes based on successful completion of games. Rewards include allowance money, either for use in real life (the parent can arrange to have the money deducted to a credit card) or in the virtual gaming environment.[21]

The founder of Dimension U, "NT" Etuk, came to America from Nigeria. As he first tried to teach math to others, he stumbled. He began to realize that "there is a whole generation of kids that are being lost in the education system because . . . the way they process information, the way [they] get engaged in anything . . . none of this comes into the classroom."

Etuk puts it this way: "The vast majority of education systems around the world ask the question, 'What do we have to do to give every child who wants one a great education?' This is a supply side question, where the supply is the number of teachers, number of schools, amount of funding, etc."

Etuk has a different way of framing his role: "We ask, 'How do we get every child to ask for a great education?' This is a fundamentally different approach, a paradigm shift, that allows for a completely different set of solutions."

The Dimension U experiment looked at the psychology behind

videogames. Kids were motivated to solve problems in the game. For instance, the game can apply a practical challenge: "Imagine you're at 14th Street and 3rd Avenue and I want you to use the coordinal system map to figure out how to get to Central Park." Early tries with this technique helped children at an elementary school in Mobile, Alabama.[22]

Many more experiments like these are underway. As one Columbia University professor explains, "Learning looks very different today, so we need to move away from the Industrial Revolution one-size-fits-all model that still plagues much of education."[23]

The Educational Design Toolkit: No. 2—Adaptive Advising and Learning

OpenStudy is a social learning network enabling students to ask questions, give help, and connect with others studying the same subjects—a collection of "massively multi-player study groups." The college-level online study groups, based on content from MIT's OpenCourseWare, provides such gamification features as badges for students who give consistently useful answers in discussion forums. The free service includes a scoreboard, chat rooms, and a drawing board where other students can walk each other through problems. In 2011 OpenStudy transitioned from research team to company, with 250,000 students from 180 different countries visiting its site each month.[24]

The next stage in a learner-driven system is to gather and use information the learner provides about how the person engages the material, the strengths or weaknesses, and areas where a teacher can most effectively help. Courses can then be customized around the learner.

Data-based eAdvisor programs are now being used at Arizona State University and Georgia State University. They help students choose majors, remain on their degree path, discover valuable courses, and seek the specific help they need.

Knewton is an "adaptive learning" system. It was created to

answer the question "Given what we understand about a student's current knowledge, what should that student be working on right now?"[25] The learning platform is a toolkit. It allows educators to create online course materials; once those materials are online, the platform recognizes where the student is doing well or is having problems. The software then guides the learner to skip what is already understood and get more help overcoming the tough spots.[26]

This tool has been tried out at Arizona State University, in combination with other tools. The goal was to find a better way to teach freshman math.

Thousands of students used the system. ASU discovered that there was an enormous number of ways that different students worked their way through the material. The customized approach worked better. The system halved the number of students quitting the course. Pass rates improved from 64 percent to 75 percent. Many of the students even finished the course early, ready to move on immediately to more advanced work.

On their own, none of these innovations work miracles. Together, they do inspire a sense of the possibilities.

The Educational Design Toolkit: No. 3—Help Learners Juggle Life with Constant Learning

In chapter 5 we talked about the world of someone like Debra Burton, trying in her 40s to plug the old gaps in her education and add new knowledge. We hope everyone will imagine or remember what can be involved in going to classes at fixed times, fighting traffic, and finding a parking place and hurrying to class lugging your course materials in rain or snow.

Imagine or remember doing this on fixed days, in a fixed place, running for a fixed semester, in classes that award a fixed number of credits. And all that is before one gets to the actual studying and course work. This is a structure that, in its basic elements, has not changed all that much in the last hundred years.

For most Americans, it is a bit of a luxury to be able to take years out of one's life to concentrate entirely on education. Nor is at all clear that the only, or even best, time for everyone to do this is between the ages of 18 and 21.

Sometimes it is unaffordable. Sometimes the would-be students are not yet ready to gain the full benefit from such costly and extended immersions, or not ready or able to do it in a block of time lasting four years or more. Many young people, however "bright" they are, may display much greater promise later, once they have spent some time at work, understanding more about what they need to learn—and why.

Our current structures mainly assume the traditional setting of a residential high school or college. Many forms of advanced education in business and the professions are already innovating well beyond this. Among business executives, one example is the success of "executive" MBA programs that blend remote and personal instruction. In medicine a busy doctor might use a similar mix in order to recertify in a specialty.

As we argued earlier in this chapter, we do not believe that digital education—alone—is a cure-all. What it does do, however, is enable educators to consider more flexible models, with more on-ramps at many points in life. The top two issues that older prospective students (aged 18–55) worried about most were (1) taking on too much debt and (2) balancing work and family responsibilities with the demands of school.[27]

The State University of New York (SUNY) is the largest comprehensive state university system in the United States. When Nancy Zimpher became chancellor in 2009, she was determined to turn its size into an asset in delivering value to students: "We're so big, if we get good ideas, we're the kind of place that can really take it to scale."

SUNY has scale, across its 64 campuses, 90,000 faculty and staff and some 460,000 students. Zimpher's "Open SUNY" initiative is an experiment that tries to leverage technology and innovation to expand access to as many students as possible—college-age and adult—and improve student outcomes in the workforce.

Open SUNY integrates all of the more than 400 online degree programs across SUNY campuses in a degree "Navigator" to help students find the right program and course options. It includes a first-of-its-kind Center for Online Teaching Excellence, to support faculty in online course design and delivery.

The initiative already recognizes that online education alone is not enough. People need to be ready to help students at every stage. The initiative is building support to member campuses, including 24/7 help desks, online tutoring, and "concierge" services. The SUNY team talked to thousands of students about their plans, consulting with hundreds of stakeholders. Zimpher hopes that this initiative, launched in 2014, will provide access to higher education for 100,000 new online students over the next three to five years.

Zimpher believes her efforts must be part of a larger, generational vision. "On the horizon is this massive expectation that we are going to educate more people, we're going to educate a much more diverse population, a global population. And it's time. It's high time. We've done this pretty much the same way for, not decades but centuries, and I think the door opened by the digital revolution is opening us to a whole new clientele that's really going to change the profile of higher education for the better."

"The past few years have been tough on the economy," Zimpher adds. "But there's only one solution. We are going to have to educate ourselves out of this mess."[28]

The Educational Design Toolkit: No. 4—Modularity

At the same time SUNY is trying to stretch the envelope in the way it delivers education, the MIT is joining the effort to redefine what a "course" means. The standard course is defined in terms of credit units, in a semester. Thus subjects tend to be converted into units taught over, say, thirteen weeks.

Analyzing experience with online learning at MIT and Harvard, the scholars noted that students tended to mine the material for what they thought they really needed. "The way in which students are accessing material," an MIT task force concluded, "points to the need for the modularization of online classes whenever possible."

The conclusions of this task force, commissioned and endorsed by MIT's president, Rafael Reif, are worth quoting at length.

> The very notion of a "class" may be outdated. This in many ways mirrors the preferences of students on campus. The unbundling of classes also reflects a larger trend in society—a number of other media offerings have become available in modules, whether it is a song from an album, an article in a newspaper, or a chapter from a textbook. Modularity also enables "just-in-time" delivery of instruction, further enabling project-based learning on campus and for students worldwide.[29]

A survey of MIT's faculty and instructors found that they thought about a quarter of their current classes would actually benefit from such an approach. Students, who were also surveyed, thought the faculty estimate was rather low.

A further benefit of such a modular approach was the ability to use the modules as "Lego bricks" in a variety of applications. "[A] module could be created in a matter of weeks and could be used as a foundation for a variety of disciplines," even "across institutions."

Part of the redesign effort should extend to the government policies that reinforce the existing models. An important example is the structure of student financial aid awarded by the federal and state governments.

The Educational Design Toolkit: No. 5—Financial Aid Systems

Government financial aid policies are currently linked tightly to the institution, to the credit unit system invented more than a hundred years ago, and to the way institutions are accredited. These links are meant to keep aid or student loan guarantees from flowing to "diploma mills," which effectively defraud students. The rules have difficulty achieving that goal. Yet they do constrain the capacity to apply federal aid for new and promising educational models.

The federal government is conscious of the rigidity of its current system. It recently granted financial aid regulation waivers to let some organizations "test new approaches."[30]

A revised federal system could open the way to deep innovation if it had the following three characteristics:

• Portability, meaning aid is tied to the individual and not the institution. This would allow an individual to pick and choose courses that are best for her or his learning goals and life situation. For example, Maria could take a five-week weekend leadership course at West Point, a short drive from her home, while she was also taking a six-month set of online statistics courses to earn a "specialization" through Coursera. The financial aid applied to these courses would not require them to be the same length or be from the same provider, but rather support the individual in pursuing both sets of skills.

• Accessibility, at any time in one's lifetime of learning. For example, Tony has enrolled in college and receives a financial aid grant. But a family member becomes ill, and he needs to drop out in order to be a caretaker and work part-time as a bookkeeper. The grant could be held in reserve for Tony to use later. With a few years of experience in this job, Tony might then still have financial aid left over from college to apply toward a preparation course to become a CPA. Structuring aid in such a way would allow Tony to obtain the skills he needs when he needs them to sustain a career path.

• Broader applicability, specifically to skills and alternative credentials—not just degrees. For example, Zina wants to take a set of courses offered through the Udacity platform that will train her to become a front-end programmer. She should be able to apply her grant to a "nanodegree" from Udacity, a set of courses designed with input from employers, and which could lead directly to a job.

These three characteristics may seem banal, but they would revolutionize the current system. Immediate policy reforms, such as decoupling federal financial aid awards from institutions and credit hours, are a way to launch such changes quickly. Corporations and nonprofits (like scholarship funds or foundations) could become disrupters to the current system by offering new types of financial aid and thus show the way.

The Educational Design Toolkit: No. 6—More Content Providers with Navigators, Coaches, and Course Developers

The definition of "educators" can become quite broad, including schools, colleges, companies, unions, libraries, museums, and community organizations. The potential resources are enormous. The challenge is to bring those resources to bear in the most learner-friendly way, "just-in-time" for when they are needed, and to do this on a large scale and with adequate structure and professional dedication.

The target audience for education and training can also be conceived very broadly. It is natural and appropriate to concentrate foundational education on young people, in part to teach them to be able to teach themselves during the rest of their life. But as life spans lengthen, as career paths proliferate, as relevant skills keep changing, Americans more and more seek education and training at many points in their lives, often to enlarge their appreciation of newfound ideas, places, and interests.

Gathering experience from this generation of technology-enhanced education programs, we want to spotlight three critical roles where caring people, much more enabled by networked technology, can join the ranks of the "new artisans" we wrote about in earlier chapters: navigators, coaches, and more course/curriculum developers.

Navigators. Sometimes aided by online avatars or networked "dashboards" integrating information about a student, navigators help guide learners among the maze of educational offerings. They probe that person's situation, background, and needs. They help with the logistics of enrollment. They explain and even provide support services. They decode unfamiliar institutions.

For example, the most famous supposed failure of a Massive Open Online Course (MOOC) experiment uses the illustration of the inability of a MOOC offered by a company called Udacity to teach math more effectively to at-risk youth in San Jose, California. But the study of that experience came up with interesting conclusions. No surprise, the key variable in student performance was the level of student effort. But in that experiment, the study reports, "[a]s students, [program officers], and faculty members explained, several factors complicated students' ability to fully use the support services, including their limited online experience, their lack of awareness that these services were available and the difficulties they experienced interacting with some aspects of the online platform."[31] These seemingly mundane problems are common, and critical.

The job description for navigators could be different from, more comprehensive than, the way school and career counselors define their roles today. Instead of being peripheral in educational institutions, they could move closer to the core. They could become important parts of a network that connects to others who care about, or have a legal duty to be involved in, a person's development.

Such navigators are not just for schools or colleges. The Workforce Innovation and Opportunity Act (WIOA) will take effect in

July 2015. The new law encourages employers to have "workplace learning advisers," individuals capable of advising other employees about the education, skill development, and credentials they will need in order to advance. The state and local workforce boards established by this law may use their federal funds to train and build networks for such advisers.[32]

Personalized Learning Coaches. Beyond the core instructional role, this kind of personal assistance is often called tutoring, or teaching assistance, but the term "coach" is more descriptive, connoting broader support. Although an online unit can be personalized to assist a student with particular problems, pointing to specific lessons that might help, students often reach a dead end. Then they need someone to help them through, providing encouragement and support.

Some massive online providers like Coursera and edX are already incorporating such coaching on an ad hoc basis, experimenting with ways to invite other online students to become "community teaching assistants" in their course. Arizona State University has taken this further in a pathbreaking partnership with the Khan Academy. The course is designed to use designated college students as "coaches" rather than the usual "teaching assistants." The student runs into trouble at an identifiable point in the course structure. Rather than lining up at the TA's door during designated office hours, the software integrates a Google feature to do just-in-time scheduling of a session with the coach in real time. The coach can then intervene just where the student is having trouble, using the online course features to intervene more strategically.

Course Developers and Knowledge Curators. Earlier in the chapter we mentioned the example of a Digital Tutor program developed for IT training, tried out by the U.S. Navy. We stressed then, and restate now, how vital and how difficult it is to do the up-front course development to achieve these results. Digital and residential education have this much in common: the quality of the input affects the quality of the output.

In other words, achieving these breakthroughs is not cheap or easy, but a larger proportion of the costs are up front, in development. The problem is not so dissimilar from the challenges involved in developing the most up-to-date versions of videogames in the computer entertainment world. To develop a videogame, the player is put into situations with many choices and possible outcomes, each leading to different pathways. Designing for all these different pathways, and programming the look and feel of the experience, is expensive and labor-intensive work.

The results, for the players, can be extraordinarily immersive. This area of technology is also advancing rapidly, as games can now incorporate physical movement (as with Kinect consoles) and new "virtual reality" technology. Some of the telepresence technologies that we mentioned earlier may also become more commonly available.

What the game developers and educators like the Khan Academy and some leading education technology companies know is that deconstructing the content in order to reconstruct it in this way is a challenging task. It calls upon experts with deep subject matter skills. There can, and should, also be a rich competitive menu of well-developed courses of this kind to choose from.

Today the job of course developer falls mostly on classroom teachers and textbook publishers. Both the teachers and the publishers are experimenting with alternatives, but it becomes one more demand on already harried teachers, who could use the help of specialized professional support. We can also imagine different numbers of course developers, with different roles, complementing the professionals now employed as instructional coordinators.

Reemploying Millions in Redesigned Systems. So imagine an educational system, organized to develop and offer courses from all the available educators in the city, the region, the nation, and even the world. Depending on the way each system is organized, and where its learners meet, the systems will still need plenty of in-person teachers. In personalized learning the teacher will have to draw on all of these assets. "Teacher" becomes a very special title (of honor).

Confronted with the challenge of economic revolutions in the second half of the 19th century, Americans undertook a breathtakingly radical series of experiments to remake and invent education systems for the entire country. By the middle of the 20th century, an entire world of high schools and universities had come into existence. The benefits for Americans of that age were incalculable.

As we experience a new economic revolution, it is our turn to develop an agenda for deep innovation. In doing this, we have an advantage the earlier makers did not. The character of the emerging networked world is inherently educational.

Navigators—Extending Helping Hands and Caring Communities

Michael Donnelly seemed like a hopeless case. He started life bouncing around the foster care system. He was adopted, but his adoptive parents divorced when he was 11. First he lived with his mother, later with his father. He had trouble in school, which eventually became just a place where he could, as he put it, "see some friends and talk to girls."

Michael and his girlfriend became parents while Michael was a junior in high school. He got married, dropped out, and found odd jobs. He then separated from his wife and began spending more time on the streets, joined a gang, and got in trouble with the law. Soon he had a felony conviction on his record and unpaid court fines. He was living in Bloomington, in McLean County, Illinois.

One day, feeling "at a complete loss," he saw a flier for a program called YouthBuild. It read, "[Y]ou could earn your GED, learn the construction trade, and leadership skills, all while earning a [modest] monthly stipend."

YouthBuild is a government program, authorized in 1992, that works through private nonprofit groups. It is managed by the U.S. Department of Labor, which makes grants on a competitive basis directly to local community-based nonprofit or public entities, like YouthBuild McLean County. The recipients must raise matching funds, at least a 25 percent local or private match. The Labor Department also partners with a national nonprofit, YouthBuild USA, Inc., to provide quality control and ensure that all the grantees stick to the program model.

After interviews with applicants to see whether they want to do this, the program puts applicants through a two-week orientation called "mental toughness training." Applicants who make it then join the full-time YouthBuild program. This means they spend half their time in an individualized alternative classroom to complete their secondary education. They spend the other half of their time in a YouthBuild hands-on practical training program, helping in the community. A common YouthBuild project is to build affordable houses or repair rundown dwellings for homeless and low-income people in their neighborhoods, using a mix of paid expert supervisors and YouthBuild students who earn a stipend for the work while they gain skills.

The program in McLean County has built 120 homes. As Michael put it, "Building a home in my community made me realize that in order to be a productive member of society, you had to be engaged and care about your surroundings."[33]

Shortly after entering YouthBuild, Michael had a sentencing hearing. Learning that he was in the program, the judge sentenced Michael to three months in the county jail, but on work release with YouthBuild during the day. Michael did his time, paid his fines, and has never been back in front of a judge.

YouthBuild has a holistic model for bringing low-income young adults back into the mainstream economy. The staff showed, as Michael put it, "a lot of love and encouragement and helped me begin to see my potential as a young man and leader."

After completion of the program, there is guidance on how to find postsecondary and employment placements. Many graduates earn AmeriCorps education awards for college on the basis of the hours of community service they have performed. Private firms such as Starbucks, Bank of America, Walmart,

Michael Donnelly, outside of the home he built for YouthBuild.

and JPMorgan Chase have helped develop training for more careers, and the government has therefore expanded the menu of eligible work in tracks like customer service, health care, and technology training. The students earn industry-recognized credentials along with the high school equivalency (GED) diploma. They receive guidance on where and how to get education or training.

In effect, YouthBuild and programs like it offer alternative sources of caring support and community for people who fell out of the standard ones. More than 130,000 former dropouts have participated in the over 270 urban and rural programs that have used this model. The cost per person per year is more than what the state would have spent on Michael if he had remained in high school for another year. The cost is far less, though, than what the state would spend on an inmate or a dependent. And few YouthBuild participants become inmates, but far fewer than their demographic profile would predict.

Suzanne Fitzgerald, the executive director of the Youth-

Build program that helped Michael, observed that the program's emphasis on practical skills gave a lot of participants a handhold lifting them back into education. "If you are someone who's more mechanically inclined, if you're someone who needs a project, to touch it, feel it, take it apart, put it back together, you don't see a lot of that available in the school systems or in the colleges. We could reach many more of our failing young people if we were able to teach in the way that they learned."

A professor at nearby Illinois Wesleyan University, Mike Seebord, adds that models like YouthBuild help students "see the relevancy of literacy and math skills. As they're learning to build homes, they're really building their lives and a future outside of construction."

But YouthBuild is not merely a design for training and education. The first-ever national survey of high school dropouts showed that academic challenge or even tough life circumstances were not the leading reasons young people left school. Instead, these young people missed a connection between what they were learning in school and what they wanted to be in life. They longed for more relevance, for supporting adults who could help show them paths from learning to careers, and higher expectations and more rigor in course work that made those connections.[34]

The core of the YouthBuild program is therefore actually the caring staff at the center, engaging with the person, building a positive peer group and a sense of community. Meanwhile the program helps to figure out ways that the program can fit with complicated individual lives. If Michael or another participant did not show up for class or work, people would notice and follow up, caring about him in ways that would surprise him and motivate him to care about himself.

We think of this function as that of a "navigator," which goes beyond the more commonly used terms like "counselor," although sometimes the staff do counsel young people dealing with the effects of childhood trauma. This function need not be unique to YouthBuild. YouthBuild only proves that such an investment can earn strong returns to society even for people society may wrongly consider hopeless. The model has much wider potential applicability, if it can be fully scaled up with more funds.

The program turned Michael's life completely around. He reunited with his wife, and they have now been married for 20 years. His oldest son has started college; his second child is finishing high school, and his third boy is still in school. His wife is a writer. Michael himself no longer relies on carpentry. His fellow participants elected him to leadership positions in the organization; he is a sought-after leader now in his community and works as a manager for United Way.

We detail the YouthBuild example because, over and over again, in program after program, we have found that the designs of the most effective education and training systems are those that find a better balance between subject matter instruction (which usually gets the vast majority of the attention and resources) and this navigator function, which directly engages the person being taught.

We can illustrate in another context what we mean. Many Americans have been puzzled why so few high-achieving low-income students apply to selective colleges in the way that more-affluent high-achieving students do. They are less likely to apply even though the generous aid programs at those colleges would make it cheaper for them to go to college.

A recent study by Caroline Hoxby and Sarah Turner demonstrated that the critical element was not just setting up a generous aid program. It was to engage the students directly, giving them some more information about their options and easing the waivers of application fees. This engagement had a modest cost of only about six dollars per student. The response to even this modest effort was excellent; the low-income students enrolled much more often, and they did well.[35]

There are many more such stories. All have in common the value of putting more weight on a more holistic approach to helping the student, balancing subject matter instruction with the role of the navigator. But navigation help is a low priority in most American education systems, especially the public ones. "Counseling is seen as an extra layer, a luxury," comments one expert on the subject. In secondary schools the ratio of students to counselors is currently about 500 to 1 and one in five high schools have none at all.[36]

YouthBuild and other programs that want to provide this kind of support thus face a challenge: How can that kind of caring outreach be scaled up and its quality preserved?

As we investigate the interface of technology, we again recall the history of Taylorism in American manufacturing. If technology is viewed as an instrument of deskilling in education, as Taylorism sought to do in the factory, we will not successfully adapt our educational system to the new networked age.

Similarly, as we detail later in this book, the goal in education as in other areas of the economy should be to open up more *and* better jobs. The new roles we envision in education should be designed to support rewarding professional careers in every sense. No one will be well served if functions like coaching are viewed as afterthoughts to be carried out by people without the training or the experience to provide real value to those who seek to learn.

Technology and networks are no panacea. Resources matter. But technology and network power do provide ingredients that can mobilize more caring people and extend their reach. As some large-scale educators already know, platforms can help

- mobilize the many interested and willing people in the community, coordinate the ways they can help, and link them up with participants in the right place and the right time;

• create user-friendly ways to reach staff who can help with problems;

• expand a proven model for training program staff to reach many more trainees with best practices from experienced program leaders;

• enable staff to coordinate their work with all the social agencies and public authorities that may already be involved in a young person's life; and

• guide participants through the maze of possible educational and work possibilities that could help them move forward.

Our goal is not to replace caring communities; our goal is to extend their reach.

Actions Needed

• Educators, public and private, should capitalize on the capabilities available now to teach anyone, anywhere, at any time in her or his life. More institutions should offer to provide valued educational content, and they should welcome a more inclusive vision of whom they can reach.

• Educators should blend appropriate mixes of in-person instruction with educational materials that also reach students effectively in the ways they find most engaging, adapting as much as possible to individual circumstances and learning styles.

• Educators can help students balance education throughout their lives with their other obligations through more flexible options, low-cost and able to be completed rapidly, including more modular educational units.

• Policymakers should adjust financial aid systems to make them portable and flexible enough to encourage educational institutions to innovate.

• Educational leaders should enlarge the usual job classifications in schools to ease the burden on traditional classroom teachers with added attention to other kinds of professionals who may have larger roles in redesigned systems.

• Policymakers should expand support for programs that provide caring mentors, designs to reach at-risk young people with untapped potential, and development of valued skills.

Chapter 9

Drift or Mastery

We propose a goal for this revolutionary age in our economy: pick up the tools that these times bring to hand and use them to rework America, to rebuild the American Dream.

To persuade, we cite evidence that these tools are already working, if on too small a scale.

And we embrace values that offer hope for more Americans, and suggest practical strategies for action, on a broad front.

Who will lead? Every American can play a part. From the start of this book we have stressed that although government support is vital, Americans cannot wait for government leaders to tell us what to do. This kind of revolution touches small businesses and huge multinational enterprises; it calls for creative thinking by schoolteachers and city bankers, by young entrepreneurs and aging executives.

We have offered many examples of people who are already making a difference. Most of the people we have mentioned are not government officials. Even where government is getting involved, local governments—mayors and county executives—are often leading the action. The networked world really is more decentralized.

When Americans remade their country for success during the 20th century, what stands out as we look back was the restless ambition and overlapping visions of Americans who rose to prominence from all sorts of backgrounds, often obscure ones. What they had in common was that they knew their country needed a radical overhaul.

Consider just a few representative American leaders of that era:

- A small-town banker from Utah, Marriner Eccles, who became the head of the Federal Reserve System and helped craft several of the carefully balanced designs for public and private finance.
- A former high school chemistry teacher and social worker, Frances Perkins, who helped design the new system for Social Security.
- A poor Russian immigrant who had to drop out of school after the eighth grade, David Sarnoff, who as the longtime head of a firm called RCA did more than any other single person to bring radio and television into every American home.
- A New Englander trained as an electrical engineer, Vannevar Bush, who became the leading bridge between the world of science and the world of government, handicapping a colossal bet to build an atomic bomb and another that built a National Science Foundation.
- A black minister's son from Florida who moved to New York as a teenager, A. Philip Randolph, who went to night school, joined the Socialist Party, organized the first successful trade union of black workers, and became the most powerful organizer of black laborers in America, pushing one U.S. president after another to break down segregation first in defense industries and later in the armed forces.
- A Texas cotton broker, Will Clayton, who became a

top diplomat instrumental in designing both the new
and more open world trading system and the Marshall Plan.

What is striking in reading about the lives of these and many
other mostly forgotten leaders is how broadly these men and
women seemed to comprehend the context of their work. They
felt the survival of the American way of life was at stake in their
lifelong struggles.

All of them were alive to the connection of their work to a
broader agenda for the future of the country. They could see and
discuss the links among topics as seemingly diverse as small-town
banking, world trade, telecommunications standards, or brand-
new housing developments. In this breadth they sometimes had
the advantage over many more learned but specialized scholars.
They were united only by a common wish to build—factories,
homes, institutions—to build an America different from the one
in which they had grown up.

They are not household names to us today. Then again, few of
the other Americans we have discussed in this book are household
names either. They are just trying to do their part.

In this concluding chapter we present two challenges for lead
ership that cut across almost all of the topics we have discussed so
far. One is the character of work and economic security. The other
is the delivery of government services in a networked age.

The Character of Work and Economic Security

In America's history, the relationships between employers and
employees have always been a balance. Governments sometimes
set the structures for these conversations or arguments, sometimes
through laws and often through courts and the legal system.

In the early era of markets and manufactures, most Americans
worked on farms or in small towns. The great issues surrounding
work in that age tended to be about "free labor." At one extreme

was the issue of slavery. At the other extreme, people could sell their labor much as they do today. In between, many Americans worked under contracts. The arguments tended to be about how much the contracts could lawfully constrain the workers and about what duties each side in the relationship owed to the other. The balance in America inclined toward more freedom, partly because workers back then could often just pick up and leave. It was a big country.

For employers this meant that they had to try to hold employees, especially the skilled ones, voluntarily or involuntarily. Another alternative was to design their businesses in ways that did not rely too much on being able to hold on to their skilled workers. Hence Francis Lowell coped with the shortage of skilled weavers by developing mechanical looms and a factory method of production, spurring the once-enormous New England textile industry. Much of the early history of American industry was a story of adapting to the mismatches in a rapidly changing economy, shortages here and surpluses there, at least until the era of mass immigration was well underway.

After World War II, at the height of the era of mass production, with mass immigration having been almost entirely cut off for more than twenty years, and after decades of intense struggle between unions and management, there emerged another kind of labor-management balance. Sometimes called the era of the "treaty of Detroit," after a landmark accord of 1950, this structure had a few key features:

- elaborate rules, mainly privately arranged but some also dictated by laws and court rulings, to govern the employer-employee relationship;
- some provisions for employee security (items like just-cause dismissal and severance pay); and
- significant benefit systems—especially for health care and pensions—that ran with the job and were organized around the workplace.[1]

In the early 21st century the assumptions surrounding the world of work are going through another historic shift.

Aside from all the issues about jobs lost, jobs redefined, and jobs gained, the networked economy creates three profound sets of issues. They are issues of freedom, organization, and economic security.

Freedom. The revolutionary change could empower frontline workers. It could give them more freedom to work remotely or freelance. It could give them more capabilities, as we discussed in chapter 5. It could give them more flexibility in finding jobs and training. Or technology could be a powerful enabler of employer-employee relationships that diminish employees' autonomy and erase the distinction between work time, rest time, and time with families.

An early illustration of the complexities of these issues has arisen in trucking. Truck driving became a middle-class occupation in the 1950s, when trucking was heavily regulated and largely unionized. Since deregulation the incomes of many truckers have fallen. Many truckers seek to add hours to their work schedules to make up for falling wages. At the same time, trucking companies seek to be able to monitor where truckers are and what they are doing at all times, with the aim of increasing labor productivity and managing risk, by means of electronic on-board recorders. Governments have entered this discussion, seeking to require on-board recorders as a public safety measure to keep drivers from driving beyond the point of exhaustion, in the wake of accidents like the one in New Jersey in 2014 involving a Walmart contract driver that nearly killed the comedian Tracy Morgan and did kill one of his companions. Both proponents and opponents of electronic on-board recorders say they are trying to protect the freedom and dignity of truck drivers.

As it was in the past, the argument about the scope of employee freedom will be settled in the private sector, in the back-and-forth between the two sides, and in public policy, through laws and court cases. In the trucking example, governments are already stepping in, for they see it as an argument about public safety.

Organization. People are always drawn to collective action to meet common needs. This impulse is what drives many social institutions where people gather. It is the basis for our democracy. And, as we have noted in this book, Americans must tackle serious challenges as they make the kind of transitions we advocate. We are still trying to create new models for collective action suited to a networked economy.

In the industrial economy, employers, unions, and government provided ways to meet collective needs. Today unions remain very important in some jobs, sectors, and regions, but union membership has been declining as a percentage of the working population for generations and is now 7 percent of the private workforce, 35 percent of workers in government jobs. The trend toward a more atomized, disorganized workforce is supercharged by the rise of the sharing economy.

The sharing economy offers opportunities to part-time, independent, and freelance workers. The physical workplace is often the home or the car. It is itself the node of a network.

As independent contractors in a service like Uber, drivers are responsible for their own expenses. Many may be unaware of the true costs of providing their service, including wear and tear on their own vehicle, fuel, insurance, and taxes. Insurance is a particularly tricky point. The car services provide an insurance policy that covers drivers while they are actually transporting passengers, but requires them to rely on their own personal insurance the rest of the time. However, insurance companies usually do not allow people using personal policies to use their vehicle for business. And, as independent contractors, drivers are missing key protections like workers' compensation, in the event that they are injured on the job.[2]

The question arises whether, and how, collective bargaining will need to be reinvented in a world where workers no longer work for an employer, but are independent contractor "partners" with a network and platform business like Uber. What is good for the customer is not always good for everyone.

Long-established unions, new types of worker organizations, and alliances between "old" and "new" are seeking to organize some of these new kinds of workers. But existing laws and union structures both orient unions to a workplace, or a company, as a site of organization. Organizations such as the Freelancers Union, the Drivers Network, the Taxi Workers Alliance, and the Domestic Workers Alliance all seek to build collective power among independent contract workers by moving beyond the focus on particular workplaces that is embedded in U.S. labor law. Also, employees of highly networked companies like Walmart have adopted networked models of their own to organize the workers.

The Freelancers Union now has about a quarter of a million members. Membership is free, but members do pay fees to utilize the group products, like health insurance opportunities. The Freelancers Union does not yet concentrate on traditional union roles, like negotiating wages and work rules.

Instead, it has much in common with trade associations of small businesses. It helps the freelancers pool their purchasing power in order to get strong group options for buying health insurance, retirement plans, and other commonly needed services. It is a forum for freelancers, who see themselves both as workers and as independent businesses, to join a networked community of people who share their challenges, and who can compare ideas and insights and organize for political action.

The Freelancers Union has much in common with unions in the preindustrial era, when workers were less bound to specific employers and more to the traditions of their craft. One of the legacies of this history is the traditional commitment of those unions to training. This legacy is well suited to the emerging networked economy.

Unions, after all, are just one type of employee organization. We live in an age of professional associations of doctors, lawyers, or architects. Such groups seek to set wages, set standards for certification and control entry, and lobby governments for laws that prevent unlicensed workers from plying the certified trade. But none of these organizations were built with a networked world in mind. Their future relevance will depend on whether they can reinvent themselves to meet the needs of employees in that new world.

The efforts of disorganized workers to organize, to develop a greater sense of community, are natural, healthy, and inevitable. Network power helps them organize. Network power limits their leverage.

We cannot yet see how this dynamic process will turn out. All Americans share an interest, though, in being sure that the labor laws and rules that were designed to give workers voice and to regulate disputes in one economic era, oriented to a physical workplace, are adapted to serve this purpose in a new era of networked work.

Security. In this new economy, many people will have a job with an employer and many will work more independently. A job can be much more than work. It signifies a regular structure, with predictable requirements and with organized benefits: paid leaves, health insurance, and retirement plans. Many Americans are therefore anxious, and justifiably so, that the networked economy will be one of piecework, desperate freelancing, and fewer "jobs."

We should not allow the outcome of the rise of the networked economy to be a decline in the economic and personal security of the American people. An absolutely fundamental achievement of America's political and economic struggles during the 20th century was the search for greater personal security. It is the dominant theme, for instance, of David Kennedy's Pulitzer Prize–winning history of America from 1929 to 1945, *Freedom from Fear*.[3]

We do not think that most Americans will regard an adaptation to this economic era as a successful rebuilding of the American Dream if they believe that the fundamental gains in personal security attained during the 20th century are eroding away. How, then, to adapt those structures?

We have no neat policy prescription. We do have a common theme. The structures should fit the new economy.

- They should be portable, moving with the individual, less tied to a workplace and less tied to where the person lives.
- They must be flexible, adjusting to a person's choice in where or how to work, leveraging the capabilities of a networked world.
- There must be roles for employees, employers, and government.

Several precedents offer some experience and inspiration. Both Social Security and Medicare have proven to be relatively portable and flexible, as many retirees living in Florida can attest. Employers and employees both contribute to funding these programs, and government manages them, with substantial roles for private contractors.

Another example is the Earned Income Tax Credit. The idea for it originated in a once-controversial Milton Friedman proposal of the 1960s for something he then called a "negative income tax." It was meant to provide a source of income support that constantly adjusted to how much a person earned, adjusting in ways that always maintained an incentive to work. The current version of the EITC has been effective, and there is broad interest, in both parties, in looking at how it might be expanded.

The other great issues may be in how to handle health care and other benefits that now are handled primarily by and through employers and the workplace. Although early in the 20th century both Theodore Roosevelt and Woodrow Wilson were moving (as Germany had) toward national health insurance approaches, the large industrial employers after the Second World War preferred employer-based health insurance and pensions, and that led to private-public alliances to handle these huge benefit programs.

That alliance evolved in the middle of the 20th century at the height of the era of mass production. Back then it was a radical departure from past practice—which was not to provide either health insurance or pensions to most employees at all. But major companies set the trend, mainly in the 1940s and 1950s, because it helped them attract and hold on to workers and was an alternative to other proposals that the business leaders liked even less.[4]

Nonetheless, even at the height of the postwar system, millions of Americans received their health insurance and retirement benefits through plans that were not tied to specific employers. Multi-employer health and pension plans were the rule in industries such as construction, trucking, and entertainment where workers changed employers frequently. And it was during this period that TIAA-CREF emerged as the dominant provider of retirement security in higher education.

Whatever views people may have on the most recent episode of health care reform and the workings of the Affordable Care Act, the changed system does provide additional portability. The recent debates over health care reform signal how difficult any significant further move would be, but neither political party seems content with the status quo.

The current system, left unchanged, may present Americans with the worst possible set of combinations. Business is currently feeling more burdened by the designs of the mid-20th-century era in both health care and retirement security. Some firms also fear being compromised in global competition. It is clear that small businesses are not suited to be insurers or managers of employee benefits. Most Americans may be stressed more and more by the transition to a networked economy, fearing as well as desiring the opportunities it could bring.

The Nature of Government in a Networked Age

Large majorities of the American public no longer trust public institutions to be able to deliver workable and cost-effective solutions to the nation's problems. Today's delivery of government services is in so many ways out of date, based on a 20th-century model of centralized and hierarchal power and an outdated model of service delivery that makes it nearly impossible for government to keep up with the pace of technology in the private sector.

Jennifer Pahlka is the founder and executive director of the nonprofit Code for America, which brings teams of talented technologists to cities to work with them for a year. She asked one of her colleagues why he'd chosen to leave Apple for a year at Code for America. He replied, "Because I believe interfaces to government can be simple, beautiful, and easy to use." Conversely, when digital interfaces to government programs are obscure and difficult, or simply fail to work, the good intentions behind government programs fail to achieve their desired results. Good government policy can be completely thwarted by bad implementation.

For example, working with San Francisco in 2013, Code for America learned how easy it is for individuals to lose food stamp (CalFresh) benefits if they fail to respond to a confusing renewal notice in a timely way. Participants often did not learn they had not requalified until the embarrassing moment when their Cal-Fresh card did not work at the store. The Code for America team built a text-message reminder system to make it easy for the city to remind participants about benefit expiration, or failure to meet requirements.

That fix sounds simple. But it took a lot of work. The agency had not collected cell phone numbers or e-mail addresses for its clients. There were privacy and other issues to be considered. But by putting themselves in the shoes of the actual consumer of government services, the team was able to build a service that really makes a difference in people's lives.

This story illustrates that the problem is not just technology itself. What has to be learned from Silicon Valley is consumer technology's relentless focus on user needs first. In the world of the consumer Internet, if no one picks up your app, you lose. If no one keeps using it, you lose. If it is too hard to get through, you lose. If it does not meet customers' needs, you lose.

Those in government who don't understand just how much implementation matters to the ultimate success of their policies are doomed to create terrible user experiences for citizens. Government has long gotten away with this because there was no alternative to its services. It is all too easy to forget that there is an alternative. It's called apathy, distrust of government, and a failure of the programs.

There are no easy policy prescriptions that will make everything better. Organizational transformation—which is what we are really talking about here—is hard work. But there are some guiding principles:

- For successful implementation of government services that use digital tools, digital leaders need a voice in policy. In top Silicon Valley companies, the management is deeply involved both in the framing of the problems to be solved and in the implementation of those solutions. The leaders are deeply technical and deeply concerned with user experience. Even in companies that are not led by engineers, top engineering management has a seat at the highest levels of decision making. And executives who are not themselves technical understand that they must gain a level of technical familiarity at least akin to their understanding of law, finance, marketing, and PR, so that they can engage in meaningful conversations with those who have a deeper understanding than they do.
- Hiring technical, design, and project management talent into government is too difficult. Normal personnel processes are slow and often make it impossible to bring in the right people for the job before they move on to other opportunities. Federal, state, and local govern-

ments should create special hiring authorities for digital workers and empower competent leaders to hire the talent they need.

• "Waterfall" methodologies of project management, which assume that planners can anticipate everything in advance, should give way to the agile style of development that has taken over in the cloud era. Phased rollouts, constant testing, and learning as you go are the hallmarks of modern software development. Yet government procurement, budgeting, and planning processes continue to encourage antiquated methodologies that do not work.

• User-centric design is essential. But we must replace the term "user-centric" with "citizen-centric," to drive home the point that systems must be designed to meet the needs of the citizens and other residents of our country who are the intended "customer" of government programs. Overly complex business rules and processes can strangle government's ability to deliver on its mission.

Needed are not flashy apps but rather *simplicity*: a paring down, and reordering of priorities to create online experiences of government that currently are still a distant dream for the United States, even with good programmers. Those who write policies to achieve important government goals must work in partnership with developers, and those developers in turn must adopt methodologies that let them release, test, and learn in quick cycles till they get things right.

There are hopeful signs that governments see the need for change. The Obama administration knows that there is a need for more technical leadership in the federal government and is working hard to bring it in—and not just for emergency rescue efforts like the one that turned around the healthcare.gov site. The Presidential Innovation Fellows program, established in 2012 and closely modeled on Code for America, actively recruits teams of technologists from outside the normal Washington contractor ecosystem to work with federal agencies on new approaches to digital services. The aim is to make them simple, beautiful, and easy to use. In 2014 two new groups were established—the United States Digital Service, part of the Office of Management and Budget, and 18F, part of the General Services Administration—to make a home for these new approaches in the federal government. The USDS is a partner to policymakers in designing digital services; 18F would be the implementation arm.

Also heartening are civic innovation efforts in cities around the country, led by people in both government and the private sector who realize that in the increasingly networked world of the 21st century, current governance models are not keeping up with the pace of technological change. John Micklethwait and Adrian Wooldridge contend, in their book *The Fourth Revolution: The Global Race to Reinvent the State*, that the next revolution in governance will be about more participation, using technology for transformed delivery of social services, and more innovation.[5] The two main drivers are data resources and the use of platforms.

These tools are connecting citizens in ways not available even two or three years ago. In the spring of 2014 an app saved the life of Drew Basse, a 57-year-old truck driver from Portland. The app, PulsePoint, was developed by a group of emergency services professionals in California.

These medics had watched an ambulance crew try to save someone next door to the restaurant where they were eating. The ambulance crew did not know that qualified rescuers were only a few yards away, and the medics did not know about the problem. So they created PulsePoint on a shoestring budget as a way to alert interested medics and other emergency responders if there was a problem nearby. Thousands have signed up to help their communities.

So when Drew Basse had a heart attack, an off-duty firefighter named Scott Brawner got a "ping" on PulsePoint. He saw he was close by. He saved Drew's life.

In this and many other ways, the networked world is extending community and public services and in the process reinventing government itself. The Internet commentator Tim O'Reilly calls this Government 2.0, when government is itself a platform for solving public problems. He writes, "This is the right way to frame the questions of Government 2.0. How does government itself become an open platform that allows people inside and outside government to innovate? How do you design a system in which all the outcomes aren't specified beforehand, but instead evolve through interactions between government and its citizens, as a service provider enabling its user community?"[6]

Government is, at bottom, a mechanism for collective action. We band together, make laws, pay taxes, and build the institutions of government to manage problems that are too large for us individually and whose solution is in our common interest. But in the old model of service delivery, government agencies like the fire department in San Ramon, California, which originally developed PulsePoint, directly deliver emergency services. The role of citizens was to provide funding and some degree of governance through the political process. But in the new model, government can extend and enrich its offerings by building a networked platform that allows citizens themselves to aid in delivering those services.

The vision is that Internet technologies could allow Americans to rebuild the kind of participatory government envisioned by our nation's founders. In that vision, as Thomas Jefferson wrote in a letter to Joseph Cabell, "every man . . . feels that he is a participator in the government of affairs, not merely at an election one day in the year, but every day."[7]

The most exciting work so far has been pioneered in several American cities. The mayor of San Francisco, Gavin Newsom (now lieutenant governor of California), saw so many possibilities in the programs he was trying out that he wrote a book about them, *Citizenville*. Newsom adapts the name from the title of a popular online social-networking game, FarmVille. In FarmVille, created by the gaming company Zynga, friends tend virtual farms, they cooperate in various ways, and they see who can harvest the most crops.

Prodded by a friend in the social-networking business world, Newsom and his friends came up with a game idea (also perhaps inspired a bit by another popular game, SimCity) in which they "combine the fun of a game with the social good of solving real problems."

> Here's one way it could work: Let's say you live in a neighborhood of twenty blocks. If four people there want to play the game—let's call it Citizenville—you can divide the neighborhood into four areas delineated by an interactive map on the Citizenville web site. Each player takes responsibility for his or her area, and if others living there decide they want to play too, they can either join forces and create a team or subdivide into even smaller areas.

The way to "win" Citizenville is to amass points by doing real-life good. If a player contacts the city to report a pothole and get it fixed, he gets one hundred points.[8]

And so on. The more Newsom thought about his game idea, Citizenville came to feel to him "like a kind of shorthand for how the government needs to adapt to this new technological age."

It would be Government 2.0. It would be an approach to government with five themes: have maximum transparency and open data; encourage people to use the data; communicate with people on their own terms, including digital media; allow people to bypass government where appropriate; and make government more change oriented and entrepreneurial, inspired by the technological possibilities.

Newsom is not the only mayor to have been energized by

these possibilities. Many others are stepping up. A former mayor of Indianapolis and a deputy mayor in the Bloomberg administration in New York City, Stephen Goldsmith, has joined with his co-author, Susan Crawford, to offer another blueprint of suggestions in their book, *The Responsive City*.[9] Bloomberg Philanthropies now devotes its efforts to fostering innovation "to help mayors solve problems and improve city life."

This ferment is a symptom of the excitement that can come at such a historical crossroads. A hundred years ago, thrown around by upheaval and inventions, every mayor of a large American city felt a bit like a bull rider in a rodeo ring. Those mayors of the past would be able to empathize with those today, embracing the wonderment of imagining what can be done along with the anxiety of trying to figure how to do it: to unite the "wow" and the "how."

In chapter 6 we discussed the significance of data as a resource. The proliferation of data—and the need for analytics to extract meaning from the data—has created a new discipline of study called urban informatics, using information to better understand how cities function. At New York University's Center for Urban Science and Progress, researchers tap into large publicly released databases to see the city anew. Ongoing projects include an effort to develop an infrared picture of Manhattan's skyline to evaluate heat and energy efficiency in buildings. NYU has partnered with a developer of a new 28-acre housing complex to build the nation's first "quantified community." Thousands of sensors will collect information on pedestrian traffic, air quality, energy production and consumption, waste management, and the health of workers and residents.[10]

Cities like New York, Boston, Chicago, and San Francisco are utilizing in-house data analytics teams, pioneered by a program in Baltimore that was called CitiStat, to tackle traffic, public safety in vulnerable neighborhoods, fire risk in buildings, and failures in social service programs. Chicago's Smart Data Project will try to identify trends and offer problem-solving predictions, connected to a WindyGrid hub, a resource collecting data from every city department in real time. The Los Angeles Police Department is using an algorithm that analyzes years of data to monitor crime hot spots and predict the probability of certain types of crimes.[11] In Philadelphia city authorities use a tool called HunchLab that collects data on crime, weather, special events, and other factors to map areas where crime and drug-related activities are most (or least) likely to occur in the short and the long terms.

The U.S. government has invested significant resources in supporting the research and development of big data. The White House released a 2014 report, called *Big Data: Seizing Opportunities, Preserving Values*, that evaluated the state of the field and made policy recommendations for how to harness big data for the public good. In 2012 six federal agencies launched the Big Data Research and Development Initiative. As part of this, the National Institutes of Health plan to spend up to $656 million by 2020 to determine how best to use data the government collects related to health.[12]

"In all these efforts," writes Steven Johnson, "you can see the emergence of a new political philosophy." He goes on,

> It takes seriously Hayek's insight about the power of decentralized systems to outperform top-heavy bureaucracies, but it also believes that innovation and progress can come from forms of collaboration beyond the market. I like to call the members of this movement "the peer progressives." . . . Peer networks are a practical, functioning reality that already underlies the dominant communications platform of our age. They can do things as ambitious as writing a global encyclopedia or as simple as fixing a pothole.[13]

The "pothole" example is no longer just in Newsom's imaginary Citizenville game. Johnson is referring to an app called SeeClick-Fix. A resident drives by a pothole and clicks on a map in the app that uses GPS to locate the position. The city is alerted to the pothole (and there is a record that it has been alerted, which heightens the incentive to fix it). Hundreds of thousands of potholes have been filled.

Textizen, originally a Code for America project done with the city of Philadelphia and now an independent start-up company, enables citizens to use their cell phones to text feedback to City Hall on projects or initiatives. The New Urban Mechanics, which operates within the city of Boston and the city of Philadelphia, uses technology for "civic innovation focused on delivering transformative city services to residents."[14] One of their projects is Citizens Connect, which—like SeeClickFix—enables residents to alert city agencies to service problems, like graffiti, potholes, or broken streetlights, by simply snapping a photo and sending it in. Participatory budgeting is next.[15]

In 2013 the Hurricane Sandy Rebuilding Task Force, overseen by the U.S. Department of Housing and Urban Development, launched Rebuild by Design. This was a multistage global competition to crowdsource the most innovative solutions for the Sandy-affected East Coast region. Instead of a top-down process where federal agencies determined the solution and requested proposals, $930 million was awarded to six teams with innovative solutions around a regional, community-driven approach.

As a more generalized solution to creating a new digital social fabric, a social-networking start-up called Nextdoor provides a private social network for the people who lived in a geographically defined neighborhood. As the company describes it, "Nextdoor's mission is to use the power of technology to build stronger and safer neighborhoods." Nextdoor lets neighbors quickly get the word out about break-ins or other public safety risks, get recommendations for local services, share, sell, or give away unneeded items, find lost animals, and get to know one another.

That is Citizenville not as a thought experiment but as a real-life Silicon Valley start-up. What is even more interesting, local police departments and other local agencies have become active participants on Nextdoor, using this private-sector platform to extend their own capabilities and reach into the community.

In their book Goldsmith and Crawford discuss such "networked citizenship" in which residents are active participants in designing how their cities operate and function. Citizens are the eyes and ears of the urban street. Digital platforms and social media are enabling citizens to voice concerns; public officials get up-to-the-minute information.

In these innovative uses of data, public data—compiled by government agencies—is effectively blended with private data. This can be the citizen noting the pothole in his neighborhood. Or it can be local communities coming together to help government agencies contribute to solutions, as with the neighborhoods hit by Hurricane Sandy.

"We've got to simplify, pull back all these layers of supposed complexity, and get down to the essentials," Newsom explains. "If we want people to engage with government, we should use the same tools that are getting them engaged with companies and institutions in private life."[16]

Quite an Agenda

The premise of this book is that America is in an age of transition to a new economic era. We should get ready and gear up for it. Americans have done this before. It is our turn to do it again.

The tools and trends are at hand to rework America and rebuild the American Dream. If we do get ready, this new era could turn out very well for Americans. We can create many more opportunities for good work. It can open up many more valued career paths. It has never been easier—in theory—for Americans to start and grow a business. It has never been easier—in theory— for Americans to connect to opportunities and get the education and skills they will need. There are myriad ways for us to connect theory to reality:

- We can link to a world of buyers as never before.
- We have the money to invest in Main Street America.
- We can network our knowledge and innovate millions of jobs on the frontlines.
- We can center more producers in our country, globally competitive and customizing products for local markets, in strong, healthy ecosystems of talented people, innovative research, and advanced networks.
- We can create exciting new ways to match Americans to opportunities.
- We can help Americans prepare for the lives they want with transformative tools that can build up our human capital and extend our caring communities, anywhere, anytime, and always.

In the summer of 1914 Walter Lippmann was 24 years old. He was beginning a career that would make him perhaps the best-known and most influential journalistic commentator on public issues in America for the next fifty years.

During his young lifetime the country had already been torn by debates over how to adjust to wrenching changes: the growth of giant corporations, the mobilization of an angry labor movement, the rise of huge cities and the struggles of farmers, and the influx of millions of unassimilated immigrants. The era of full-out mass production—and mass consumerism—was just getting underway. Henry Ford was just beginning to roll out his cars from an assembly line.

The new president, Woodrow Wilson, acknowledged, in words a president today could borrow,

> There is one great basic fact which underlies all the questions. . . . That singular fact is that nothing is done in this country as it was done twenty years ago. We are in the presence of a new organization of society. Our life has broken away from

the past. . . . We have changed our economic conditions, absolutely, from top to bottom; and, with our economic society, the organization of our life. The old political formulas do not fit the present problems. . . . [17]

Lippmann had grown up amid debates about how to adapt. First he had rejected the conservatism of his parents. He became the leader of the Socialist Club at Harvard. Then he became disillusioned with Marxism.

Putting pen to his frustrations, he wrote a set of essays called *Drift and Mastery*. People read the book. The Republican president who had just left office, Theodore Roosevelt, enthusiastically praised the young ex-Socialist for showing "the folly alike of the persons who believe in the non-existent virtues of a non-existent golden past and of the persons who merely dream of a golden future without making any sane effort to better conditions in the present."

Lippmann thought America had entered a new world, yet many of its leaders were just reacting. In his view they were not leading. They were not trying hard enough to shape the future. He thought Wilson was a man stuck in the past, longing to restore an America of little businesses, a vision unduly romanticized and irretrievably gone.

"Institutions have developed a thousand inconsistencies. Our schools, churches, courts, governments were not built for the kind of civilization they are expected to serve," Lippmann wrote. He warned his fellow Americans that they should "adjust their thinking to a new world situation." Otherwise they would just "drift along at the mercy of economic forces that we are unable to master."

In 1914 he had no easy prescription. Too much was new.

"We are," he admitted, "all of us immigrants in the industrial world, and we have no authority to lean upon." So "[i]n a real sense it is an adventure. We have still to explore the new scale of human life which machinery has thrust upon us."

That was written just more than a hundred years ago. Once again America is entering a new world, not only for its economy but also for its society. We are today perhaps not quite so far along on the new path as the industrial age was in 1914. Perhaps our situation now is more akin to that of America in about 1890, as it was just entering the most turbulent phase of industrial acceleration and transition.

Of course, the circumstances today are very different. We might now use technology in ways that actually might make life *less* centralized, *less* standardized, with goods and services more fitted to our needs. It may be an era both more global and yet more local too.

What resonates best from remembering Lippmann's argument of a century ago is to think back about the intensity of that articulate young man, sensing that his country was at a crossroads. We identify with his earnest plea that his leaders try to drive the forces of the future rather than be driven by them.

Lippmann knew he did not have all the answers. "All we can do is to search the world as we find it, extricate the forces that seem to move it, and surround them with criticism and suggestion."[18]

That is what we have tried to do in this book.

We have tried to outline some of the great forces at play, the tools that can be used for good. We are optimistic about America because we are optimistic about Americans. The talent and the energy are there. We live in a system that grants exceptional scope for liberty and ingenuity.

But many of the structures and institutions of America today need to be remade. Most of them were radical innovations in their day. They have served well.

But at this time of historic transition, we recall the scale and ambition our countrymen possessed. It is our turn.

In some ways it is easier for our generation of Americans. We have more information to work with. We no longer exclude people from our political system or our workplaces because of the color of their skin or their gender.

In other ways it is harder for us, hardest of all because of the inertia of past success. The old ways are set. People are used to them. Interest groups protect them. For a successful country, it can be easy to feel a bit complacent, easy to feel anxious about the uncertainties of change.

That would be the path of drift: uncertain, divided, and unmoved. We prefer another American tradition: the restless desire to master our fate, joined in our community of freedom.

Acknowledgments

This book is the result of a unique process that was created to tackle one of the most daunting challenges of our time. We are enormously grateful to the members of Rework America who brought their experience and commitment, to the substantive experts who engaged with us, and for the support of the Markle staff. Together we met, debated, drafted, and ultimately collaborated on a collective product that we hope will improve the future for millions of Americans.

The initiative, chaired by Zoë Baird and Howard Schultz, met together regularly and in groups of various sizes over an 18-month period to develop this book and the actions we are taking to effect our recommendations. Members shared views about the issues in three full plenary meetings, in Colorado (July 2013), New York (February–March 2014), and California (January 2015). The plenary meetings were augmented by two active working groups—one focused on Personal Development (co-chaired by Michael Crow and Cheryl Mills) and one focused on Business Development (co-chaired by Michael Leavitt and Michael Spence). Based on these discussions and debates, all the members were given three successive working drafts of the manuscript to review before it went to the publisher. Beyond their direct participation in these processes, several members made further notable contributions to the manuscript, especially John Bridgeland, Erik Brynjolfsson, Michael

Crow, James Dempsey, Lew Kaden, Gilman Louie, James Manyika, Andrew McAfee, Craig Mundie, Tim O'Reilly, Walter Robb, Elizabeth Shuler, Matthew Slaughter, and Dorothy Stoneman.

Without access to a group of deep subject matter experts this work would not have been possible. In addition to the commissioned research and input from the individuals acknowledged in the endnotes, including the McKinsey Global Institute, we held two expert workshops to go over the initial book manuscript in detail, one hosted by MIT and the other by the McKinsey Global Institute. These workshops were extraordinary and produced extremely valuable contributions that were instrumental in shaping this manuscript. Our gratitude goes to Dan Breznitz, Brynjolfsson, Michael Chui, Brendan Curry, Dempsey, Ellen Dulberger, Drew Erdmann, James Fallows, Bill Galston, Shane Green, Keith Hennessey, Gary Horlick, Chris Howard, Louis Hyman, Zachary Karabell, Jonathan Law, Eli Lehrer, Louie, Susan Lund, Manyika, McAfee, Mundie, Paul Osterman, Jaana Remes, Miriam Sapiro, Slaughter, Richard Swart, Zeynep Ton, David Verrill, and other MIT and McKinsey staff.

Fallows, Lehrer, Wan-Lae Cheng, Yuanxia Ding, Andre Dua, Alec Gewirtz, Julian Gewirtz, Slade Gorton, Peter Haynes, Hyman, Law, Lund, Sree Ramaswamy, Damon Silvers, and Vivek Varma offered further detailed suggestions of great value as the manuscript evolved and deserve special thanks. Among the many experts we met with in the course of the initiative's work, some offered particularly formative suggestions for the book, notably David Autor, Brian Balogh, Bill Bradley, Arthur Brooks, Beth Comstock, Ping Fu, Jeff Jonas, Vivek Kundra, Michael Levi, Amy Liu, Karen Mills, Dan Wagner, and Gavin Wright. Neither these experts nor those who participated in the workshops are individually responsible for what we ultimately chose to use.

This book is the result of the collaboration and considerations of a broad collective effort. Zoë Baird and Philip Zelikow had the final editorial pen and took the lead to engage and debate text, working through the sometimes disparate and varied views of our members. The credit for turning this all into a compelling narrative, providing the historical context, and developing the stories and the factual support goes to Philip. The Markle staff and our advisers are the enabling foundation for all the initiative's work, including this book. Max Elder provided much of the daily support and coordination. Katherine Rowland, Kadi Davis, and Stefaan Verhulst played important roles in the research. Carol Diamond, Lisa MacSpadden, and Ash Carter were vital advisers. Other staff directly involved in supporting this book project included Angela Bowens-Gamble, Karen Byers, William Herbig, Brandon Kist, Julian Mancuso, Michael Napolitano, and Steven Sypa. Finally, none of this work would have been possible without the unstinting support this project has received from the Board of Directors of the Markle Foundation: Lew Kaden (chair), Slade Gorton, Suzanne Nora Johnson, Gilman Louie, Herbert Pardes, Edward Rover, Stanley Shuman, and Debora Spar.

Notes

Preface

1 We saw this compelling phrase in James Fallows, "'Career Technical' Education: More Middle in the Middle Class?," *Atlantic*, March 29, 2014. Fallows was reacting to a comment from an anonymous reader on the profile of a Georgia high school system that we describe in chapter 7.

Chapter 1

1 Carmen DeNauas Walt and Bernadette Proctor, *Income and Poverty in the United States: 2013*, U.S. Census Bureau, Current Population Reports P60–249, September 2014, p. 23, table A-1. Figures on median income (through 2012) are also depicted in the graph below, using numbers from the Census Bureau's Current Population Survey, Historical Income Tables, Table H-5.

Real Median Household Income (1967–2012)

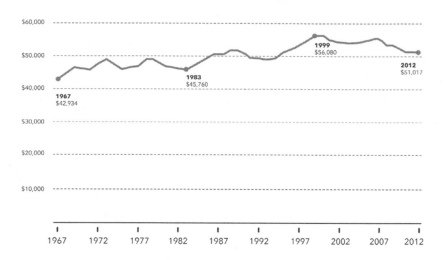

2 From 2009 through 2011, for example, net household wealth continued to decline, in real terms, for 87 percent of Americans. The wealth of the 13 percent of Americans with net worth (after debts) of half a million dollars or more improved by 21 percent. Richard Fry and Paul Taylor, Pew Research Center, *A Rise in Wealth for the Wealthy; Declines for the Lower 93%: An Uneven Recovery, 2009–2011*, April 23, 2013, at http://www .pewsocialtrends.org/files/2013/04/wealth_recovery_final.pdf.

This is because most of the economic gains in the recovery have not come in wages; they have come from appreciation of capital assets, mainly holdings of stocks and bonds through mutual funds. This capital income accrues to a small minority of Americans. Two-thirds of all holdings of financial assets, like stocks and bonds, are held by 5 percent of the households. Federal Reserve System chair, Janet Yellen, "Perspectives on Inequality and Opportunity from the Survey of Consumer Finances," October 17, 2014, p. 7 and fig. 7, at http:// www.federalreserve.gov/newsevents/speech/yellen20141017a.pdf.

This general depiction of flat real income growth holds true whether one looks at income before or after taxes, or before or after accounting for government transfer payments. Neil Irwin, "You Can't Feed a Family with G.D.P.," *New York Times*, September 16, 2014.

Per Capita GDP / Median Household Income

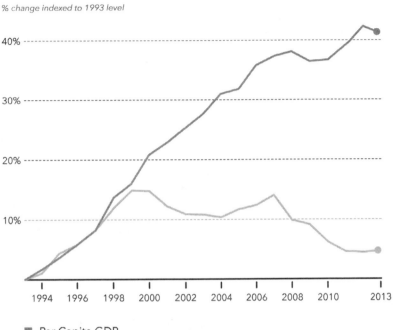

% change indexed to 1993 level

- ■ Per Capita GDP
- ■ Median Household Income

SOURCE: Census; Bureau of Economic Analysis

See also the figure below, produced by McKinsey & Company based on data from the U.S. Bureau of Labor Statistics (BLS) and Moody's Analytics (ECCA) forecast.

Median Household Income

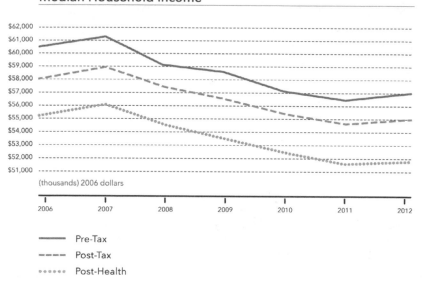

SOURCE: U.S. Bureau of Labor Statistics and Moody's Analytic Forecast

3 Chart from presentation by Alan Blinder for the Hamilton Project, November 15, 2014.

Productivity and Real Hourly Compensation

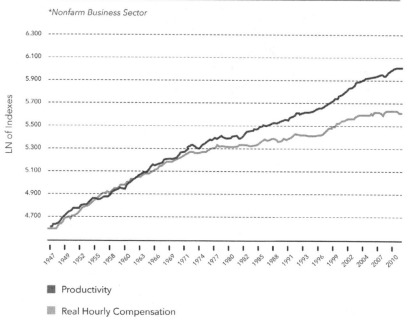

4   John Winthrop, "A Modell of Christian Charity" (1630), in *Collections of the Massachusetts Historical Society*, 3rd ser. (Boston: MHS, 1838), p. 47, available at https://history.hanover.edu/texts/winthmod.html. Spellings have been modernized.

5   *Washington Post*–Miller Center Poll, "American Dream and Economic Struggles," *Washington Post*, November 25, 2013.

6   The classic statement is David Potter, *People of Plenty: Economic Abundance and the American Character* (Chicago: University of Chicago Press, 1958).

7   James Truslow Adams, *The Epic of America* (Boston: Little, Brown, 1931).

8   On the War of 1812 and that era's interruption of British trade as a turning point stimulating the growth of American manufactures, see Stanley Engerman and Kenneth Sokoloff, "Technology and Industrialization, 1790–1914," in Engerman and Robert Gallman, eds., *The Cambridge Economic History of the United States*, vol. 2, *The Long Nineteenth Century* (Cambridge: Cambridge University Press, 2000), pp. 372–73.

9   To take advantage of what historians later called a "market revolution" in American commerce, Clay would have the government sell off public lands it owned to make internal improvements, like roads and canals, connecting farms to markets. He would levy tariffs—another source of government revenue—to protect American producers and manufacturers from predatory British traders. By raising the price of land, he would discourage uncontrolled settlement of the West, thereby opposing many slaveholders eager to get more land on which they could grow cotton to sell across the Atlantic. See Charles Sellers, *The Market Revolution: Jacksonian America, 1815–1846* (New York: Oxford University Press, 1991); Daniel Walker Howe, *What Hath God Wrought: The Transformation of America, 1815–1848* (New York: Oxford University Press, 2007), pp. 270–75; Sean Wilentz, "Society, Politics, and the Market Revolution, 1815–1848," in Eric Foner, ed., *The New American History*, rev. ed. (Philadelphia: Temple University Press, 1997), pp. 62–70.

10 See the recent summary in Sven Beckert, *Empire of Cotton: A Global History* (New York: Knopf, 2014), chaps. 5 and 6.

11 These issues were all connected. Until well into the 20th century the national government had little money, except what it could get from sales of public lands and from tariff revenue. So a good Southern Democrat might denounce tariff hikes as a way of standing up for free world trade (especially in cotton), and this position had the added virtue of keeping the national government from having much money.

12 Stuart Bruchey, *Enterprise: The Dynamic Economy of a Free People* (Cambridge: Harvard University Press, 1990), p. 195.

13 Daniel Walker Howe, *Making the American Self: Jonathan Edwards to Abraham Lincoln* (Cambridge: Harvard University Press, 1997), pp. 107–56, quotation from p. 126.

14 The chronologies of the American economic eras outlined in this chapter are linked to the two global economic revolutions, often called *industrial* revolutions, usually dated to the 18th and 19th centuries. Most historians refer to a first industrial revolution that emerged in the late 1700s and grew in

importance during the first half of the 1800s. Some see this emerging very gradually, over centuries. Others date this first industrial revolution more technologically, associating it with the steam engine and growing use of fossil fuels for energy. Historians agree that this first economic revolution reached its height between about 1750 and 1850. Emblems of this era were coal, steam engines, and big machines to run "factories," drive ships, and create railroads.

Most historians then observe another profound period of economic change, sometimes called a "second industrial revolution" or "second economic revolution." It was actually as much about ways of organizing society as about technologies. This was the age of very large-scale production of steel, new materials created by industrial chemistry, and the harnessing of electromagnetism to generate electricity and communicate through wires. Emblems of this era were electrification, high explosives, the internal combustion engine, giant mass production enterprises, and piped systems to distribute clean running water.

This second revolution occurred more rapidly than the first. It took off during the last quarter of the 19th century and was already globe spanning by the early 1900s. Jürgen Osterhammel, *The Transformation of the World: A Global History of the Nineteenth Century*, trans. Patrick Camiller (Princeton: Princeton University Press, 2014). In a vast literature on these economic revolutions, Osterhammel's dense and masterly survey is a marvel of distillation, esp. chap. 12. There are excellent related chapters on labor (chap. 13), networks (chap. 14), and knowledge (chap. 16). It is this second revolution, the "great acceleration" toward the end of the 19th century, that is the global side of what the text calls an American "era of mass production." The term "great acceleration" was an observation of contemporaries as diverse as Lenin, who used this phrase, and Henry Adams. See also the last section of C. A. Bayly, *The Birth of the Modern World, 1780–1914: Global Connections and Comparisons* (London: Wiley-Blackwell, 2004).

15 Garfield and Howells quoted in the wonderful essay by Allen Guelzo, "A War Lost and Found," *American Interest*, September/October 2011, pp. 6, 9. For a persuasive case on the role of the Civil War in accelerating the rise of powerful corporations in American life, see Sean Patrick Adams, "Soulless Monsters and Iron Horses: The Civil War, Institutional Change, and American Capitalism," in Michael Zakim and Gary J. Kornblith, eds., *Capitalism Takes Command: The Social Transformation of Nineteenth-Century America* (Chicago: University of Chicago Press, 2012), pp. 249–76.

16 Quoted in Robert MacDougall, *The People's Network: The Political Economy of the Telephone in the Gilded Age* (Philadelphia: University of Pennsylvania Press, 2013), p. 260. The original authors of the famous Muncie study of 1924, Robert and Helen Lynd, returned there in 1935. They also noticed, and were bothered by, the widespread acceptance of—or resignation to—the big structures dominating modern life. See Robert Lynd and Helen Lynd, *Middletown in Transition: A Study in Cultural Conflicts* (New York: Harcourt, Brace, 1937).

17 Richard McCormick, "Public Life in Industrial America, 1877–1917," in Foner, ed., *The New American History*, p. 108. This is a collection of historiographical essays published for the American Historical Association. See also Matthew D. Lassiter, "Political History beyond the Red-Blue Divide," *Journal of American History* 98, no. 3 (December 2011): 760–64.

18 See the excellent introductory discussion in Brian Balogh, *The Associational State: American Governance in the Twentieth Century* (Philadelphia: University of Pennsylvania Press, 2015).

19 Debora L. Spar, *Ruling the Waves: Cycles of Discovery, Chaos, and Wealth from the Compass to the Internet* (New York: Harcourt, 2001), pp. 8, 10.

20 There is a lively summary in John F. Stover, *American Railroads* (Chicago: University of Chicago Press, 1961); the Minnesota land-grant number is on p. 92.

21 Especially valuable on the evolution of the older generation of network communication is Richard John, *Network Nation: Inventing American Telecommunications* (Cambridge: Harvard University Press, 2010).

22 Quoted ibid., p. 23.

23 Enrico Moretti, *The New Geography of Jobs* (New York: Houghton Mifflin Harcourt, 2012), pp. 3–4.

24 Thoughtful examples include the Economic Opportunity Index, developed by the Hope Street Group, at http://www.hopestreetgroup.org/our-work/big-idea/economic-opportunity-index; the survey-based American Dream Composite Index and its five subindices, developed by Xavier University's Center for the Study of the American Dream, at http://www.americandreamcompositeindex.com; and the Opportunity Index developed by Opportunity Nation and Measure of America, which is a project of the Social Science Research Council, at http://opportunityindex.org/#4.00/40.00/-97.00/.

25 For those who are interested, here are some more details on these metrics.

Relevant Surveys of Public Opinion. If you want to know whether Americans are more hopeful about the economic future, then ask them. Many surveys do. The answers have been getting consistently more pessimistic for at least ten years. For example, consumer attitudes are regularly polled by the University of Michigan with Thomson Reuters. This includes a question asked since 1998 about whether respondents believe they will have a real income gain during the next five years. At the end of the 1990s the percentage of expectant "yes" answers were in the low to mid 40s. By 2004 that number had dropped into the 30s. It kept dropping. By 2011 it fell even into the 20s. The number has recovered, but so far only into the low 30s. In other words, only about one-third of Americans say they are hopeful that their real income will improve during the next five years. Chart 16, March 2014, Thomson Reuters and University of Michigan, "Surveys of Consumers," at http://www.sca.isr.umich.edu/get-chart.php?y=2014&m=3&n=16h&f=pdf&k=b369a586a4c295f6100c8e1da76167d2.

Net Job Creation. If more American businesses grow, we will regard this as a success if it creates more opportunities for Americans to contribute. An indirect measure of this is the unemployment rate. A more direct measure of that success would be the creation of new jobs. In a dynamic and innovative economy, many jobs will be created and many will be lost. In a dynamic and healthy economy, more will be created, for a net plus. The number of net jobs created, as a proportion of the labor force, is therefore an indicator of both growth and energy.

Since the early 1980s the American economy has gradually become less dynamic. The current trend is one of "anemic job creation." In 2011, with the recovery well underway, about three million fewer jobs were created than had been created in any of the years between 1980 and 2006. For an eloquent recent statement on the importance of economic dynamism, and contemporary reflections on creative destruction, see Edmund Phelps, *Mass Flourishing: How Grassroots Innovation Created Jobs, Challenge, and Change* (Princeton: Princeton University Press, 2013).

The chart below indicates the general trend in the job creation rate and a sense of the net job creation rate, since 1980. Note the apparent decline in overall dynamism and the trend toward rough equilibrium in creation and destruction.

U. S. Annual Job Creation and Destruction Rates, 1980–2011

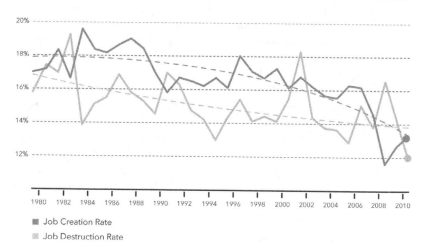

■ Job Creation Rate

▨ Job Destruction Rate

SOURCE: Author calculations from the U. S. Census Bureau's Business Dynamics Statistics
NOTES: The filter is Hodrick-Prescott with multiplier 400. The vertical axis does not begin at zero.

Fig. 3 in Ryan Decker, John Haltiwanger, Ron Jarmin, and Javier Miranda (the authors in the "author calculations" mentioned in the source), "The Role of Entrepreneurship in US Job Creation and Economic Dynamism," *Journal of Economic Perspectives* 28, no. 3 (Summer 2014): 3, 14. See also

John Haltiwanger, Javier Miranda, and Ron Jarmin, "Anemic Job Creation and Growth in the Aftermath of the Great Recession: Are Home Prices to Blame?," U.S. Census Business Dynamics Statistics Briefing, Kauffman Foundation, July 2013, p. 2 and fig. 1.

More Young Firms. There is a broad consensus among experts that many young firms are a strong measure of a growing, healthy, and vibrant economy. Older firms are vital, of course. About half of U.S. employment is provided by under 1 percent of America's companies. And most business start-ups exit in the early years. But a small fraction of young firms become high-growth enterprises. They play a disproportionate part in creating jobs, innovation, and productivity. Their growth also signals good availability of credit and capital for entrepreneurs. "Business ownership," the Fed chair Janet Yellen recently underscored, "is associated with higher levels of economic mobility." Yellen, "Perspectives on Inequality and Opportunity," p. 16.

The best measures focus not just on start-ups but also on the start-ups that survived, establishments that are five years old or less, whether or not they have remained under the original management. The role of such young firms in the U.S. economy has been declining slowly for about thirty years. The decline accelerated after 2000.

Despite much publicity about start-ups in Silicon Valley and sensational prices paid for them, one group of experts recently concluded, "A critical factor in accounting for the decline in business dynamics is a lower rate of business startups and the related decreasing role of dynamic young businesses in the economy. . . . These trends suggest that incentives for entrepreneurs to start new firms in the United States have diminished over time." Decker, Haltiwanger, Jarmin, and Miranda, "The Role of Entrepreneurship," p. 4. The following charts depict the trend.

Declining Share of Activity from Young Firms (Firm Age Five or Less) U.S. Private Sector, BDS

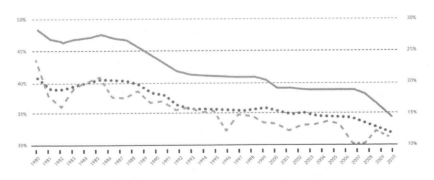

——— Share of firms that are young

- - - - Share of job creation from young firms

•••••• Share of employment from young firms (right-axis)

Chart adapted from fig. 3 in John Haltiwanger, Ron Jarmin, and Javier Miranda, "Where Have All the Young Firms Gone?," U.S. Census Business Dynamics Statistics Briefing, Kauffman Foundation, May 2012.

Rising Real Median Income. If more Americans are contributing more value, they are likely to earn more. The effect should be visible in gains at the median point, right at the middle of America's middle class. We think it is also important, however, to look for higher median income *within* groups of similar education and gender. One of the striking illustrations of the mismatched economy is how much income is skewed even when such factors are held constant. See, e.g., David Autor, Lawrence Katz, and Melissa Kearney, "Trends in U.S. Wage Inequality: Revising the Revisionists," *Review of Economics and Statistics* 90, no. 2 (May 2008): 300–323.

A More Fluid Labor Market. In a dynamic economy with a lot of job creation and innovation, an ideal labor market should also feature a lot of mobility. People would be adjusting their skills and moving to better opportunities. Employers would be getting optimal matches of people for their needs. Just such patterns marked periods of economic advancement in America's history.

Job and worker reallocation rates, especially among younger Americans, are a good measure of the fluidity of the labor market. Yet, despite the profound changes accompanying the rise of a networked economy and the digital revolution, a recent study noted, "Summing up, the United States underwent a large, broad-based decline in the pace of labor market flows in recent decades. The decline holds across major industry sectors, across all states, and across age and education groups for both men and women." Steven Davis and John Haltiwanger, "Labor Market Fluidity and Economic Performance," National Bureau of Economic Research, NBER Working Paper 20479, September 2014, p. 8.

Improved Adult Job Skills. Americans are used to reading measures of how they stack up in academic achievement. While all academic attainments can be enriching, some kinds of education are most relevant to potential earnings in the workplace. The Paris-based Organization for Economic Cooperation and Development (OECD) is well known for its survey of student achievement. It has now added an ambitious effort to identify the kind of skills adults need in 21st-century work and directly measure those "adult competencies" in the 29 member countries. Their assessments of literacy, numeracy, and "problem-solving in technology-rich environments" may sound similar to some academic categories, but the measures are not the same.

In 2013, the first time these skills were measured, Americans were assessed as significantly below the average in *all* of these categories, compared with the other 28 developed countries. Only two other countries in this group ranked so low. OECD, *OECD Skills Outlook 2013: First Results from the Survey of Adult Skills* (Paris: OECD, November 2013), fig. 2.13, p. 97. The other two countries with below-average assessments in all categories were Ireland and Poland. It is possible that Italy and Spain also would have been below average in all categories, but data was incomplete. The four countries that were above average in all categories were Finland, the Netherlands, Norway, and Sweden. For corroboration and elaboration of these OECD findings, see Madeline Goodman, Anita Sands, and Richard Coley, *America's Skills Challenge: Millenials and the Future*, Educational Testing Service, 2015.

    Participation by Young Americans in the Labor Force. Although general participation in the labor force has dropped a bit over the decades, some of this drop can reflect the aging of the workforce and other factors that may not be a source of concern. But large dropouts of younger Americans from the workforce should be a disturbing "canary in the mineshaft." It reflects the availability of entry-level jobs, the dynamism of the economy, the fluidity of the labor market, the availability of relevant education and skills, and whether educational structures have the flexibility to adjust to the lives of young people who wish to work at least part-time. When young people put off any participation in the labor force, their lack of experience influences their lifelong prospects.

    The drop in labor force participation by young people, age 16 to 24, is most worrying. In 1992, when the numbers of young people successfully completing high school and college had already plateaued, the proportion of this age group who were at least working part-time was 66 percent. Twenty years later that number had fallen to 55 percent and was expected to keep dropping. Table 3, "Labor Force Projections to 2022: The Labor Force Participation Rate Continues to Fall," *Monthly Labor Review*, December 2013, at http://www.bls.gov/opub/mlr/2013/article/labor-force-projections-to-2022-the-labor-force-participation-rate-continues-to-fall.htm.

26 We have not included import-export numbers, for example, because there are serious data collection problems that obscure the contribution of U.S. value to the networked production of "imports" or the contribution of foreign value to "exports." Nor did we include data for public or private spending on research and development, because spending alone is not a reliable metric of effect, and alternatives, like counting numbers of patents or counting research citations, are also problematical.

27 Robert F. Kennedy, *To Seek a Newer World* (Garden City, NY: Doubleday, 1967), p. 231.

Chapter 2

1 Anne Fisher, "Brooklyn Startup Plays Manufacturing Matchmaker," *CNNMoney*, March 7, 2014, at http://money.cnn.com/2014/03/07/smallbusiness/makers-row-manufacturers/.

2 Karen Klein, "When Designers Want Their Clothes 'Made in the USA,'" *Bloomberg Businessweek*, November 19, 2013.

3 Erica Swallow, "Maker's Row and the Future of American Manufacturing," *Mashable*, March 12, 2013.

4 Ibid.

5 Hayley Phelan, "How Tech Startup Maker's Row Is Revolutionizing American Manufacturing," *Fashionista*, June 19, 2013.

6 Ibid.; Jordan Kushins, "Maker's Row: A Comprehensive Database of American Manufacturers," *Fast Company*, November 26, 2012.

7 Ingrid Lunden, "To Give U.S. Manufacturing a Boost, Maker's Row Gets $1M from Index, Comcast, Alexis Ohanian & More," *Tech Crunch*, July 19, 2013; Joseph Flaherty, "'Maker's Row' Bridges Daunting Gap between Design and Manufacturing," *Wired*, November 26, 2012.

8 Milstein Commission on New Manufacturing, "Building a Nation of Makers: Six Ideas to Accelerate the Innovative Capacity of America's Manufacturing SMEs," Miller Center, University of Virginia, June 2014, p. 26, at http://web1.millercenter.org/conferences/milstein/ MilsteinReport-Manufacturing.pdf; Phelan, "How Tech Startup Maker's Row Is Revolutionizing American Manufacturing"; Lunden, "To Give U.S. Manufacturing a Boost."

9 Walter Isaacson, *The Innovators: How a Group of Hackers, Geniuses, and Geeks Created the Digital Revolution* (New York: Simon & Schuster, 2014).

10 See the further discussion in Erik Brynjolfsson and Andrew McAfee, *The Second Machine Age: Work, Progress, and Prosperity in a Time of Brilliant Technologies* (New York: Norton, 2014).

11 Nelson Lichtenstein, *The Retail Revolution: How Wal-Mart Created a Brave New World of Business* (New York: Picador, 2009), pp. 53–56.

12 J. H. Saltzer, D. P. Reed, and D. D. Clark, "End-to-End Arguments in System Design," *ACM Transactions on Computer Systems* 2, no. 4 (1984): 277–88.

13 While the technical standards of the Internet have been unregulated, the early commercial Internet benefited from a regulatory scheme that respected these competition-enhancing principles of interconnection and nondiscrimination. Since early in the 20th century, the Bell System operated as a common carrier.

Under the principle of interconnection, it was bound to accept the calls originating with any independent provider. And under the principle of nondiscrimination, a telephone company could not favor the traffic of one content provider over the content of another.

When the first ISPs began to emerge, this requirement proved crucial. The telephone company may have been suspicious of the new technology. But it could not decline the ISP's request for lines. It could not treat data traffic any less favorably than voice. (Another regulatory choice, flat-rate pricing for local calls, was also enormously important to the takeoff of the dial-up Internet.) See Tim Wu, *The Master Switch: The Rise and Fall of Information Empires* (New York: Random House, 2011).

A critical policy choice was made in 1996 when Congress adopted Section 230 of the federal Communications Act. Section 230 says that ISPs, web hosts, social media platforms, blogs, search engines, and other intermediaries are not liable for the conduct of their users. They cannot be sued for the third-party content that they host or transmit. Without this shield from liability, countless Internet platforms could face burdensome lawsuits for providing opportunities for individuals to share their own ideas or launch small businesses.

Another crucial set of Internet policies revolves around the issue of trust. To use the Internet for commerce and interpersonal communication requires a degree of confidence in its privacy and security. Even before the Internet became widely available, Congress adopted the Electronic Communications Privacy Act (ECPA) of 1986. ECPA established the principle that e-mail in transit would have the same legal protection traditionally accorded to telephone calls. ECPA is outdated today, but the crucial decision to place data communications on the same footing as voice communications fostered trust in a fledgling technology.

The debate most occupying Washington today is over "net neutrality." The narrowband, dial-up Internet was an open platform. It offered equal treatment to all users and all content providers, based in part on the regulation of telephone companies as common carriers.

Today's broadband market is concentrated among a small number of major carriers. The issue is whether those carriers can restrict access or charge differential prices for access to the networks, these new commanding heights. Although the Internet has not needed much regulatory protection so far, the "net neutrality" debate has opened up arguments about direct regulation, antitrust law, a return to "common carrier" standards, or other authorities.

14 A leading skeptic, Northwestern's Robert Gordon, argues instead, "Invention since 2000 has centered on entertainment and communication devices that are smaller, smarter, and more capable, but do not fundamentally change labor productivity or the standard of living in the way that electric light, motor cars, or indoor plumbing changed it." Gordon, "Is U.S. Economic Growth Over? Faltering Innovation Confronts the Six Headwinds," NBER Working Paper 18315, August 2012, p. 2, at http://www.nber.org/papers/w18315.

There was actually a broad improvement in productivity, attributed to the initial introduction of the personal computer and networking technologies. "Industry-level data show that the recent U.S. acceleration in productivity is a broad-based phenomenon that reflects gains in a majority of industries through the late 1990s. . . . Nearly two-thirds of these industries show a productivity acceleration. . . . This suggests the U.S. productivity revival is not narrowly based in only a few IT-producing industries." Kevin Stiroh, "Information Technology and the U.S. Productivity Revival: What Do the Industry Data say?," *Federal Reserve Bank of New York*, January 24, 2001, p. 2.

Then the productivity improvements appeared to subside after about 2005; hence the Gordon argument: the bubble has burst. In the text we discuss an important answer to this position: the time lag, often in decades, after the introduction of new general-purpose technologies, which did not fully begin coming together until the 1990s and 2000s.

As is already becoming apparent, it was premature to view these solely as information and communications innovations, any more than the initial introduction of electric lighting was the climactic chapter in the productive use of electricity. That said, we do not take a techno-utopian view of the ultimate potential. Effective and productive diffusion of innovation is not predetermined.

Historical experience shows that country, sector, and business-level choices can make large differences in how ably and innovatively new technology is employed. We wrote this book, in part, precisely because of that concern.

There are some significant technical concerns with the Gordon argument. It relies heavily on data from a short time period that included the worst global downturn since the Depression. The numerator for all productivity calculations is output; when it plunges, it often has a tendency to drag productivity growth down with it. Previous stretches of great technological advance, such as the era of electricity and internal combustion, also included several years of slow or even negative productivity growth.

We are concerned as well with the use of statistics about productivity, specifically total (or multi) factor productivity (TFP), as the measure of impact from the third economic revolution. The TFP numbers are derived from residual GDP gains not explained by other inputs, such as capital and labor. As we discuss later in this chapter, the GDP metric itself was an adaptation responding, in the 1930s and 1940s, to the second economic revolution. It is well designed for that purpose, an insightful measure of conventional production, especially of traditional goods. As we will point out, the current GDP metric does not appear to be so well suited to measure the impact of the third economic revolution.

15 This helpful concept was developed among a group of scholars during the late 1990s. General-purpose technologies, or GPTs, have been described as technologies or system designs that offer great scope for further improvement, are applicable in many ways, and complement both existing technologies and new ones. See the collection in Elhanan Helpman, ed., *General Purpose Technologies and Economic Growth* (Cambridge: MIT Press, 1998); and Paul David and Gavin Wright, "General Purpose Technologies and Productivity Surges: Historical Reflections on the Future of the ICT Revolution," in David and Mark Thomas, eds., *The Economic Future in Historical Perspective* (Oxford: Oxford University Press, 2003).

16 See Nathan Rosenberg and Manuel Trajtenberg, "A General-Purpose Technology at Work: The Corliss Steam Engine in the Late Nineteenth-Century United States," *Journal of Economic History* 64, no. 1 (March 2004): 61–99.

17 See Andrew Atkeson and Patrick Kehoe, "Modeling the Transition to a New Economy: Lessons from Two Technological Revolutions," *American Economic Review* 97, no. 1 (2007): 64–88.

18 Throughout the Depression years labor input was flat, and double-digit unemployment reigned. Private capital inputs actually declined. Yet U.S. output rose by nearly 40 percent between 1929 and 1941. The innovations of the 1930s were a foundation for America's wartime victory and its postwar boom. The seminal work by Alexander Field (building especially on earlier work by John Kendrick) is now pulled together in his *A Great Leap Forward: 1930s Depression and U.S. Economic Growth* (New Haven: Yale University Press, 2011). What were some of these innovations?

- More than twenty years after the initial widespread introduction of electric power into cities, during the 1920s and continuing in the 1930s, electrification worked its way into general-purpose use in industries and homes. Governments designed private-public utilities to enable this advance.
- More than a decade after the large-scale production of self-propelled vehicles had begun with Ford's Model T, the 1930s were the decade in which automobile technology decisively advanced (power steering, hydraulic brakes, inflated rubber tires, etc.). Tractors began revolutionizing and depopulating American farms.
- A built-out U.S. route system finally created intercity networks of paved roads. Bridges were built; tunnels were blasted. A trucking industry became viable. As government broke down barriers to freight carriage among competing railroads, intermodal transportation mingling railroads and trucks became feasible. The extension of this containerization to oceangoing shipping later extended intermodal transport across the seas.
- During the Depression years, electrical engineering spanned the electromagnetic spectrum. A telecommunications age began: portable radios, televisions, radar.
- Petrochemical engineering during these same years created new materials: nylon, Lucite, Teflon.
- The 1930s were the breakthrough for learning to tame and mold light metals like aluminum—exemplified by a breakthrough passenger aircraft, the DC-3. Many future military aircraft were among the immediate results.

19 Richard R. Nelson, *The Sources of Economic Growth* (Cambridge: Harvard University Press, 1996), p. 198; see also the essay by Nathan Rosenberg in Helpman, *General Purpose Technologies and Economic Growth*, pp. 167–92.

20 See Niall Ferguson, "Networks and Hierarchies," *American Interest*, June 2014, at http://www.the-american-interest.com/articles/2014/06/09/net works-and-hierarchies/.

21 Thomas Malone, Joanne Yates, and Robert Benjamin, "Electronic Markets and Electronic Hierarchies," *Communications of the ACM* 30, no. 6 (June 1987): 484–97, quoted in the excellent essay by Richard Adler, *Frag-*

mentation and Concentration in the New Digital Environment (Washington, DC: Aspen Institute Communications and Society Program, 2014).

22 Andrei Hagiu, "Strategic Decisions for Multisided Platforms," *MIT Sloan Management Review*, December 19, 2013, at http://sloanreview.mit.edu/article/strategic-decisions-for-multisided-platforms/.

23 Levie's tweet of August 22, 2013, at https://twitter.com/levie/status/370776444013510656; on the Goldman investment of $1.6 billion and Uber's current valuation, Kia Kokalitcheva, "Goldman Sachs Confirms $1.6B Investment in Uber," *Venture Beat*, January 21, 2015, at http://venturebeat.com/2015/01/21/goldman-sachs-confirms-1–6b-investment-in-uber/.

24 Jonathan Hall and Alan Krueger, "An Analysis of the Labor Market for Uber's Driver-Partners in the United States," draft paper prepared for Uber, January 22, 2015, available at https://s3.amazonaws.com/uber-static/comms/PDF/Uber_Driver-Partners_Hall_Kreuger_2015.pdf. Hall works for Uber; Krueger is a well-known economist now teaching at Princeton who states that Uber granted him full discretion to decide what to say in this report.

25 The Boston numbers were reported in Jordan Graham, "Data: 10,000 Uber Cars Dwarf Licensed Taxis in Boston," *Boston Herald*, January 22, 2015. The San Francisco numbers were reported in Henry Blodget, "Uber CEO Reveals Mind-Boggling New Statistic That Skeptics Will Hate," *Business Insider*, January 19, 2015, at http://www.businessinsider.com/uber-revenue-san-francisco-2015–1.

26 Hall and Krueger, "An Analysis of the Labor Market," pp. 2–3.

27 Ibid., pp. 7–8.

28 Figures from presentation by Stephane Kasriel of Elance-oDesk at the MIT Digital Platforms Strategy Summit hosted by the MIT Media Lab, July 15, 2014.

29 Elance-oDesk, "U.S. Online Work Report," June 2014, at http://elance-odesk.com/sites/default/files/media_coverage/reports/us-online-work-report-2014-ytd.pdf.

30 Ruth Simon, "One Week, 3,000 Product Ideas," *Wall Street Journal*, July 3, 2014.

31 Liz Stinson, "Quirky and GE Partner to Conquer the Internet of Things." *Wired*, November 19, 2013, at http://www.wired.com/2013/11/how-ge-and-quirky-want-to-smarten-up-your-home/.

32 John Biggs, "GitHub Adds 3D Modeling Features That Make It a Printer-Agnostic Choice for Object Sharing," *TechCrunch*, September 18, 2013, at http://techcrunch.com/2013/09/18/github-adds-3d-modeling-features-that-make-it-a-printer-agnostic-choice-for-object-sharing/.

33 Hal Varian, "Micromultinationals Will Run the World," *Foreign Policy*, August 15, 2011, at http://www.foreignpolicy.com/articles/2011/08/15/micromultinationals_will_run_the_world.

34 See, e.g., Daisuke Wakabayashi, "Apple, Samsung Call Patent Truce outside U.S." *Wall Street Journal*, August 5, 2014.

35 Sean Ekins and Antony Williams, "Reaching Out to Collaborators: Crowdsourcing for Pharmaceutical Research," *Pharmaceutical Research* 27, no. 3 (March 2010) 393–95.

36 See James Manyika, Michael Chui, Diana Farrell, Steve Van Kuiken, Peter Groves, and Elizabeth Almasi Doshi, *Open Data: Unlocking Innovation and Performance with Liquid Information*, McKinsey Global Institute, October 2013, available at http://www.mckinsey.com/insights/business_ technology/open_data_unlocking_innovation_and_performance_with_ liquid_information.

37 Charles Fishman, "The Insourcing Boom," *Atlantic*, December 2012.

38 Ibid. GE has sold its now more valuable consumer appliance division to Electrolux for a hefty price. For some time to come the products will keep the GE brand. On Nucor and DiMicco's views, see Dan DiMicco, *American Made* (New York: Palgrave Macmillan, 2015), pp. 14, 116.

39 See the detailed articles by Andrew Rice, "American Giant Guns for Gap by Doubling Down On the USA," and Max Chafkin, "Warby Parker Sees the Future of Retail," and the briefer sketch on Cree by Jon Gertner, all in *Fast Company*, March 2015.

40 Quoted in Rice, "American Giant."

41 Michael Kremer, "The O-ring Theory of Economic Development," *Quarterly Journal of Economics* 108, no. 3 (August 1993): 551, quotation on p. 553.

42 Sources for the Boeing story are Christopher Tang and Joshua Zimmerman, "Managing New Product Development and Supply Chain Risks: The Boeing 787 Case," UCLA Business School study, published in *Supply Chain Forum* 10, no. 2 (2009), available at http://www.supplychain-forum.com/ article.cfm?num=19&art=170&CFID=9844940&CFTOKEN=48619538; Dominic Gates, "A 'Prescient' Warning to Boeing on 787 Trouble," *Seattle Times*, February 5, 2011; the leaked paper by L. J. Hart-Smith, "Out-Sourced Profits—The Cornerstone of Successful Subcontracting," presented at Boeing symposium in St. Louis, February 2001, at http://seattletimes.nwsource .com/ABPub/2011/02/04/2014130646.pdf; two essays by Steve Denning, "The Boeing Debacle: Seven Lessons Every CEO Must Learn," *Forbes*, January 17, 2013, and "What Went Wrong at Boeing?," ibid., January 21, 2013; and Christopher Harress, "Boeing (BA) Choose Everett for 777X Wing Production Sustaining Jobs in Seattle," *International Business Times*, February 18, 2014. The major orders for the 777X were announced in July 2014 from Emirates and from Qatar Airways.

One of the interesting sidelights of our argument is its implications for the way the U.S. government buys many of its innovative and complex products. Partly for political reasons, the networked supply chains for complex defense systems are extremely elaborate, spreading the work around, and the products are notorious for delays and cost overruns. Hart-Smith's analysis of why Boeing had done the 787 process the way it had showed that it was because it had been influenced by McDonnell-Douglas practices in its defense work. Hart-Smith noted that these practices eventually destroyed the Douglas commercial business and may have seemed viable for companies because "[t]he military approach didn't require you to risk your own money." Gates, "A Prescient Warning."

43 James Manyika, Jeff Sinclair, Richard Dobbs, Gernot Stubbe, Louis Rassey, Jan Mischke, Jaana Remes, Charles Roxburgh, Katy George, David O'Halloran, and Sree Ramaswamy, *Manufacturing the Future: The Next Era of Global Growth and Innovation*, McKinsey Global Institute, November 2012, pp. 37–38.

44 "Making It in America," *Economist*, July 7, 2011; see also Andrew Liveris and Dick Hill, *Make It in America: The Case for Re-inventing the Economy* (New York: Wiley, 2011).

45 See Daniel Yergin, *The Prize: The Epic Quest for Oil, Money, and Power* (New York: Simon & Schuster, 1991), pp. 248–69; David S. Painter, *Oil and the American Century: The Political Economy of U.S. Foreign Oil Policy, 1941–1954* (Baltimore: Johns Hopkins University Press, 1986).

46 Gavin Wright, "The Origins of American Industrial Success, 1879–1940," *American Economic Review* 80, no. 4 (September 1990): 651–68. Back in 1990 Wright was pessimistic about America's ever regaining its former high ground in natural resource abundance. He has since revised his views.

47 See the summary in David Petraeus and Robert Zoellick, chairs, and Shannon O'Neil, director, *North America: Time for a New Focus*, Council on Foreign Relations Independent Task Force Report No. 71, October 2014, pp. 15–28, available at http://www.cfr.org.

48 See Brandon Owens, *The Rise of Distributed Power*, GE Ecomagination Whitepaper, 2014 at http://www.eenews.net/assets/2014/02/25/document _gw_02.pdf.

49 Richard Dobbs, Jeremy Oppenheim, Fraser Thompson, Marcel Brinkman, and Marc Zornes, *Resource Revolution: Meeting the World's Energy, Materials, Food, and Water Needs*, McKinsey Global Institute, November 2011, pp. 1–2; see also pp. 10–14.

50 Manyika et al., *Manufacturing the Future*, p. 93. Also, on "green manufacturing," ibid., pp. 90–91.

51 Ibid., pp. 85–86.

52 Quoted in James Fallows, "Made in America, Again," *Atlantic*, October 2014.

53 Manyika et al., *Manufacturing the Future*, p. 73.

54 Ibid., p. 80.

55 Ailbhe Coughlan, "Is Your Company Ready for the IoT?" *Forbes*, June 3, 2014, at http://www.forbes.com/sites/ptc/2014/06/03/is-your-company-ready-for-the-iot/.

56 IBM, "What Is Big Data," at http://www-01.ibm.com/software/data/bigdata/what-is-big-data.html; Brad Brown, Michael Chui, and James Manyika, "Are You Ready for the Era of 'Big Data'?," *McKinsey Quarterly*, October 2011, at http://www.mckinsey.com/insights/strategy/are_you_ready_for_the_era_of_big_data.

57 Stefaan Verhulst, Beth Simone Noveck, Robyn Caplan, Kristy Brown, and Claudia Paz, *The Open Data Era in Health and Social Care*, Report for NHS England (New York: Governance Lab, 2014), p. 12, at http://images.thegovlab.org/wordpress/wp-content/uploads/2014/10/nhs-full-report-21.pdf.

58 Manyika et al., *Open Data*.

59 "G8 Open Data Charter Released 2013," at http://opensource.com/government/13/7/open-data-charter-g8.

60 "A New Goldmine," *Economist*, May 18, 2013.

61 Robert L. Grossman, Yunhong Gu, Joe Mambretti, Michal Sabala, Alex Szalay, and Kevin White, "An Overview of the Open Science Data Cloud," 2010, at http://datasys.cs.iit.edu/events/ScienceCloud2010/p02.pdf.

62 On the genomic initiative, see Broad Institute, "Global Alliance for Genomics and Health Members Meet to Advance Genomic Data Sharing," October 20, 2014, at https://www.broadinstitute.org/news/6147.

63 Christopher Steiner, *Automate This: How Algorithms Came to Rule Our World* (New York: Penguin, 2012), p. 5; John MacCormick, *Nine Algorithms That Changed the Future: The Ingenious Ideas That Drive Today's Computers* (Princeton: Princeton University Press, 2011), p. 3.

64 Steiner, *Automate This*, p. 127.

65 Solon Barocas, "Big Data: A Tool for Inclusion or Exclusion? Framing the Conversation," Center for Information Technology Policy Presentation, September 15, 2014.

66 Federal Trade Commission, "Data Brokers: A Call for Transparency and Accountability," May 2014, at http://www.ftc.gov/system/files/documents/reports/data-brokers-call-transparency-accountability-report-federal-trade-commission-may-2014/140527databrokerreport.pdf.

67 Parmy Olson, "Apple's iPhone Just Stepped Closer to Shaping Your Health Costs," *Forbes*, October 1, 2014.

68 Alex Knapp, "First Zero-G 3D Printer Is on Its Way to the Space Station," *Forbes*, September 22, 2014, at http://www.forbes.com/sites/alexknapp/2014/09/22/first-zero-g-3d-printer-is-on-its-way-to-the-space-station/.

69 "2013 Shapeways 3D Printing Year in Review," *Shapeways Blog*, December 20, 2013, at http://www.shapeways.com/blog/archives/2394–2013-shapeways-3d-printing-year-in-review.html.

70 Tim Adams, "The 'Chemputer' That Could Print Out Any Drug" *Guardian*, July 21, 2012.

71 Sarah Zhang, "Visit This House Being 3D Printed in Amsterdam Right Now," *Gizmodo*, March 14, 2014, at http://gizmodo.com/visit-this-house-being-3d-printed-in-amsterdam-right-no-1543503640.

72 John Hagel, John Seely Brown, and Duleesha Kulasooriya, *A Movement in the Making* (Deloitte University Press, January 2014), pp. 2, 13, at http://dupress.com/articles/a-movement-in-the-making/.

73 The senator was Robert LaFollette Jr. of Wisconsin. Two important recent summaries are Diane Coyle, *GDP: A Brief But Affectionate History* (Prince-

ton: Princeton University Press, 2014), pp. 11–23, and, on GDP and much more, Zachary Karabell, *The Leading Indicators: A Short History of the Numbers That Rule Our World* (New York: Simon & Schuster, 2014), with his introduction of the history of GDP at pp. 48–90.

74 Karabell, *The Leading Indicators*, p. 72.

75 See Erik Brynjolfsson and JooHee Oh, "The Attention Economy: Measuring the Value of Digital Services on the Internet," *Proceedings of the International Conference on Information Systems*, December 2012.

76 Brynjolfsson and McAfee, *The Second Machine Age*, p. 109. Brynjolfsson has been involved in much of the recent work on problems with GDP measurement. For a summary of the concerns, see ibid., pp. 109–24.

77 Coyle, *GDP*, p. 91.

78 Richard Stone quoted in Coyle, *GDP*, p. 105.

79 William Nordhaus's wonderful paper on the "price of light" is "Do Real-Output and Real-Wage Measures Capture Reality? The History of Lighting Suggests Not," Cowles Foundation (Yale) Paper No. 957 (1998), at http://cowles.econ.yale.edu/P/cp/p09b/p0957.pdf.

Chapter 3

1 "Cash Cow, Taobao," *Economist*, May 24, 2014.

2 See U.S. National Intelligence Council, *Global Trends 2030: Alternative Worlds* (Washington, DC: Office of the Director of National Intelligence, December 2012), pp. 9–11; Bradford Jensen, "Expanding Service Exports Background," working paper prepared for the Rework America initiative of the Markle Foundation, February 28, 2014.

3 See Hal Varian, "Micromultinationals Will Run the World," *Foreign Policy*, August 15, 2011, at http://foreignpolicy.com/2011/08/15/micromulti nationals-will-run-the-world/.

4 The chart is from *Global Trends 2030*, p. 10.

5 See Anthony Williams, Dan Herman, and Warren Clarke, "Winning in the Global Services Economy: A 21st Century Export Strategy for Job Creation and Growth," Centre for Digital Entrepreneurship and Economic Performance, June 2014, available at http://deepcentre.com/ publications.

6 At the request of the Senate Finance Committee (which oversees trade issues), the International Trade Commission recently concluded the most extensive effort to measure online commerce conducted so far, surveying tens of thousands of firms. Online commerce can happen in two forms.

> • Firms can go online to reach buyers (or sellers), then deliver physical goods or services—like shipping a toy or picking up a rental car.
> • Or firms can go online to reach buyers, then deliver something to them that is also delivered online—like music or a banking service.

U.S. International Trade Commission, *Digital Trade in the U.S. and Global Economies, Part 2*, No. 4485 (Washington, DC: August 2014), pp. 41–45. On the estimate in the text about this kind of trade tripling in size: looking at markets in six countries, including the U.S. and China, 94 million online shoppers were spending $105 billion, expected to rise to 130 million shoppers spending more than $300 billion by 2018. Ibid., p. 203, citing data compiled by PayPal.

7 Ibid., pp. 45–46. These figures are superior to those compiled by the Census Bureau through its "E-Stats" reports and are also more comprehensive than the data compiled by the Department of Commerce. See ibid., p. 41 n. 39; compare with Jessica Nicholson and Ryan Noonan, *Digital Economy and Cross-Border Trade: The Value of Digitally-Deliverable Services*, ESA Issue Brief 01–14 (Washington, DC: U.S. Department of Commerce, 2014). at http://www.esa.doc.gov/sites/default/files/reports/documents/digitaleconomyandtrade2014-1-27final.pdf. For more analysis of the problems of measuring online trade, see also Michael Mandel, "Data, Trade, and Growth," Progressive Policy Institute Working Paper, August 15, 2013, at https://southmountaineconomics.files.wordpress.com/2013/09/datatradegrowth-8-15-13.pdf.

8 Andreas Lendle, "An Anatomy of Online Trade: Evidence from eBay Exporters," draft paper, August 2013, at http://www.etsg.org/ETSG2013/Papers/206.pdf; see also Andreas Lendle, Marcelo Olarreaga, Simon Schropp, and Pierre-Louis Vezina, "There Goes Gravity: How eBay Reduces Trade Costs," World Bank Policy Research Working Paper No. 6253, October 1, 2012, at http://papers.ssrn.com/so13/papers.cfm?abstract_id=2167187.

9 Trade Benefits America, "Opening Markets and Increasing Exports for SMEs: A Case Study of the eBay Platform," March 25, 2014, at http://tradebenefitsamerica.org/resources/opening-markets-and-increasing-exports-smes-case-study-ebay-platform.

10 See Jennifer Wells, "Lavasa: Indian Industrialist Bets $30 Billion on Building a Private City," *Toronto Star*, May 13, 2013; see also Angela Saini, "21st Century, Hi-tech India: The Smartest Country on the Planet," *Observer*, March 5, 2011.

11 Jensen, "Expanding Service Exports Background."

12 Farhad Manjoo, "Microsoft HoloLens: A Sensational Vision of the PC's Future," *New York Times*, January 21, 2015.

13 Quoted in Shalene Gupta, "Skip the Waiting Room by Visiting Doctors Virtually," *Fortune*, November 6, 2014.

14 Williams, Herman, and Clarke, "Winning in the Global Services Economy," pp. 12–13.

15 Jensen, "Expanding Service Exports Background."

16 See Ryan Santacrose, U.S. Chamber of Commerce Foundation, "Overwhelming Majority of American Businesses Still Not Exporting," July 11, 2013, at http://www.uschamberfoundation.org/blog/post/overwhelming-majority-american-businesses-still-not-exporting/34010.

17 U.S. International Trade Commission, *Small and Medium-Sized Enterprises: Characteristics and Performance*, (Washington, DC: November 2010), pp. xvi, 6.

18 Joshua Meltzer, "Growing Service Exports by Small and Medium-Sized Enterprises," paper prepared for the Markle Foundation Economic Initiative, November 2014.

19 Brian Bieron, testimony to the Subcommittee on Commerce, Manufacturing, and Trade of the House Committee on Energy and Commerce, September 17, 2014, at http://democrats.energycommerce.house.gov/sites/default/files/documents/Testimony-Bieron-CMT-Cross-Border-Data-Flows-2014-9-17.pdf.

20 John Grossman, "When Plan to Help Others Sell in China Fails, a Start-up Changes Tack," *New York Times*, September 17, 2014.

21 These elements are drawn from suggestions ibid., pp. 19–23.

22 The data is from James Manyika, Jacques Bughin, Susan Lund, Olivia Nottebohm, David Poulter, Sebastian Jauch, and Sree Ramaswamy, *Global Flows in a Digital Age: How Trade, Finance, People, and Data Connect the World Economy*, McKinsey Global Institute, April 2014, pp. 6, 23.

23 This particular story was illustrated in detail by a team of journalists with National Public Radio's program *Planet Money*, at http://www.npr.org/series/248799434/planet-moneys-t-shirt-project. The project was inspired by Pietra Rivoli, *The Travels of a T-Shirt in the Global Economy* (New York: Wiley, 2005).

24 See Richard Baldwin and Anthony Venables, "Spiders and Snakes: Offshoring and Agglomeration in the Global Economy," *Journal of International Economics* 90, no. 2 (2013): 245–54.

25 Marcel Timmer, Abdul Azeez Erumban, Bart Los, Robert Stehrer, and Gaaitzen de Vries, "Slicing Up Global Value Chains," *Journal of Economic Perspectives* 28, no. 2 (Spring 2014): 99, 104, and table 1. They place the financial/managerial factor under a general heading of "capital," which really is a place they lump the money that goes to everything from machinery to real estate to intellectual property to whatever goes to the financiers and shareholders. Ibid., p. 102.

26 See Chris Reiter, "BMW Makes Lone Shift to Carbon Fiber to Gain Auto Edge," *Bloomberg*, November 15, 2013, at http://www.bloomberg.com/news/print/2013-11-14/bmw-makes-lone-shift-to-carbon-fiber-to-gain-auto-edge.html; Jeff Sloan, "Market Outlook: Surplus in Carbon Fiber's Future?," *Compositesworld*, March 1, 2013, at http://www.compositesworld.com/articles/market-outlook-surplus-in-carbon-fibers-future. Unfortunately, the ecosystem for centering such work in America is still limited. Only one of the top five private firms producing carbon fiber is based in the United States. The American-based supplier was Zoltek (in St. Louis). The mass production cost issue is linked to the source material from which the carbon fiber is derived, which has mainly been expensive acrylics, with a dominant producer community for them centered in Japan.

27 Robert Koopman, William Powers, Zhi Wang, and Shang-Jin Wei, "Give Credit Where Credit Is Due: Tracing Value Added in Global Production Chains," NBER Working Paper no. 16426, September 2010, appendix p. 7, 38, at http://www.nber.org/papers/w16426.pdf.
28 The Mary Huang illustration and the cyberlaw expert's statement are both from Shawn Donnan, "Digital Trade: Data Protectionism," *Financial Times*, August 4, 2014.
29 See the OGC website, http://www.opengeospatial.org/ogc.
30 International Trade Commission, *Digital Trade in the U.S. and Global Economies*, pp. 206–8.

Chapter 4

1 The descriptions of Chinese textile investment in South Carolina are drawn from Linly Lin, "Textile Manufacturing Returns to Carolinas—by Way of China," *Charlotte Observer*, August 8, 2014; "JN Fibers to Set Up Manufacturing Plant in Richburg, S.C.," *Textile World*, October 1, 2013, at http://www.textileworld.com/Articles/2013/October/Textile_News/JN_Fibers_To_Set_Up_Manufacturing_Plant_In_Richburg-S.C.; and the short film *Made by China in America*, in the interesting series *We the Economy*, produced by Vulcan Productions and Cinelan. This episode, No. 17, was directed by Miao Wang, available at https://wetheeconomy.com.
2 Joel Kurtzman, *Unleashing the Second American Century: Four Forces for Economic Dominance* (New York: Public Affairs, 2014), pp. 145–48 (emphasis in original).
3 The concept of net private capital as a ratio of national income is detailed in Thomas Piketty, *Capital in the Twenty-First Century*, trans. Arthur Goldhammer (Cambridge: Harvard University Press, 2014), chap. 5. The particular numbers in the text are from his supplemental table C5.1, at http://piketty.pse.ens.fr/files/capital21c/en/pdf/supp/TS5.1.pdf.
4 Almost all these financial assets are held by the wealthiest 20 percent of American households, and the holdings are highly concentrated within the upper end of that quintile. The fees that go with such numbers are the main reason why the proportion of national income going to pay for financial services has more than doubled since 1970 (that portion of national income now amounts to about 9 percent of GDP, or $1.4 trillion). Figures for assets under management and much more are from Robin Greenwood and David Scharfstein, "The Growth of Finance," *Journal of Economic Perspectives* 27, no. 2 (Spring 2013): 3–28. See also Alan Blinder, Andrew Lo, and Robert Solow, eds., *Rethinking the Financial Crisis* (New York: Russell Sage Foundation, 2012), esp. the essay by Thomas Philippon.
5 Greta Krippner, *Capitalizing on Crisis: The Political Origins of the Rise of Finance* (Cambridge: Harvard University Press, 2011), pp. 29–57. Krippner does not believe these large changes to have been the result of purposeful government policy. Instead, she finds the shift to be the inadvertent prod-

uct of various U.S. efforts to cope with economic and political problems during the 1970s and early 1980s.

6 Tallies of stock buyback sums are not readily available in public sources. The numbers cited in the text are drawn from the data in historical tables of the U.S. Census Bureau's Quarterly Financial Report, 2000–2015. Dollar numbers are nominal, not constant, and the calculations are across Q4 numbers. In 2014 these reports showed a remarkable drop in business cash holdings, from more than $2.6 trillion down to just under $2 trillion in one year. If our calculations are correct and the Census estimates are accurate (and the Census estimates are just that, based on surveys and sampling), it would be by far the largest one-year drop in these cash holdings recorded in more than fifteen years. That could be a promising sign of dramatically higher business spending—or an anomaly of some kind.

7 Net domestic investment is calculated after allowing for depreciation of things like buildings and equipment. These numbers are from Thomas Piketty and Gabriel Zucman, "Capital Is Back: Wealth-Income Ratios in Rich Countries, 1700–2010," Chartbook, 2013, table A113, at http://www.gabriel-zucman.eu/files/capitalisback/F130.

8 Luke Stewart and Robert Atkinson, *Restoring America's Lagging Investment in Capital Goods*, Information Technology & Innovation Foundation, October 2013, figs. 4 and 10, pp. 11, 14, at http://www2.itif.org/2013-restoring-americas-lagging-investment.pdf.

9 Òscar Jordà, Moritz Schularick, and Alan Taylor, "The Great Mortgaging: Housing Finance, Crises, and Business Cycles," NBER Working Paper 20501, September 2014, p. 2.

10 Kurtzman, *Unleashing the Second American Century*, p. 148.

11 The Glass-Steagall bill proposed the separation of commercial and investment banking. It would create a new Federal Deposit Insurance Corporation (FDIC) that protected ordinary depositors against the regular, predictable failures of hundreds of banks. The American Bankers Association fought this deposit guarantee, saying it was "unsound, unscientific, unjust, and dangerous." Arthur M. Schlesinger Jr., *The Age of Roosevelt: The Coming of the New Deal, 1933–1935* (Boston: Houghton Mifflin, 1958), p. 443.

Nonetheless, the law passed in June 1933. It rescued and revived a system with thousands of local banks. Perhaps the biggest impact of the FDIC was to set national standards for bank accounting and regular audits. The FDIC mitigated risks without eliminating them. It facilitated the ready windup of failed banks as if they were, in effect, just another kind of bankrupt business.

12 Both Herbert Hoover and Franklin Roosevelt were attuned to housing finance as a potential enabler for American growth. In the 1920s only about 45 percent of Americans lived in their own home, which they could only buy for cash, or with large down-payments (at least 30 percent) and a 5- or 10-year note.

So the Roosevelt administration and Congress devised a cluster of agencies—the Home Owners' Loan Corporation (HOLC); the Federal Housing Administration (FHA); a Federal National Mortgage Association (Fannie Mae) created within the Reconstruction Finance Corporation in 1938; and, after World War I, a Veterans Administration (VA) program. After providing some emergency relief to refinance troubled mortgages and slow the wave of defaults, what these organizations did, in effect, was to provide national standards for appraising home value and set minimum standards for home construction. They also gave lenders additional sources of mortgage insurance since the uncertainties inherent in long-term mortgages—like a 20- or 30-year note—are difficult for any single lender to manage.

13 Marriner Eccles, *Beckoning Frontiers: Public and Personal Recollections* (New York: Knopf, 1966), p. 145.

14 See Louis Hyman, *Borrow: The American Way of Debt* (New York: Random House, 2012); see also Hyman's more detailed historical treatment of this evolution in *Debtor Nation: The History of America in Red Ink* (Princeton: Princeton University Press, 2011).

15 Jordà, Schularick, and Taylor, "The Great Mortgaging," p. 12, and table 2, p. 13.

16 See Atif Mian and Amir Sufi, *House of Debt: How They (and You) Caused the Great Recession, and How We Can Prevent It from Happening Again* (Chicago: University of Chicago Press, 2014).

17 Screenplay from *Sabrina* (1954) by Billy Wilder and Ernest Lehman, adapted from the play by Samuel Taylor.

18 William Lazonick and Mary O'Sullivan. "Maximizing Shareholder Value: A New Ideology for Corporate Governance," *Economy and Society* 29, no. 1 (2000): 13–35.

19 James W. Michaels, foreword to David Callahan, *Kindred Spirits: Harvard Business School's Extraordinary Class of 1949 and How They Transformed American Business* (New York: Wiley, 2002), pp. vi–vii. See also Rakesh Khurana, *From Higher Aims to Hired Hands: The Social Transformation of American Business Schools and the Unfulfilled Promise of Management as a Profession* (Princeton, N.J.: Princeton University Press, 2010).

20 William Lazonick, "Profits without Prosperity," *Harvard Business Review*, September 2014.

21 For Fink's open letter to corporate chairmen and CEOs, March 21, 2014, see http://online.wsj.com/public/resources/documents/blackrockletter.pdf.

22 Paul Polman, "Business, Society, and the Future of Capitalism," *McKinsey Quarterly*, May 2014.

23 For recent summaries of the data on these points, see Hyman, *Borrow* (on consumer debt); Daniel Pinto, *Capital Wars: The New East-West Challenge for Entrepreneurial Leadership and Economic Success* (London: Bloomsbury, 2014) (on investments for short-term stock performance); and "Rise of the Distorporation," *Economist*, October 26, 2013 (on partnership ownership structures).

24 Dominic Barton and Mark Wiseman, "Focusing Capital on the Long

Term," *Harvard Business Review*, January 2014. The authors cite a *McKinsey Quarterly* survey conducted by McKinsey and the Canada Pension Plan Investment Board (CPPIB) in 2013 of more than 1,000 board members and C-Suite executives around the world. In that survey 86 percent of respondents "declared that using a longer time horizon to make business decisions would positively affect corporate performance in a number of ways, including strengthening financial returns and increasing innovation."

25 Ibid.

26 "Most important factor": Suzanne Berger, at rollout of an MIT report on Production in the Innovation Economy, September 24, 2013, at http://newsoffice.mit.edu/2013/mit-pie-conference-0924; see also *A Preview of the MIT Production in the Innovation Economy Report*, February 22, 2013, p. 11, at http://web.mit.edu/pie/news/PIE_Preview.pdf. Similar arguments are in the National Research Council report edited by Charles Wessner and Alan Wm. Wolff, *Rising to the Challenge: U.S. Innovation Policy for the Global Economy* (Washington, DC: National Academies Press, 2012).

27 Polman in "Three Perspectives on 2012," *Wall Street Journal*, January 3, 2012; and idem, "Business, Society, and the Future of Capitalism."

28 Group of Thirty (chaired by Jean-Claude Trichet and board chair Jacob Frenkel), Working Group on Long-Term Finance (chaired by Guillermo Ortiz), *Long-Term Finance and Economic Growth* (Washington, DC: Group of 30, 2013), at http://www.group30.0rg/images/PDF/Longterm_Finance_hi-res.pdf.

29 See Bureau of Labor Statistics, Business Employment Dynamics, "Entrepreneurship and the U.S. Economy," chart 6, at http://www.bls.gov/bdm/entrepreneurship/entrepreneurship.htm; see also James Manyika, Susan Lund, Byron Auguste, Lenny Mendonca, Tim Welsh, and Sreenivas Ramaswamy, *An Economy That Works: Job Creation and America's Future*, McKinsey Global Institute, June 2011, p. iv.

30 Karen Gordon Mills and Brayden McCarthy, "The State of Small Business Lending: Credit Access during the Recovery and How Technology May Change the Game," Harvard Business School Working Paper 15–004, July 22, 2014, p. 4. The 51 percent to 29 percent figures, derived from FDIC data, are also in the Mills and McCarthy paper. The Federal Reserve's regional banks hear and report on the loud chorus of small-business complaints. See, e.g., Ann Marie Wiersch and Scott Shane, "Why Small Business Lending Isn't What It Used to Be," Federal Reserve Bank of Cleveland, August 14, 2013.

31 Steven Davis and John Haltiwanger, "Labor Market Fluidity and Economic Performance," National Bureau of Economic Research, NBER Working Paper 20479, September 2014, p. 14.

32 National Venture Capital Association, "VC Investments Q3 '14—MoneyTree—National Data" at http://nvca.org/index.php?option=com_content&view=article&id=344&Itemid=103.

33 Federal Reserve Bank of New York, "Key Findings Small Business Credit Survey, Q4 2013," February 2014, pp. 3, 10.

34 Robert Dilger, Congressional Research Service, *Small Business Administration 7(a) Loan Guaranty Program*, (Washington, DC: GPO, May 1, 2013), p. 13.

35 Ibid., p. 4.

36 The initial plan uses loans extended by microfinance institutions owned by Alibaba. Those loans are then packaged into a special purpose vehicle with a credit guarantee from Shangcheng Guarantee, another firm owned by the Alibaba Group. Those packages are then divided into three tranches. The lowest-risk tranche offers about a 6 percent rate of return to investors; the middle group about an 11 percent return; and the weakest group is bought directly by Alibaba Financial. Because of Alibaba's experience with many of these businesses, and investments in data analytics, the company believes it can provide adequate risk assessment.

37 Edward Robinson, "Lenders Disrupt U.K. Finance Funding Borrowers Banks Snub," *Bloomberg*, September 28, 2014.

38 See Donna Kelley, Abdul Ali, Candida Brush, Andrew Corbett, Thomas Lyons, Mahdi Majbouri, and Edward Rogoff, *2013 United States Report: Global Entrepreneurship Monitor—National Entrepreneurial Assessment for the United States of America* (Wellesley, MA: Babson College, 2014), at http://www.gemconsortium.org/docs/download/3375; and Robert Fairlie, *Kauffman Index of Entrepreneurial Activity, 1996–2013* (Kansas City, MO: Ewing Marion Kauffman Foundation, April 2014), at http://www.kauffman.org/~/media/kauffman_org/research%20reports%20and%20covers/2014/04/kiea_2014_report.pdf. Although rates of entrepreneurial activity declined slightly in 2014, overall rates viewed over the last 18 years are relatively constant. Recent declines may reflect a reduction of "forced" entrepreneurship as more payroll jobs are available and layoffs decline.

39 "An Entrepreneurial Generation of 18-to-34-Year-Olds Wants to Start Companies When Economy Rebounds, According to New Poll," November 10, 2011, at http://www.kauffman.org/newsroom/2012/11/an-entrepreneurial-generation-of-18-to-34yearolds-wants-to-start-companies-when-economy-rebounds-according-to-new-poll.

40 John Haltiwanger, Ron Jarmin, and Javier Miranda, "Who Creates Jobs? Small versus Large versus Young," *Review of Economics and Statistics* 95, no. 2 (May 2013): 347.

41 Amir Sufi, "Bernanke's Failed Mortgage Application Exposes the Flaw in Banking," *Financial Times*, October 13, 2014. The original Bernanke statement is from his essay "Nonmonetary Effects of the Financial Crisis in the Propagation of the Great Depression," in his collection *Essays on the Great Depression* (Princeton: Princeton University Press, 2004).

42 James Dornbrook, "This Man Is Out to Change the Way You Get Paid,"

Kansas City Business Journal, October 10, 2014, at https://c2fo.com/wp-con
tent/uploads/2014/11/Kansas-City-Business-Journal_C2FO-Cover-
Story-10.10.201411.pdf; current transaction volume is from C2FO reports.

43 Sarah Max, "More Likes, More Cash? Kabbage Provides Working Capital for Online Merchants," *Time,* July 13, 2012, at http://business.time
.com/2012/07/13/more-likes-more-capital-kabbage-looks-at-every-
thing-from-sales-history-to-social-media-to-determine-whether-online-
merchants-are-credit-worthy/.

Chapter 5

1 See Seth Robson, "Smartphone Upgrade Keeps Troops Plugged In on
the Battlefield," *Stars and Stripes,* April 12, 2013, at http://www.stripes.
com/news/smartphone-upgrade-keeps-troops-plugged-in-on-the-
battlefield-1.216407. The downside of this achievement was that, for reasons more organizational than technological, it took more than ten years
of effort for the operating business, the Army, to work through the issues
of how to get a much sought-after capability that could save many lives
into the field. For one account of the headaches, see Spencer Ackerman,
"It Only Took the Army 16 Years and 2 Wars to Deploy This Network,"
Wired, June 28, 2012, at http://www.wired.com/2012/06/army-data-
network-war/all/. Problems in pairing the Rifleman Radio with the Nett
Warrior system—because the two components were developed in separate
processes and were not naturally compatible—still appear to constrain the
geo-location function, although this problem is reportedly being solved.

2 Based on discussions with DAQRI officials; see also http://hardware
.daqri.com/smarthelmet/. In January 2015 Microsoft unveiled a prototype
of its own augmented reality device, a HoloLens. Reporters trying out
the device began realizing, as one put it, that "interacting with holograms
could become an important part of how we use machines in the future."
Farhad Manjoo, "Microsoft HoloLens: A Sensational Vision of the PC's
Future," *New York Times,* January 21, 2015.

3 The John Deere/Farmer Jane example in this and the succeeding para-
graphs is derived from the case studies "Digital Innovations in Agriculture" and "M2M [machine-to-machine] Communications-based
Packages Delivering Agricultural Solutions," in U.S. International Trade
Commission, *Digital Trade in the U.S. and Global Economies, Part 2,* No.
4485 (Washington, DC: August 2014), pp. 164–66.

4 See Rebecca Bagley, "How the Cloud and Big Data Are Changing
Small Business," *Forbes,* July 15, 2014, at http://www.forbes.com/sites/
rebeccabagley/2014/07/15/how-the-cloud-and-big-data-are-changing-
small-business/; SMB Group, "Top 10 SMB Technology Trends for
2014," December 3, 2013, at http://www.smb-gr.com/wp-content/uploads
/2013/12/12–3-13__2014_Top_Technology_Trends.pdf; and Intuit Network, "Sizing Up Big Data for Small Business," December 18, 2012, at

http://network.intuit.com/2012/12/18/infographic-sizing-up-big-data-for-small-business/.

5 We have drawn on the useful summary in Susan Lund, James Manyika, Scott Nyquist, Lenny Mendonca, and Sreenivas Ramaswamy, *Game Changers: Five Opportunities for US Growth and Renewal*, McKinsey Global Institute, July 2013, pp. 69–71.

6 Gartner Survey, September 17, 2014, at http://www.gartner.com/news room/id/2848718.

7 Rachael King, "Salesforce.com Debuts Analytics Cloud Product at Dreamforce," *Wall Street Journal*, October 13, 2014.

8 In 2013, 78 percent of office-based physicians used any type of electronic health record (EHR) system, up from 18 percent in 2001; Chun-Ju Hsiao and Esther Hing, "Use and Characteristics of Electronic Health Record Systems among Office-Based Physician Practices: United States, 2001–2013," National Center for Health Statistics, Centers for Disease Control and Prevention, *Data Brief Number 143*, January 2014.

9 Pamela Anderson and Terri Townsend, "Medication Errors: Don't Let Them Happen to You," *American Nurse Today*, March 2010, p. 27.

10 Over the spring and summer of 2014, physicians in Beth Israel Deaconess Medical Center in Boston's emergency department engaged in a four-month pilot project using heavily modified versions of Google Glass to look up patient records. The emergency physician Steve Horng is spearheading the project. "Emergency medicine is a very information-intensive specialty where even small nuggets of information available immediately really matter," he says. "Having information one minute earlier can actually be quite life-saving." See also Susan Rojahn, "Why Some Doctors Like Google Glass So Much," *MIT Technology Review*, May 6, 2014; Oliver Muensterer et al., "Google Glass in Pediatric Surgery: An Exploratory Study," *International Journal of Surgery* 12, no. 4 (April 2014): 281–89; Urs-Vito Albrecht, "Google Glass for Documentation of Medical Findings: Evaluation in Forensic Medicine," *Journal of Medical Internet Research* 16, no. 2 (February 12, 2014).

11 Zeynep Ton, *The Good Jobs Strategy: How the Smartest Companies Invest in Employees to Lower Costs and Boost Profits* (New York: New Harvest/Houghton Mifflin Harcourt, 2014).

12 Ibid., fig. 1.1, p. 12.

13 Adi Ignatius, "'We Had to Own the Mistakes,' An Interview with Howard Schultz," *Harvard Business Review*, July–August 2010, pp. 108–15.

14 The Hitachi Foundation calls these companies who innovate the jobs "pioneer employers." See Jonathan Levine with Mark Popovich and Tom Strong, "Doing Well and Doing Good: Pioneer Employers Discover Profits and Deliver Opportunity for Frontline Workers," p. 17 (on traditional training investment), at http://www.hitachifoundation.org/storage/documents/DWDG_Web_Final.pdf; for details about Marlin Steel Wire, see materials on that and other manufacturing case studies at http://www.hitachifoundation.org/our-work/good-companies-at-work/pioneer-

employers/the-pioneers-of-manufacturing. The foundation has also developed a set of case studies in health care.

For a useful analysis from the HR side of how companies can recruit and manage their workforce in more customized, individualized ways, by two leading consultants at Accenture, see Susan Cantrell and David Smith, *Workforce of One: Revolutionizing Talent Management through Customization* (Boston: Harvard Business Press, 2010).

15 Ray Marshall and Marc Tucker, *Thinking for a Living: Education and the Wealth of Nations* (New York: Basic Books, 1992), p. xvi.

16 See "Q&A: Sitting Down with John Venhuizen, CEO of Ace Hardware," *Hardware Retailing*, January 2014, at http://www.hardwareretailingarchive.com/i/230961/73; Brigid Sweeney, "How Ace Hardware Profits in a Home Depot World," *Crain's*, June 21, 2014, at http://www.chicagobusiness.com/article/20140621/ISSUE01/306219989/how-ace-hardware-profits-in-a-home-depot-world.

17 Based on interviews by Katherine Rowland of the Markle Foundation with staff at the Paraprofessional Healthcare Institute, September 23, 2014.

18 Carl Benedikt Frey and Michael Osborne, "The Future of Employment: How Susceptible Are Jobs to Computerization?," September 17, 2013, at http://www.oxfordmartin.ox.ac.uk/downloads/academic/The_Future_of_Employment.pdf.

19 Alexander Keyssar, *Out of Work: The First Century of Unemployment in Massachusetts* (Cambridge: Cambridge University Press, 1986), p. 15.

20 Claudia Goldin, "Labor Markets in the Twentieth Century," in Stanley Engerman and Robert Gallman, eds., *Cambridge Economic History of the United States* (Cambridge: Cambridge University Press, 2000), p. 550.

21 Warren D. Devine, "From Shaft to Wires: Historical Perspective on Electrification," *Journal of Economic History* 43, no. 2 (June 1983): 347–72.

22 Claudia Goldin and Lawrence Katz, "Human Capital and Social Capital: The Rise of Secondary Schooling in America, 1910 to 1940," NBER Working Paper 6439, March 1998, at http://www.nber.org/papers/w6439.

23 Marco Iansiti and Karim Lakhani, "Digital Ubiquity: How Connections, Sensors, and Data Are Revolutionizing Business," *Harvard Business Review*, November 2014, pp. 3–11, quotation on p. 8. GE sells less hardware in this paradigm, but it is selling more of a partnership.

24 Ibid., p. 5.

25 Both the "quality of the service" quotation and the reference to Katz are from David Autor, "Polanyi's Paradox and the Shape of Employment Growth," NBER Working Paper 20485, September 2014, p. 40 and n. 42.

26 Lund et al., *Game Changers*, p. 86.

27 See Timothy Bresnahan, Erik Brynjolfsson, and Lorin Hitt, "Technology, Organization, and the Demand for Skilled Labor," in Margaret Blair and Thomas Kochan, eds., *The New Relationship: Human Capital in the American Corporation* (Washington, DC: Brookings Institution, 2000),

pp. 145–93; Adam Seth Litwin, "Technological Change at Work: The Impact of Employee Involvement on the Effectiveness of Health Information Technology," *ILR Review* 64, no. 5 (October 2011): 863–88. Thomas Kochan called this work to our attention.

28 Eve Glicksman, "Wanting It All: A New Generation of Doctors Places Higher Value on Work-Life Balance," *Association of American Medical Colleges Reporter*, May 2013.

29 The Hitachi Foundation case studies, cited earlier, illustrate specifically how this can be done in the health care field.

30 Based on interviews by Kadi Davis and Max Elder of the Markle Foundation with Cheryl Feldman, executive director of the fund, November 4, 2014.

31 See generally James Heckman, John Eric Humphries, and Tim Kautz, eds., *The Myth of Achievement Tests: The GED and the Role of Character in American Life* (Chicago: University of Chicago Press, 2014), esp. chap. 5.

32 The information about Debra Burton is from the AFL-CIO. Markle Foundation staff also interviewed participants in the Training Fund program to flesh out some of the details. See Robert Wood Johnson Foundation, "Jobs to Careers: Transforming the Front Lines of Health Care," December 13, 2012, at http://www.rwjf.org/content/dam/farm/reports/program_results_reports/2012/rwjf403395.

33 Robert Wood Johnson Foundation, "Jobs to Careers."

34 Helen Nissenbaum, *Privacy in Context: Technology, Policy, and the Integrity of Social Life* (Stanford: Stanford University Press, 2010), p. 127 (emphasis in original).

35 Stefaan Verhulst, Beth Simone Noveck, Robyn Caplan, Kristy Brown, and Claudia Paz, *The Open Data Era in Health and Social Care*, Report for NHS England (New York: Governance Lab, 2014), p. 38.

36 White House, *Consumer Data Privacy in a Networked World: A Framework for Protecting Privacy and Promoting Innovation in the Global Digital Economy* (2012), at http://www.whitehouse.gov/sites/default/files/privacy-final.pdf.

Chapter 6

1 On Jay Rogers, see the Local Motors website; also the profile of Rogers by Neal Gabler, "Crowdsourcing the Car of the Future," *Playboy*, January 11, 2013, at http://www.playboy.com/articles/crowdsourcing-the-car-of-the-future; Geoff Manaugh, "A Visit to Local Motors, Badass Innovators of Future Vehicle Design," *Gizmodo*, January 6, 2014, at http://gizmodo.com/a-visit-to-local-motors-badass-innovators-of-future-ve-1495859889; Rogers address at LinuxCon + CloudOpen North America, August 21, 2014, at https://www.youtube.com/watch?v=GjuIM8xzYL4&list=PLbzoR-pLrL6qmJ5_7hf64Uku-sGt5nLKs&index=4.

2 Suzanne Berger with the MIT Task Force on Production in the Inno-

vation Economy, *Making in America: From Innovation to Market* (Cambridge: MIT Press, 2013), p. 25; Enrico Moretti, *The New Geography of Jobs* (Boston: Houghton Mifflin Harcourt, 2012), pp. 23, 47.

3 For some powerful reflections on the pernicious social divide between so-called knowledge workers and other kinds of producers or practical skills, see Matthew Crawford, "The Case for Working with Your Hands," *New York Times Magazine*, May 24, 2009; elaborated in Crawford's book, *Shop Class as Soulcraft: An Inquiry into the Value of Work* (New York: Penguin, 2009), e.g., chap. 2, "The Separation of Thinking from Doing."

4 James Manyika, Jeff Sinclair, Richard Dobbs, Gernot Strube, Louis Rassey, Jan Mischke, Jaana Remes, Charles Roxburgh, Katy George, David O'Halloran, and Sreenivas Ramaswamy, *Manufacturing the Future: The Next Era of Global Growth and Innovation*, McKinsey Global Institute, November 2012, p. 87.

5 See, e.g., the data in ibid., pp. 73–74.

6 John Zysman, Stuart Feldman, Kenji E. Kushida, Jonathan Murray, and Niels Christian Nielsen, "Services with Everything: The ICT-Enabled Digital Transformation of Services," in Dan Breznitz and John Zysman, eds., *The Third Globalization: Can Wealthy Nations Stay Rich in the Twenty-First Century?* (New York: Oxford University Press, 2013), p. 100.

7 Manyika et al., *Manufacturing the Future*, p. 38. See also Michael Mandel, "Beyond Goods and Services: The (Unmeasured) Rise of the Data-Driven Economy," Progressive Policy Institute Policy Memo, October 2012, at https://southmountaineconomics.files.wordpress.com/2013/06/10–2012-mandel_beyond-goods-and-services_the-unmeasured-rise-of-the-data-driven-economy-f.pdf.

8 Berger et al., *Making in America*, p. 2.

9 On Taylor, see Robert Kanigel, *The One Best Way: Frederick Winslow Taylor and the Enigma of Efficiency* (Cambridge: MIT Press, 2005). The quotation from Drucker is on p. 11.

10 Mike Rose, *The Mind at Work: Valuing the Intelligence of the American Worker*, 10th anniversary ed. (New York: Penguin, 2014), p. xv.

11 Philip Scranton, *Endless Novelty: Specialty Production and American Industrialization, 1865–1925* (Princeton: Princeton University Press, 1997).

12 Mike Rose in the forum "How Finance Gutted Manufacturing," *Boston Review*, March 6, 2014; see also Richard Florida, *The Rise of the Creative Class, Revisited* (New York: Basic Books, 2011), chap. 4, which discusses creativity in the "machine shop and the hair salon."

13 Hope Street Group and Alcoa Foundation, *Missing Makers: How to Rebuild America's Manufacturing Workforce* (2014), p. 13, at http://www.hopestreetgroup.org/sites/default/files/docs/resources/MissingMakers_0.pdf.

14 Dan Breznitz, "Why Germany Dominates the U.S. in Innovation," *Harvard Business Review*, May 27, 2014, at http://blogs.hbr.org/2014/05/why-germany-dominates-the-u-s-in-innovation/.

15 Hope Street Group and Alcoa Foundation, *Missing Makers*, pp. 29, 26.

16 Summarized in Joel Kurtzman, *Unleashing the Second American Century: Four Forces for Economic Dominance* (New York: Public Affairs, 2014), pp. 171–75.

17 Tom Krisher, "Auto Industry Hiring Spree Will Likely Result in 35,000 More Jobs This Year," Associated Press, June 9, 2013, at http://www .huffingtonpost.com/2013/06/09/auto-industry-hiring-spree_n_3411531 .html.

18 Gary P. Pisano and Willy C. Shih, *Producing Prosperity: Why America Needs a Manufacturing Renaissance* (Boston: Harvard Business Review Press, 2012).

19 Suzanne Berger, "How Finance Gutted Manufacturing," *Boston Review*, April 1, 2014.

20 For a thought-provoking analysis of how the rising power of financial managers is setting in motion major changes in U.S. corporate structures since the 1970s, see Gerald F. Davis, *Managed by the Markets: How Finance Re-shaped America* (New York: Oxford University Press, 2009).

21 Jacob Bunge, "Investors Weigh Bid to Break Up DuPont," *Wall Street Journal*, September 18, 2014.

22 Berger, "How Finance Gutted Manufacturing."

23 Jacob Bunge and David Benoit, "At DuPont, Gains Didn't Ward Off Trian," *Wall Street Journal*, January 10–11, 2015. Sonnenfeld's comments were originally published on ChiefExecutive.net.

24 For a recent summary, see Mercedes Delgado, Michael E. Porter, and Scott Stern, "Clusters, Convergence, and Economic Performance," NBER Working Paper 18250, July 2012, at http://www.nber.org/papers/w18250.

25 Greater Houston Partnership (hereinafter GHP), "Houston: The Economy at a Glance," September 2014, pp. 1–2 (using data from the U.S. Bureau of Labor Statistics), comparing major metropolitan areas. Houston was second to the New York City metro area in the absolute number of jobs added, but the increase was about twice as large in proportion to the base population. The other major metro areas with double-digit employment growth rates in the last five years were—in order—Dallas–Fort Worth, San Francisco, Seattle (another leader in manufacturing employment growth, as narrowly defined), Minneapolis, San Diego, Detroit, and Atlanta.

26 These and other data about Houston employment given below are from ibid.; GHP, "2014 Houston Employment Forecast," December 3, 2013; and GHP, "Houston Economic Indicators," September 22, 2014. The numbers on relative employment growth in the last year between sectors use a year-to-date average. During 2014 the average Houston unemployment rate, using standard U.S. metrics, has been 6.3 percent; the national average has been 7.7 percent.

27 GHP, "2014 Houston Employment Forecast," p. 6. The report also observed that many construction workers have taken themselves off the

statistical payroll data by becoming independent contractors, in order to avoid "immigration and benefits issues."

28 "Houston: The Economy at a Glance," September 2014, p. 10.

29 Moretti, *The New Geography of Jobs*, p. 60.

30 Berger and MIT Task Force, *Making in America*, p. 4; see also Robert D. Atkinson, Luke A. Stewart, Scott M. Andes, and Stephen Ezell, "Worse Than the Great Depression: What the Experts Are Missing about American Manufacturing Decline," Information Technology and Innovation Foundation Report, March 2012.

31 Dan Breznitz, "Why Silicon Valley Shouldn't Be the Model for Innovation," *Harvard Business Review*, November 18, 2014, at https://hbr .org/2014/11/why-silicon-valley-shouldnt-be-the-model-for-innovation.

32 Manyika et al., *Manufacturing the Future*, p. 36.

33 Mark Muro and Bruce Katz, "The New 'Cluster Moment': How Regional Innovation Clusters Can Foster the Next Economy," Brookings Institution, Metropolitan Policy Program, September 2010.

34 Susan Lund, James Manyika, Scott Nyquist, Lenny Mendonca, and Sreenivas Ramaswamy, *Game Changers: Five Opportunities for US Growth and Renewal*, McKinsey Global Institute, July 2013, exhibit 14, p. 65.

35 This description of the Golden Triangle of Mississippi is based on reporting work by James and Deborah Fallows, along with further details supplied directly to Markle Foundation staff by Brenda Lathan and her colleagues. See James Fallows, "The New Industrial Belt: The Deep South," *Atlantic*, April 25, 2014; idem, "Theories of History: Joe Max Higgins and the Golden Triangle of Mississippi," ibid., May 23, 2014; idem, "Heavy Industry in the Mississippi 'Prairie': Why Are These Factories Here?," ibid., May 30, 2014; idem, "Raj Shaunak and the Economic Boom in Eastern Mississippi," ibid., July 2014; and Deborah Fallows, "A Mississippi School Striving for Excellence," ibid., May 2014, all at http:// theatlantic.com.

36 Yolanda Kodrzycki and Ana Patricia Muñoz, "Lessons from Resurgent Cities," *2009 Annual Report*, Federal Reserve Bank of Boston, pp. 9–31.

37 Fallows, "Heavy Industry in the Mississippi 'Prairie.'"

38 Tamar Jacoby, "Why Germany Is So Much Better at Training Its Workers," *Atlantic*, October 2014.

39 A vast literature arguing the nuances of this statement exists, much of it rooted in a classic essay by Robert M. Solow, "Technical Change and the Aggregate Production Function," *Review of Economics and Statistics* 39, no. 3 (August 1957): 312–20.

40 For a persuasive evolutionary interpretation of technological progress, see generally Richard R. Nelson, *The Sources of Economic Growth* (Cambridge: Harvard University Press, 1996), which also compiles some of the work Nelson did with Sidney Winter and with Gavin Wright. For a follow-on emphasis on the role of private-sector innovation, see Edmund Phelps,

Mass Flourishing: How Grassroots Innovation Created Jobs, Challenge, and Change (Princeton: Princeton University Press, 2013), or, for an account emphasizing instead the role of government-sponsored R&D, see Mariana Mazzucato, *The Entrepreneurial State: Debunking Public vs Private Sector Myths* (London: Anthem, 2013).

41 Bradford Goldense, "Applied Research & Advanced Development Processes Come of Age," *Machine Design*, June 23, 2014.

42 Andy Harris, "Young, Brilliant and Underfunded," *New York Times*, October 2, 2014.

43 Sally Rockey, "Comparing Success Rates, Award Rates, and Funding Rates," Office of Extramural Research, National Institutes of Health, March 5, 2014.

44 National Science Board, "Science and Engineering Indicators Digest," February 2014.

45 Report of the President's Council of Advisors on Science and Technology, "Transformation and Opportunity: the Future of the U.S. Research Enterprise," November 2012.

46 Allison Proffitt, "Robots for Hire: Emerald Launches Robotic Laboratories for Life Sciences," *Bio-IT World*, July 1, 2014, at http://www.bio-itworld.com/2014/7/1/emerald-launches-robotic-laboratories-life-sciences.html; Sachin Rawat, "Emerald Cloud Lab: Taking Biotech to the Cloud," *Synbiobeta*, July 25, 2014, at http://synbiobeta.com/emerald-cloud-lab-taking-biotech-cloud/.

47 There are several options that can be considered. One reason the tax credit is not permanent now is that a permanent credit would weigh heavier in calculating budget scores. But that issue is secondary to the haphazard character of corporate taxation and the differential tax rates that apply to dividends and capital gains. The underlying goal is a tax system that rewards genuine business investment, encouraging a perspective of long-term, sustainable growth. Within the current patchwork, an increase in the R&D tax credit could help. But larger gains might be possible in a more comprehensive reform that simplified the whole system.

48 Valuable research on R&D tax credits includes Nirupama Rao, "Do Tax Credits Stimulate R&D Spending? The Effect of the R&D Tax Credit in Its First Decade," NYU Wagner School research paper, April 2013, at http://isites.harvard.edu/fs/docs/icb.topic1258829.files/RAO-Nirupama_Tax-Credits_April2013.pdf; Bronwyn H. Hall and John Van Reenen, "How Effective Are Fiscal Incentives for R&D? A Review of the Evidence," NBER Working Paper 7098, April 1999, at http://www.nber.org/papers/w7098.pdf; Rachel Griffith, Stephen Redding, and John Van Reenen, "Measuring the Cost-Effectiveness of an R&D Tax Credit for the UK," *Fiscal Studies* 22, no. 3 (2001): 375–99; Ross DeVol and Perry Wong, "Jobs for America: Investments and Policies for Economic Growth

and Competitiveness," Milken Institute, January 2010, pp. 24–31, at http://assets1b.milkeninstitute.org/assets/Publication/ResearchReport/PDF/JFAFullReport.pdf; and Dan Wilson, "The Rise and Spread of State R&D Tax Credits," Federal Reserve Bank of San Francisco Economic Letter, October 14, 2005, at http://www.frbsf.org/economic-research/publications/economic-letter/2005/october/the-rise-and-spread-of-state-research-development-tax-credits/.

49 Robert D. Atkinson, "Create Jobs by Expanding the R&D Tax Credit," Information Technology and Innovation Foundation, January 26, 2010, at http://www.itif.org/files/2010–01–26-RandD.pdf.

50 Nelson, *The Sources of Economic Growth*, p. 264 (this chapter was originally co-authored by Gavin Wright).

51 Clayton M. Christensen, *The Innovator's Dilemma: When New Technologies Cause Great Firms to Fail* (Boston: Harvard Business Review Press, 1997).

52 Peter F. Drucker, *Management: Tasks, Responsibilities, Practices* (New York: E. P. Dutton, 1986), p. 541. Chap. 61 of the book, on innovative business organization, still holds up very well today.

53 Harvey E. Wagner, "The Open Corporation," *California Management Review* 33, no. 4 (Summer 1991): 46–60.

54 Michael A. Bernstein, *The Great Depression: Delayed Recovery and Economic Change in America, 1929–1939* (Cambridge: Cambridge University Press, 1989).

55 See Gerald T. White, *Billions for Defense: Government Financing by the Defense Plant Corporation during World War II* (Birmingham: University of Alabama Press, 1980).

56 Lund et al., *Game Changers*, exhibit 27, p. 101; see also box 8 on p. 102.

57 Ibid., pp. 106–7.

58 Louise Story, "As Companies Seek Tax Deals, Governments Pay High Price," *New York Times*, December 1, 2012.

59 Nathan Jensen, "Evaluating Firm-Specific Location Incentives: An Application to the Kansas PEAK Program," Ewing Marion Kauffman Foundation, 2014, at http://www.kauffman.org/~/media/kauffman_org/research%20reports%20and%20covers/2014/04/jensen%20whitepaper_final.pdf.

60 E.g., Paige Williams, "Drop Dead, Detroit!," *New Yorker*, January 27, 2014, profiling the executive of one of the neighboring counties.

61 Based on reporting by James Fallows; see also Bruce Smith, "SC Inland Port Praised as Good for Jobs, Environment," *The State*, January 24, 2014, at http://www.thestate.com/2014/01/24/3226068/sc-inland-port-praised-as-good.html.

62 Diana Carew and Michael Mandel, "Infrastructure Investment and Economic Growth: Surveying New Post-crisis Evidence," Progressive Policy Institute, March 2014, at http://www.progressivepolicy.org/wp-content/uploads/2014/03/2014.03-Carew_Mandel_Infrastructure-Investment-

and-Economic-Growth_Surveying-New-Post-Crisis-Evidence.pdf. PPI singled out a 2007 study by Robert Crandall, William Lehr, and Robert Litan of Brookings, which examined broadband penetration data over 2003–05 and found it had a positive effect on employment.

63 Akamai issues quarterly reports on the "State of the Internet" that are a valuable source for broad comparisons. See also Klaus Schwab, "The Global Competitiveness Report, 2013–2014," World Economic Forum, pp. 514–16; OECD Broadband Portal, at http://www.oecd.org/sti/broadband/oecdbroadbandportal.htm; Broadband Commission, "The State of Broadband 2014: Broadband for All," September 2014, pp. 96–98; Household Download Index, Ookla Speedtest, at http://www.netindex.com/download/allcountries/.

64 Bill Snyder, "U.S. Lags in Broadband Speed Due to Serious Lack of Competition," *CIO Magazine*, October 1, 2014.

65 "China to Invest $323 Bln to Expand Broadband to All," Reuters, September 18, 2013.

66 "Obama Rolls Out Wireless Internet Plan," *International Business Times*, February 11, 2011; Jason Mick, "Obama Reveals National Wi-Fi Plans, Claims It Will Cut Deficit by $10B USD," *Daily Tech*, February 10, 2011.

67 "Community Network Map," Institute for Local Self-Reliance, at http://www.muninetworks.org/communitymap.

68 George Ford and Thomas Koutsky, "Broadband and Economic Development: A Municipal Case Study from Florida," *Review of Urban & Regional Development Studies* 17, no. 3 (2005): 219–29. See also Lynne Holt and Mark Jamison, "Broadband and Contributions to Economic Growth: Lessons from the US Experience," *Telecommunications Policy* 33, nos. 10–11 (November–December 2009): 575–81.

69 George Ford, "Do Municipal Networks Offer More Attractive Service Offerings Than Private Sector Providers?," *Phoenix Center Perspectives*, January 27, 2014 (finding that municipal systems typically charge consumers substantially more than their private-sector rivals for very similar triple-play offerings).

70 J. Stricker, "Casting a Wider Net: How and Why State Laws Restricting Municipal Broadband Networks Must Be Modified," *George Washington Law Review* 81 (2013): 589–627; Alex Wilhelm, "FCC Chairman Tom Wheeler: Internet Will Not Be Divided into 'Haves' and 'Have-Nots,'" *Tech Crunch*, April 30, 2014.

71 "Google Fiber," at https://fiber.google.com/about2/.

72 President's Council of Advisors on Science and Technology, *Report to the President: Realizing the Full Potential of Government-Held Spectrum to Spur Economic Growth*, July 2012, at http://www.whitehouse.gov/sites/default/files/microsites/ostp/pcast_spectrum_report_final_july_20_2012.pdf. These recommendations were accepted by President Obama, and are being followed up by the Federal Communications Commission and the relevant

agency of the Department of Commerce. See "Presidential Memorandum—
Expanding America's Leadership in Wireless Innovation," June 14, 2013, at
http://www.whitehouse.gov/the-press-office/2013/06/14/presidential-mem
orandum-expanding-americas-leadership-wireless-innovatio.

73 See Jessica Rosenworcel, "Remarks at the Marconi Society Anniversary
Symposium, National Academy of Sciences, October 2, 2014," at https://
apps.fcc.gov/edocs_public/attachmatch/DOC-329734A1.pdf; "The Race
to 5G Is On," *Re/code*, October 27, 2014, at http://recode.net/2014/10/27/
the-race-to-5g-is-on/.

Chapter 7

1 Materials provided by Burning Glass, 2014. Burning Glass analyzed New
York City job postings between July 2013 and July 2014 and also the characteristic middle-skill IT career ladder.

2 For individuals between the ages of 25 and 64. Census Bureau, "Educational Attainment of the Population," table 1, 2013. An oft-cited figure is
that about 30 percent of Americans have completed college. This may be
based on numbers for how many Americans have completed four years of
college. The number cited here is for the proportion who earned a bachelor's
degree.

3 In one set of numbers for late 2013, unemployment among bachelor's
degree holders between 20 and 29 years of age was 11.5 percent; more than
40 percent of those who had jobs were doing work that did not traditionally
require a college degree. Nearly half of the underemployed recent graduates were working only part-time or in low-wage jobs. Accenture (Jennifer
Burrowes and Alexis Young), Burning Glass Technologies (Dan Restuc-
cia), and Harvard Business School (Joseph Fuller and Manjari Raman),
Bridge the Gap: Rebuilding America's Middle Skills, November 2014, p. 5, at
http://www.hbs.edu/competitiveness/Documents/bridge-the-gap.pdf.

4 Ibid., p. 2.

5 Two enormous demographic changes gathered strength from the 1970s into
the 2000s. One was that women entered the workforce on a massive scale.
The growing participation of women in the labor force rose slowly from
about 1890 to 1930, picked up more between 1930 and 1960, and then really
took off in the 1960s and, even more, in the 1970s. It has only recently
started to plateau. See Claudia Goldin, "Labor Markets in the Twentieth
Century," in Stanley Engerman and Robert Gallman, eds., *Cambridge Economic History of the United States*, vol. 3, *The Twentieth Century* (Cambridge:
Cambridge University Press, 2000), pp. 576–79 and fig. 10.7.

The other large demographic change in the late 20th century was
that, after imposing tight limits for about fifty years, the United States
reopened its gates and again began allowing mass immigration. The tidal
flows of European and Asian immigration that accompanied the rise of

less expensive steamship travel in the 1840s were first limited by restrictions on Asian immigration beginning in the 1880s. In 1914 World War I began interfering with European immigration, and the U.S. government followed with a series of increasingly stringent legal restrictions enacted in 1917, 1924, and 1929.

As historians of the United States know, the curtailment of mass immigration from Europe had the effect of increasing the bargaining power of labor unions. Another effect of the limits was to open many more job opportunities for poorer Americans (many being pushed off of increasingly low-wage, mechanized, or unproductive farms) to find work in the industrial cities. This was a particular opening for blacks in the American South, who moved to the North and West in the millions between the 1910s and 1960s. See Joshua Rosenbloom and William Sundstrom, "Labor-Market Regimes in U.S. Economic History," in Paul Rhode, Rosenbloom, and David Weiman, eds., *Economic Evolution and Revolution in Historical Time* (Stanford: Stanford University Press, 2011), pp. 293–97.

The percentage of Americans who were foreign-born was as high as about 15 percent in 1910 and 13 percent in 1920. It then steadily dropped. By the 1960s the percentage of foreign-born Americans reached a historic low, at about 5 percent. In 1965 a federal law opened up avenues for family unification. This led to a vast and largely unforeseen return of mass immigration, both legal and illegal. As one historian concluded, "it is the case that a law designed to preserve the established profile of the American population inadvertently contributed to its radical modification." By 2010 the percentage of foreign-born Americans had jumped all the way back up to 12 percent, returning to proportions last seen a hundred years earlier. See generally Aristide Zollberg, *A Nation by Design: Immigration Policy in the Fashioning of America* (Cambridge: Harvard University Press, 2006), pp. 295, 338; Mae Ngai, "Immigration and Ethnic History," in Eric Foner and Lisa McGirr, eds., *American History Now* (Philadelphia: Temple University Press, 2011), p. 369.

The return of mass immigration has created new opportunities for tens of millions of immigrants. It has also, as economists would expect, added a large supply of labor. That has had foreseeable effects on wages in those jobs that do not require formal skills or credentials. For a recent summary, see George Borjas, "Immigration and the American Worker: A Review of the Academic Literature," Center for Immigration Studies, April 2013, available at http://www.hks.harvard.edu/fs/gborjas/publications/popular/CIS2013.pdf.

Each of these changes—women, immigrants—added tens of millions of additional workers into the labor supply. Civil rights laws and changing norms made more and more jobs open to all Americans.

6 Population growth rates are for the "civilian noninstitutional population," a term used to define people who are 16 and over, and not incarcerated.

Data drawn from Mitra Toossi, "A Century of Change: The U.S. Labor Force, 1950–2050," *Monthly Labor Review*, May 2002, table 2, p. 18. We updated that information for the period since 2000 by using historical labor force data provided to us by Dr. Toossi at the Bureau of Labor Statistics (hereinafter BLS), plus the population data from the U.S. Census Bureau. See also the BLS data on labor force and population growth compiled at http://research.stlouisfed.org/fred2/series/CIVPART and http://research.stlouisfed.org/fred2/series/CNP160V.

Dr. Toossi published a different estimate of historical annual labor force growth for the 2000–2010 period (0.8 percent) in another source. "Labor Force Projections to 2020: A More Slowly Growing Workforce," *Monthly Labor Review*, January 2012, p. 44, table 1. But the underlying data appears to yield the annualized growth rate we provide in the text.

7 At the beginning of 2012 Toossi, in "Labor Force Projections," projected only 0.7 percent labor force growth in the 2010s. An earlier BLS projection had expected only 0.2 percent labor force growth between 2015 and 2025. See BLS, "Working in the 21st Century," at http://www.bls.gov/opub/working/page1b.htm.

8 To offset all this added labor supply and still maintain the old tightness between labor supply and demand, the economy would have needed some enormous, appropriately disproportionate expansion. One option might have been many more foreign buyers of American goods. Just the opposite trend occurred.

Another option would be to juice up internal demand from, say, lowering credit barriers in order to enable much more debt-fueled consumer spending. After the Great Recession few believe that jacking up consumer indebtedness holds much promise. Some believe there is more scope for government spending that would create more employment. Whatever the merits of that argument, to us it seems more like a possible palliative, not a lasting solution.

9 A useful summary of recent data is provided in Brad Plumer, "Three Reasons the U.S. Labor Force Keeps Shrinking," *Washington Post*, September 6, 2013.

10 BLS, "TED: The Economics Daily—Youth Employment and Unemployment, July 2014," August 19, 2014.

11 For some suggestive numbers, see Rosabeth Moss Kanter, "To Create Jobs, Break the ICE—Innovate, Collaborate, Educate," *Huffington Post*, June 24, 2012; "The Employment Situation—September 2014," BLS release, October 3, 2014; "Job Openings and Labor Turnover Summary—August 2014," BLS release, December 9, 2014.

12 The work started out with a particular focus on skills gaps in advanced manufacturing. It then broadened to an analysis of the middle-skills gap, defined in the broader terms we share. Compare PCAST "Report to the President, Capturing a Domestic Competitive Advantage in Advanced

Manufacturing, Report of the Advanced Manufacturing Partnership Steering Committee—Annex 3: Education and Workforce Development Workstream Report," July 2012, at http://www.whitehouse.gov/sites/default/files/microsites/ostp/amp_final_report_annex_3_education_and_workforce_development_july_update.pdf; with PCAST [letter] Report to the President, "Information Technology for Targeting Job-Skills Training and Matching Talent to Jobs," September 2014, at http://www.whitehouse.gov/sites/default/files/microsites/ostp/PCAST/PCAST_workforce_edIT_Oct-2014.pdf. A member of our Initiative, Craig Mundie, was also a member of the PCAST who was very involved in this work. Markle Foundation experts were among those consulted by the PCAST in the development of the September 2014 report and, with Mundie, proposed the framework of a "WTE Triangle" that is featured in that report, and here.

13 See PCAST Reports, *Prepare and Inspire: K–12 Education in Science, Technology, Engineering, and Math (STEM) for America's Future*, September 2010, at http://www.whitehouse.gov/sites/default/files/microsites/ostp/pcast-stem-ed-final.pdf; and *Engage to Excel: Producing One Million Additional College Graduates with Degrees in Science, Technology, Engineering, and Mathematics*, February 2012, at http://www.whitehouse.gov/sites/default/files/microsites/ostp/pcast-engage-to-excel-final_2-25–12.pdf.

14 Mona Mourshed, Diana Farrell, and Dominic Barton, *Education to Employment: Designing a System That Works*, McKinsey Center for Government, December 2012, p. 18. at http://mckinseyonsociety.com/downloads/reports/Education/Education-to-Employment_FINAL.pdf.

15 Willy Shih, "What It Takes to Reshore Manufacturing Successfully," *MIT Sloan Management Review*, Fall 2014.

In late 2014 GE decided to sell its consumer appliance production to Electrolux, based in Sweden, although the products will still be marketed with the GE brand. Electrolux has not yet announced whether it will ouo tain the commitment to Louisville's Appliance Park and the production jobs there.

16 The countries closest to, but still above, the United States in this overall survey of young adult numeracy skills are Italy and Cyprus. See figs. 2.7a and 2.7b, 2.13, in *OECD Skills Outlook 2013: First Results from the Survey of Adult Skills* (2013), pp. 82–83, 97, available with much more material at http://skills.oecd.org. The other two countries with below-average assessments in all categories were Ireland and Poland. It is possible that Italy and Spain also would have been below average in all categories, but data was incomplete. The four countries that were above average in all categories were Finland, the Netherlands, Norway, and Sweden.

The OECD work on adult workforce skills more formally defines "numeracy" as "the ability to access, use, interpret, and communicate mathematical information and ideas in order to engage in and manage the mathematical demands of a range of situations in adult life. To this end, numeracy involves managing a situation or solving a problem in a real context, by responding to mathematical content/information/ideas represented in multiple ways." For more detail see chapter 1 of the Reader's Companion to the OECD Survey of Adult Skills 2013.

Confirmation and elaboration of the OECD findings is in Madeline Goodman, Anita Sands, and Richard Coley, *America's Skills Challenge: Millenials and the Future*, Educational Testing Service, January 2015.

17 PCAST Report, "Engage to Excel: Producing One Million Additional College Graduates with Degrees in Science, Technology, Engineering, and Mathematics," February 2012, Executive Report, p. vi.

18 Thomas Hilliard, "Building the American Workforce," Working Paper, Council on Foreign Relations, July 2013, p. 4, at http://www.cfr.org/united-states/building-american-workforce/p31120.

19 Graph adapted from Catherine Rampell, "Degree Inflation? Jobs That Newly Require B.A.'s," *New York Times*, December 4, 2012.

20 Both the office and IT work analysis is from Burning Glass Technologies, "Moving the Goalposts: How Demand for a Bachelor's Degree Is Reshaping the Workforce," September 2014, at http://www.burning-glass.com/media/4737/Moving_the_Goalposts.pdf.

21 Richard Arum and Josipa Roksa, *Aspiring Adults Adrift: Tentative Transitions of College Graduates* (Chicago: University of Chicago Press, 2014). Among the thousand students being surveyed, it turned out that the selectivity of their college, their race, their gender—none of these factors were correlated to the employment outcomes. Arum and Roksa focus on the transition of colleges into places for "meandering," self-discovery, and social development. As they discussed in the previous books in this survey, and repeat in this one, in most subjects and courses the educational agendas are unfocused and not very demanding.

22 McKinsey & Co. in collaboration with Chegg, Inc., "Voice of the Graduate," May 2013, at http://mckinseyonsociety.com/downloads/reports/Education/UXC001%20Voice%200f%20the%20Graduate%20v7.pdf.

23 Melissa Korn, "A Bit of College Can Be Worse Than None at All," *Wall Street Journal*, October 13, 2014.

24 Estimates from BLS data. See also Susan Lund, James Manyika, Scott Nyquist, Lenny Mendonca, and Sreenivas Ramaswamy, *Game Changers: Five Opportunities for US Growth and Renewal*, McKinsey Global Institute, July 2013, pp. 112, 121.

25 Alina Tugend, "What It Takes to Make New College Graduates Employable," *New York Times*, June 29, 2013. For a broad critique of the growing gap between college and the workplace, see William J. Bennett with David Wilezol, *Is College Worth It?* (Nashville: Thomas Nelson, 2013).

26 See, e.g., Hilliard, "Building the American Workforce," and Mary Jo Webster, "Where the Jobs Are: The New Blue Collar," *USA Today*, September

30, 2014, at http://www.usatoday.com/longform/news/nation/2014/09/30/job-economy-middle-skill-growth-wage-blue-collar/14797413/.

27 Interestingly, they found the gap is not equally present in all states. In a recent survey, the problems were most difficult in Michigan and Texas, least difficult in Indiana and Tennessee. Burning Glass, "The Skills Gap in Production Roles," January 8, 2014, at http://www.burning-glass.com/media/3111/The%20Skills%20Gap%20in%20Production%20Roles.pdf.

Both Indiana and Tennessee have invested years of effort into unusual public-private partnerships in workforce training, and to the integration of workforce education into mainstream schooling.

28 The first survey is from James Manyika et al., *An Economy That Works: Job Creation and America's Future*, June 2011, available at http://www.mckinsey.com/insights/employment_and_growth/an_economy_that_works_for_us_job_creation. The second study was by Accenture; the third, by the Accenture, Burning Glass, Harvard Business School group. Both are discussed in that group's report, *Bridge the Gap*, p. 16.

29 See, in this context, Ian Hathaway and Robert E. Litan, "The Other Aging of America: The Increasing Dominance of Older Firms," Economic Studies at Brookings, July 2014.

30 Suzanne Berger with the MIT Task Force on Production in the Innovation Economy, *Making in America: From Innovation to Market* (Cambridge: MIT Press, 2013), pp. 188–89.

31 PCAST report, "Information Technology for Targeting Job-Skills Training and Matching Talent to Jobs," fig. 1, p. 4.

32 Felix W. Ortiz III, "The Middle-Skill Issue," *Huffington Post*, September 25, 2013.

33 Mourshed, Farrell, and Barton, *Education to Employment*, p. 18.

34 Linsey Sledge and Tiffany Dovey Fishman, "Reimagining Higher Education: How Colleges, Universities, Businesses, and Governments Can Prepare for a New Age of Lifelong Learning," Deloitte University Press, May 22, 2014, at http://dupress.com/articles/reimagining-higher-education/.

35 We borrow this language from a recommendation in Accenture, Burning Glass, Harvard Business School, *Bridge the Gap*, p. 20.

36 Shih, "What It Takes. . . ."

37 The IBEW-NECA electrical-training alliance is detailed at http://www.electricaltrainingalliance.org.

38 Burning Glass, "Moving the Goalposts."

39 PCAST report, "Information Technology for Targeting Job-Skills Training and Matching Talent to Jobs," p. 2; Mourshed, Farrell and Barton, *Education to Employment*, p. 52.

40 See the case study on AMTEC at "McKinsey on Society," at http://mckinseyonsociety.com/e2e_casestudy/amtec-united-states/.

41 See, e.g., Corinne Alfeld and Sharika Bhattacharya, "Mature Programs

of Study: A Structure for the Transition to College and Career?," *International Journal of Educational Reform* 21 (2012): 119–37 (finding that even when career-oriented programs of study were available to support the transition from high school to college-level work, less than one-fifth of such students remained in the same program of study that they had begun in high school).

42 Frederick Rudolph, *The American College & University: A History* (Athens: University of Georgia Press, 1990, orig. 1962), pp. 232, 339.

43 Laurence R. Veysey, *The Emergence of the American University* (Chicago: University of Chicago Press, 1965), pp. 115–16, quoting works by James (in 1891) and Dewey (in 1902).

44 See, e.g., the nine "Principles" at http://www.media.mit.edu/about/principles.

45 On the divide between academia and the workplace, see the reflections in Matthew Crawford, *Shop Class as Soulcraft: An Inquiry into the Value of Work* (New York: Penguin, 2009), e.g., chap. 2, "The Separation of Thinking from Doing."

46 See James Fallows, "High School in Southern Georgia: What 'Career Technical' Education Looks Like" and "Career Technical' Education: More Middle in the Middle Class?," *Atlantic*, March 27 and 29, 2014.

47 A good sense for the emerging menu of ideas can be found in a detailed conference report, Pathways to Prosperity Project and The Achievement Gap Initiative, *Creating Pathways to Prosperity: A Blueprint for Action*, June 2014, at http://www.agi.harvard.edu/pathways/CreatingPathwaystoProsperityReport2014.pdf. See esp. the discussion of work in Kentucky (p. 33), Indiana (p. 34), Cincinnati (pp. 40–41), and several countries, including Germany, Switzerland, and Denmark. See also the comments of Volker Rein, James Rosenbaum, and David Autor (pp. 42–45), the discussion of the CCTC program (p. 57), and the "ConnectEd" ideas (pp. 64–65).

48 For an example of the argument, see a recent summary of a long body of work in James E. Rosenbaum, Jennifer L. Stephan, and Janet E. Rosenbaum, "Beyond One-Size-Fits-All College Dreams: Alternative Pathways to Desirable Careers," *American Educator*, Fall 2010 (cover story), pp. 2–13, at https://www.aft.org//sites/default/files/periodicals/Rosenbaum_0.pdf.

49 Michael Mandel, "Connections as a Tool for Growth: Evidence from the Linkedin Economic Graph," November 2014, p. 3, at https://southmountaineconomics.files.wordpress.com/2014/11/mandel-linkedin-connections-nov2014.pdf. The research was supported by Linkedin, which gave Mandel access to its data.

50 A combination of New Deal programs and wartime mobilization finally broke the historical isolation of the South from the national labor market and mainstream of American economic life. Some of the initiatives were welcomed and sought by Southern business leaders; some were not. But the effects have been historic and generally raised productivity and per capita income levels across most of the South.

The New Deal programs (like the minimum wage provisions of the Fair Labor Standards Act of 1938), court decisions curtailing the practice of "peonage," wartime mobilization, and the mechanization of cotton farming together displaced millions of black Southerners from marginal work. Meanwhile, opportunities opened for daring moves to the North and West. There was a mass migration. Civil rights laws improved the quality of education and employment opportunity for black Americans everywhere, lifting their productivity and inclusion in labor markets. The sweeping account is Gavin Wright, *Old South, New South: Revolutions in the Southern Economy since the Civil War* (Baton Rouge: LSU Press, 1996).

51 Kevin Starr, *Golden Dreams: California in an Age of Abundance, 1950–1963* (New York: Oxford University Press, 2009), p. 13. The rise of the American West is a familiar story, once it is recalled. In 1900 California's population was about equal to that of Arkansas. A big farming state with a burgeoning movie business, California was growing, passing Alabama in size by about 1910. In 1940 California had the same population as the state of Ohio, one of the great states of the old union. Then came the takeoff. Between 1940 and 1970 California's population went from 6.9 million to about 20 million. It became the home of some of America's greatest universities and research institutes. It—and the state of Washington—became the center of America's most modern defense and aerospace industries, turning the wheels of the booming national security state. A magisterial summary is Kenneth T. Jackson, *Crabgrass Frontier: The Suburbanization of the United States* (New York: Oxford University Press, 1985).

52 Data drawn from U.S. Bureau of the Census, Current Population Survey, "Historical Geographical Mobility/Migration Tables, 1948–2013," table A-1.

53 Our arguments here draw from a good recent synthesis of the ingredients for a policy to reignite mobility in Eli Lehrer and Lori Sanders, "Moving to Work," *National Affairs*, no. 18 (Winter 2014): 21–35.

54 Morris M. Kleiner and Alan B. Krueger, "Analyzing the Extent and Influence of Occupational Licensing on the Labor Market," *Journal of Labor Economics* 31, no. 2, pt. 2 (April 2013): S173, S175.

55 The case, *North Carolina State Board of Dental Examiners v. FTC*, was decided by the Court in February 2015.

56 See, e.g., Eduardo Porter, "Job Licenses in Spotlight as Uber Rises," *New York Times*, January 27, 2015.

Chapter 8

1 Claudia Goldin, "The Human-Capital Century and American Leadership: Virtues of the Past," *Journal of Economic History* 61, no. 2 (June 2001): 263–92.

2 Susan Lund, James Manyika, Scott Nyquist, Lenny Mendonca, and

Sreenivas Ramaswamy, *Game Changers: Five Opportunities for US Growth and Renewal*, McKinsey Global Institute, July 2013, p. 16.

3 PCAST report, "Information Technology for Targeting Job-Skills Training and Matching Talent to Jobs," box 1, pp. 2–3.

4 The following figure was prepared from the Digest of Education Statistics of the National Center for Education Statistics, part of the U.S. Department of Education's Institute of Education Sciences, using data in table 201.20.

High School Enrollment

* As a ratio of population 14–17–year-olds

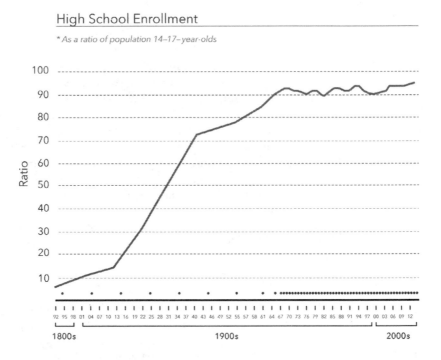

• Represents years with data

5 In 2013 more than 80 percent of the applicants to UC-Berkeley were refused admission. This exclusivity is *rewarded* by better placement in the highly publicized *U.S. News* rankings of universities.

6 Two other enormous additions to the human capital stock of the United States between 1945 and 1970 were the opening up of education and private and public employment opportunities on a scale to black Americans and then to women.

With European immigration substantially cut off after the restrictive immigration laws of 1920 (except for some refugees), African Americans had unprecedented chances to gain entry-level jobs and then be able to advance. The Civil Rights Act of 1964 and greater access to education protected those possibilities. See Gavin Wright, "The Civil Rights Revolution as Economic History," *Journal of Economic History* 59, no. 2 (June 1999): 267–89.

The charts in note 7 offer some evidence about human capital development for women. High school completion rates did not change much. College completion rates, and the opportunities that went with them, went up. See, e.g., Claudia Goldin, "The Quiet Revolution That Transformed Women's Employment, Education, and Family," *American Economic Review* 96, no. 2 (May 2006): 1–21.

For blacks and for women, the 1970s became a period of significant gains. New civil rights laws were more generally enforced. Social norms changed. In more recent years these gains have been consolidated, but the rate of advance has plateaued. The Head Start program provided preschool educational and health benefits that slowly improved the prospects of many poor children. Martha Bailey and Sheldon Danziger, eds., *Legacies of the War on Poverty* (New York: Russell Sage Foundation, 2013).

7 The following two tables, prepared by Daron Acemoglu and David Autor, track birth cohorts. Performance of a birth cohort after 1950 on the table reflects school achievement during the late 1960s and early 1970s.

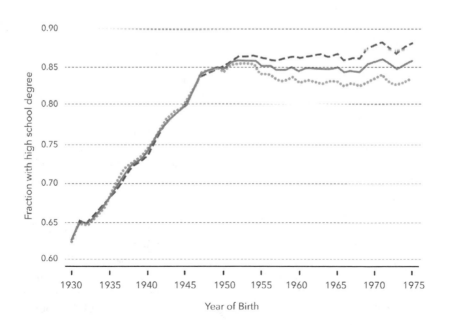

High School Completion Rates (by Birth Cohort)

College Completion Rates (by Birth Cohort)

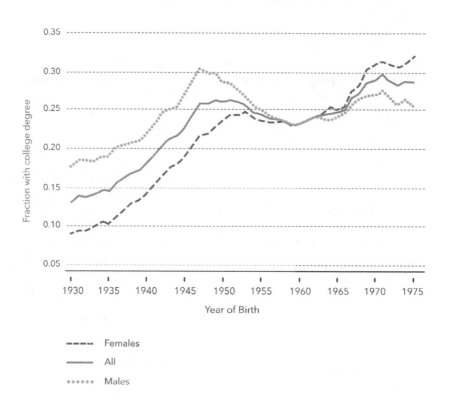

Females

All

Males

In both charts the figures for men actually tend to *decline* after about 1970. The aggregate figures stay more or less flat because of offsetting increases in completion rates for women. Daron Acemoglu and David Autor, "What Does Human Capital Do? A Review of Goldin and Katz's 'The Race between Education and Technology,'" *Journal of Economic Literature* 50, no. 2 (2012): 426–63.

8 Robert Balfanz and John Bridgeland, "Building a Grad Nation: Progress and Challenge in Ending the High School Dropout Epidemic, Annual Update," Civic Enterprises, Everyone Graduates Center at Johns Hopkins University, America's Promise Alliance, and the Alliance for Excellent Education, April 2014, at http://gradnation.org/sites/default/files/17548 _BGN_Report_FinalFULL_5.2.14.pdf. These trends may help explain why intergenerational income mobility in much of Western Europe (children earning more than their parents did) caught up to the levels of America. That happened during the 1950s and 1960s. Some of the European countries now have higher income mobility than the average community in the United States. Public education may be a key factor. Jason Long and Joseph Ferrie, "The Path to Convergence: Intergenerational Occupational

Mobility in Britain and the United States in Three Eras," *Economic Journal* 117 (March 2007): C61–C71.

9 John Bridgeland and Jessica Milano, "Opportunity Road: The Promise and Challenge of America's Forgotten Youth," Civic Enterprises and America's Promise Alliance in association with Peter D. Hart Research Associates for the Annie E. Casey Foundation, Bill and Melinda Gates Foundation, and James Irvine Foundation, January 5, 2012, at http://www.serve.gov/sites/ default/files/ctools/opportunity_road_the_promise.pdf.

10 Ibid.

11 Clive Belfield, Henry Levin, and Rachel Rosen, "The Economic Value of Opportunity Youth," Queens College, City University of New York, for the White House Council for Community Solutions, January 2012, at http://www.serve.gov/sites/default/files/ctools/econ_value_opportunity _youth.pdf.

12 "About," MIT OpenCourseWare at http://ocw.mit.edu/about/; Candace Thille, "Building Open Learning as a Community-Based Research Activity," in Toru Iiyoshi and M.S. Vijay, eds., *Opening Up Education: The Collective Advancement of Education through Open Technology, Open Content, and Open Knowledge* (Cambridge: MIT Press, 2008).

13 Tina Rosenberg, "Turning Education Upside Down," *New York Times*, October 9, 2013.

14 See Michael Crow and William Dabars, *Designing the New American University* (Baltimore: Johns Hopkins University Press, 2015). For a strong survey of ingredients coming together to create a "University of Everywhere" available to everyone, see Kevin Carey, *The End of College* (New York: Riverhead, 2015).

15 Crow and Dabars, *Designing the New American University*, p. viii.

16 University Innovation Alliance, "Who We Are," at http://www.theuia .org/#who-we-are.

17 White House (task force led by Vice President Biden), "Ready to Work: Job-Driven Training and American Opportunity," July 2014, p. 50, at http://www.whitehouse.gov/sites/default/files/docs/skills_report.pdf.

18 See Libby Nelson, "The Top-Ranked Teacher Education Program Doesn't Have Classes," *Vox*, June 18, 2014, at http://www.vox.com/2014/6/18/581 8268/why-a-top-ranked-teacher-education-program-doesnt-require- students-to. Information about student training and average is from the WGU website: http://www.wgu.edu.

19 See, e.g., Jeffrey Selingo, "Demystifying the MOOC," *New York Times*, October 29, 2014. Some of the most cutting-edge educational experiments are in business education. There the "blended" models are now proving their worth. See Jonathan Moules, "Schools Embrace Blended Teaching," *Financial Times*, March 9, 2015.

20 Institute-wide Task Force on the Future of MIT Education, "Final Report," July 28, 2014, pp. 14–15, at http://web.mit.edu/future-report/TaskForceFinal _July28.pdf.

21 Jessica Roy, "DimensionU Wants Kids to Earn Their Allowances through Educational Games," *BetaBeat*, March 23, 2012, at http://betabeat.com /2012/03/dimensionu-wants-kids-to-earn-their-allowances-through-educational-games/.

22 Tamika Moultrie, "Dimension U Introduces Video Games as an Educational Tool," *Black Enterprise*, May 31, 2012, at http://www.blackenterprise. com/technology/dimension-u-introduces-video-games-as-an-educational-tool/; the Dimension U website has data on the Mobile and other promising initial experiments.

23 Joey Lee quoted in Melanie Plenda, "Are Multiplayer Games the Future of Education?," *Atlantic*, July 11, 2014.

24 See Alexia Tsotsis, "OpenStudy Wants to Turn the World into 'One Big Study Group,'" *TechCrunch*, June 8, 2011, at http://techcrunch.com/2011 /06/08/openstudy-wants-to-turn-the-world-into-one-big-study-group/; Jeffrey Young, "'Badges' Earned Online Pose Challenge to Traditional College Diplomas," *Chronicle of Higher Education*, January 8, 2012, at http://chronicle .com/article/Badges-Earned-Online-Pose/130241/; Andrew James, "Open-Study Catapults Learning with Cash," *PandoDaily*, August 2, 2012, at http:// pando.com/2012/08/02/openstudy-catapults-learning-with-cash/.

25 "Knewton Adaptive Learning: Building the World's Most Powerful Recommendation Engine for Education," at http://www.knewton.com/ adaptive-learning-white-paper/.

26 Marc Parry, "Big Data on Campus," *New York Times*, July 18, 2012. This kind of adaptive individualized learning tool is now being tried out on a large scale in secondary school math courses. Tina Rosenberg, "Reaching Math Students One by One," *New York Times*, March 13, 2015.

27 See Public Agenda, "Is College Worth It for Me? How Adults without Degrees Think about Going (Back) to School," November 2013 (prepared with support from the Kresge Foundation), at http://www.publicagenda .org/files/IsCollegeWorthItForMe_PublicAgenda_2013.pdf.

28 Libby Nelson, "Meet Obama's Favorite College Leader," *Politico*, January 17, 2014; Interview of Nancy Zimpher by the Economist Intelligence Unit, February 27, 2014, at http://www.academicpartnerships.com/page/ nancy-zimpher-new-model-education.

29 Task Force on the Future of MIT Education, "Final Report," pp. 13–14.

30 Paul Fain, "Experimenting with Aid," *Inside Higher Ed*, July 23, 2014, at https://www.insidehighered.com/news/2014/07/23/competency-based-education-gets-boost-education-department.

31 The NSF-supported study was Elaine Collins, "Preliminary Summary SJSU+ Augmented Online Learning Environment Pilot Project," September 2013, the quotation is from p. 35. Collins is conducting a follow-on study to examine whether different forms of human mentoring can significantly broaden the reach of online courses like MOOCs.

32 See Vicki Choltz, with Louis Soares and Rachel Pleasants, *A New National Approach to Career Navigation for Working Learners*, Center for American

Progress, March 2010, at http://cdn.americanprogress.org/wp-content/uploads/issues/2010/03/pdf/career_counseling.pdf.

33 Information about Michael Donnelly is from a personal statement he prepared for YouthBuild, shared with his permission, along with the PBS *NewsHour* report on the YouthBuild program in McLean County, Illinois, reported by Paul Solman, May 21, 2012 (which include Michael Donnelly), at http://www.pbs.org/newshour/bb/american-graduate-jan-june12-amgrad_05–21/. Supplemental information was provided by Dorothy Stoneman, a member of the initiative and a leader of YouthBuild USA.

34 John Bridgeland, John J. DiIulio Jr., and Karen Morison, "The Silent Epidemic: Perspectives of High School Dropouts," Civic Enterprises in association with Peter D. Hart Research Associates for the Bill and Melinda Gates Foundation, March 2006, at https://docs.gatesfoundation.org/Documents/TheSilentEpidemic3–06Final.pdf.

35 Caroline Hoxby and Sarah Turner, "Expanding College Opportunities for High-Achieving, Low-Income Students," Stanford Institute for Economic Policy Research, SIEPR Discussion Paper No. 12–014, 2014, at http://siepr.stanford.edu/?q=/system/files/shared/pubs/papers/12–014paper.pdf.

36 Elizabeth A. Harris, "Little College Guidance: 500 High School Students per Counselor," *New York Times*, December 25, 2014.

Chapter 9

1 In a large literature, convenient summaries are Joshua Rosenbloom and William Sundstrom, "Labor-Market Regimes in U.S. Economic History," and Frank Levy and Peter Temin, "Inequality and Institutions in Twentieth-Century America," both in Paul Rhode, Rosenbloom, and David Weiman, eds., *Economic Evolution and Revolution in Historical Time* (Stanford: Stanford University Press, 2011).

2 See Jon Fingas, "Ridesharing Insurance Leaves Many Drivers in the Lurch," *Engadget*, December 23, 2014, at http://www.engadget.com/2014/12/23/ridesharing-insurance-gaps/; and Ellen Huet, "What Happens to Uber Drivers and Other Sharing Economy Workers Injured on the Job?," *Forbes*, January 6, 2015, at http://www.forbes.com/sites/ellenhuet/2015/01/06/workers-compensation-uber-drivers-sharing-economy/.

3 David Kennedy, *Freedom from Fear: The American People in Depression and War, 1929–1945* (New York: Oxford University Press, 1999).

4 The standard account is Paul Starr, *The Social Transformation of American Medicine: The Rise of a Sovereign Profession and the Making of a Vast Industry* (New York: Basic Books, 1983).

5 John Micklethwait and Adrian Wooldridge, *The Fourth Revolution: The Global Race to Reinvent the State* (New York: Penguin, 2014).

6 Tim O'Reilly, "Government 2.0," at http://www.oreilly.com/tim/gov2/.

7 Jefferson to Cabell, February 2, 1816, at http://tjrs.monticello.org/letter/332.

8 Gavin Newsom with Lisa Dickey, *Citizenville: How to Take the Town Square Digital and Reinvent Government* (New York: Penguin, 2013), p. xx.

9 Stephen Goldsmith and Susan Crawford, *The Responsive City: Engaging Communities through Data-Smart Governance* (San Francisco: Jossey-Bass, 2014).

10 "NYU CUSP, Related Companies, and Oxford Properties Group Team Up to Create 'First Quantified Community' in the United States at Hudson Yards," NYU Center for Urban Science and Progress Press Release, April 14, 2014, at http://cusp.nyu.edu/press-release/nyu-cusp-related-companies-oxford-properties-group-team-create-first-quantified-community-united-states-hudson-yards/.

11 Nate Berg, "Predicting Crime, LAPD-style," *Guardian*, June 25, 2014.

12 "NIH Invests Almost $32 Million to Increase Utility of Biomedical Research Data," National Institutes of Health Web, October 9, 2014, at http://www.nih.gov/news/health/oct2014/od-09.htm.

13 Steven Johnson, "Peer Power, from Potholes to Patents," *Wall Street Journal*, September 21, 2012.

14 "Top 25 Programs: In Detail," Ash Center for Democratic Governance and Innovation, at http://www.ash.harvard.edu/Home/News-Events/Press-Releases/Innovations/Top-25-Innovations-in-Government-Announced2/Top-25-Programs.

15 See "Participatory Budgeting in New York City," at http://pbnyc.org/; Richelle Plesse, "Parisians Have Their Say on City's First €20m 'Participatory Budget,'" *Guardian*, October 8, 2014.

16 Newsom, *Citizenville*, p. 101.

17 Woodrow Wilson, *The New Freedom: A Call for the Emancipation of the Generous Energies of a People* (New York: Doubleday, Page, 1913) (from Wilson's 1912 campaign speeches), p. 1, at http://www.gutenberg.org/files/14811/14811-h/14811-h.htm.

18 Walter Lippmann, *Drift and Mastery: An Attempt to Diagnose the Current Unrest* (Englewood Cliffs: Prentice-Hall, 1961; originally 1914), quotations from pp. 88, 118, 93, 8. Lippmann has the quotation from Wilson on p. 82; we have edited it very slightly to conform with the wording in Wilson, *The New Freedom*, cited above. For the Theodore Roosevelt commentary on Lippmann's book, see TR's review in "Two Noteworthy Books of Democracy," *Outlook* 103 (November 18, 1914): 648–51.

Index

Page numbers in *italics* refer to charts and illustrations.